HOW TO READ
A
HOROSCOPE

HOW TO READ
A
HOROSCOPE

A Scientific Model of Prediction
based on benefic & malefic analysis of planets
& bhavas as per Hindu astrology

P.V.R. RAYUDU

MOTILAL BANARSIDASS PUBLISHERS
PRIVATE LIMITED ● DELHI

First Edition : Delhi, 1997
Reprint : Delhi, 2002

ISBN: 81-208-1458-4 (Cloth)
ISBN: 81-208-1459-2 (Paper)

Also available at:

MOTILAL BANARSIDASS
41 U.A. Bungalow Road, Jawahar Nagar, Delhi 110 007
8 Mahalaxmi Chamber, 22 Bhulabhai Desai Road, Mumbai 400 026
236, 9th Main III Block, Jayanagar, Bangalore 560 011
120 Royapettah High Road, Mylapore, Chennai 600 004
Sanas Plaza, 1302 Baji Rao Road, Pune 411 002
8 Camac Street, Kolkata 700 017
Ashok Rajpath, Patna 800 004
Chowk, Varanasi 221 001

Printed in India
BY JAINENDRA PRAKASH JAIN AT SHRI JAINENDRA PRESS,
A-45 NARAINA, PHASE-I, NEW DELHI 110 028
AND PUBLISHED BY NARENDRA PRAKASH JAIN FOR
MOTILAL BANARSIDASS PUBLISHERS PRIVATE LIMITED,
BUNGALOW ROAD, DELHI 110 007

Preface

I have been studying and practising astrology for the last three decades. I was trained directly by Late Daivagna Ratna and Vidya Visaradha Sri Divakaruni Venkata Subbarao and by my beloved father Late Sri Pemmaraju Venkata Rao. I have also been trained rather indirectly by Sri B.V. Raman, the famous Indian Astrologer, by studying all his astrological books and magazines. My non-professional and research oriented scientific bent of mind has prompted me to present a new book on Astrology giving a methodology for the Benefic and Malefic percentage analysis of planets, influencing a horoscope and thereby proceeding further to analyse the benefic and malefic percentage of bhavas and planetary periods resulting in suitable predictions.

After studying various texts of astrology and based on my experience, I have picked up and chosen what I have considered best for presenting this new approach of analysis of benefic and malefic tendencies of planets and bhavas. I have enumerated the predictions of various ascendants and various planets in different rasis, bhavas and their lordship results in different bhavas, in a novel way under different topics of body, health, temperament and personality, courage, education, houses and landed property, happiness, children, diseases, enemies, debts, marriage and marital relationship, longevity, prosperity, profession, gains and income, losses and expenditure giving the benefic and malefic results separately, since many people are interested to know their future in these topics generally and it will be easy to refer to the particular topic as per their interest. Of course, these predictions will be available in many standard text books on astrology, though I have added some from my experience, but the predictions are not available under different topics in any astrological text book for easy reference as I have presented. I have also preferred to give a Model Horoscope presenting my approach.

I hope that this book will make a useful addition to the existing literature on predictive astrology. I find now a days that a lot of literate and scientific community are taking a good deal of interest in studying astrology. As such I look forward to the prospect of this book being received with interest and approbation by the students as well as scholars in the subject, particularly the scientific astrologers.

I will be thankful if any suggestions for improvement and any mistakes detected during the course of study are communicated to me so that they may be incorporated in my future endeavours.

I take this opportunity of expressing my thanks to my blessed son, Sri P.V. Kamesh, in computerising this scheme of analysis and predictions and my many friends for their valuable suggestions. My special thanks are to my wife, P. Bharati, for assistance in preparing the data with her astrological knowledge and to Sri Nair for typing the manuscript.

I am greatly indebted to Dr. A.N. Kapoor for patiently going through the entire book and improve its presentation.

My thanks are to my close friend, Dr. Y.V.S.R. Sastry, Prof. of Mech. Engg., Delhi College of Engg., Delhi, who had helped in liaisoning with the publishers. My thanks are also to Sri N.P. Jain of Messrs. Motilal Banarsidass Publishers for taking personal interest in publishing the book. Lastly my sincere prayers are to Sri Shirdi Saibaba for his constant guidance in the form of visions in my astrological research pursuits and to our family Dieties Lord Venkateswara and Alivelu Manga.

17-1-383/67 Vinayanagar,   **P.V.R. Rayudu**
Saidabad,
Hyderabad-500059, INDIA.
Phone: 4530210
email: rayadu@satyam.net.in;
         pvrrayudu@hotmail.com;
         pvrrayudu@yahoo.com;
         pvrrayudu@rediffmail.com;
         pvrrayudu@chequemail.com
website: http://www.loudoun-net.com/kamesh/rayudu.html

Abstract

Planets are positioned in different Rasis (signs) and Bhavas (houses) with respect to a particular ascendant at the particular time of birth. Accordingly, each planet is subjected to many influences as per its placement in a particular rasi and bhava with respect to the placement of other planets. As such, the benefic and malefic tendencies of each planet differ in each horoscope. For example, the benefic or malefic tendency of a planet may differ as per its placement in exaltation/debilitation rasi, own rasi/star, friendly/enemy rasi/star, different bhavas as per its own lordship and as per its associations and aspects by other friendly/enemy planets etc. Each of these placements, aspects, associations are not of equal importance and they are to be considered giving different weightages for each type of influence. Similarly each bhava is also subjected to influence of different planets.

In this book, a methodology is given to evolve the benefic and malefic percentage of a planet and bhavas in a horoscope considering all the influences that they would be subjected to along with suitable weightages for each type of influence. The predictions of all planets as per their benefic or malefic tendencies with respect to their placement in different rasis and bhavas are enumerated separately under different topics of body, health, temperament and personality, wealth, courage, education, houses and landed property, happiness, children, diseases, enemies, debts, marriage and marital relationship, longevity, prosperity, profession, gains and income, losses and expenditure. Once each planet and bhava are analysed for its benefic and malefic percentage for a particular horoscope, the predictions on all important aspects of life can be given as per the concerned ruling main, sub and interperiod planets.

The tables of the periods of the ruling main, sub and interperiod planets from the time of birth are calculated as per the Vimsottari Dasa system of Hindu astrology.

The complete scheme of analysing the planets and bhavas for a particular horoscope along with broad life predictions for each bhava and yearly predictions for the current ruling main, sub and interperiod planets, is computerised.

A model horoscope in this respect is also given for ready interpretation of this new methodology.

Contents

CHAPTER I

Introduction

Astrology is a science as well as an art. It is true that the astrological predictions simply cannot be based upon strict mathematical calculations and analysis, but a certain amount of intuitive capacity must be brought to bear upon such attempts. Nevertheless, this science has been most wonderfully cultivated by many of the astrologers for a long time, resulting in many calculations for Varga charts, Shadbala strengths of planets, Astakavarga predictions etc. Simultaneously, many predictions have also been enumerated simply on the basis of Rasi chart and sometimes coupled with Navamsa chart. It was felt that neither the predictions based on the elaborate calculations nor based on the cursory look at the Rasi chart, resulted in any real fruitful predictions. It has also been felt that it would not be really easy using the various calculations and rules of all Varga charts, Shadbala strengths of planets, inter-dependence of planets etc., in interpreting the predictions.

In view of the above, a via-media solution was found for ease of predictions by mathematically analysing the percentage benefic and malefic tendencies of each planet in a horoscope considering the various influences it was subjected to, giving suitable weightages for each type of influence The Rasi, Navamsa and Bhava charts are taken for this purpose of calculations, though the inclusion of other Varga charts may give better planetary analysis. Once the planets are analysed for their percentage benefic and malefic nature, the twelve bhavas can also be analysed for their percentage benefic and malefic tendencies with respect to the different planets influencing the bhavas. Subsequently, the benefic or malefic predictions of the ruling main planets, sub-planets and inter-planets under the circumstances can be given on the basis of their position in Rasi, Bhava and Lordship as per the standard norms laid down and the results are to be attributed to one's own social, environmental, economic/cultural circumstances. Of course, the transit results of the planets (Gochara) may be subsequently coupled as given in any standard text book on astrology.

The calculations for preparing the Rasi, Navamsa and Bhava charts and Vimsottari Dasas of planets are not dealt with, since these are given in all standard astrological books. Bhava chart is to be prepared as per the procedure given by Sri Satyacharya in ancient texts on astrology.

SOME FUNDAMENTALS

The fundamentals used in the analysis of planets and bhavas are given below for ready reference:

Planetary Ownerships, Stars, Exaltation and Debilitation Signs

Planet	Own house	Stars	Exaltation sign	Debilitation sign
Sun	Leo	Krittika Uttara Uttarashadha	Aries	Libra
Moon	Cancer	Rohini Hasta Sravana	Taurus	Scorpio

Planet	Own house	Stars	Exaltation sign	Debilitation sign
Mars	Aries Scorpio	Mrigasira Chitra Dhanistha	Capricorn	Cancer
Mercury	Gemini Virgo	Aslesha Jyeshtha Revati	Virgo	Pisces
Jupiter	Sagittarius Pisces	Punarvasu Vishakha Poorva-bhadrapada	Cancer	Capricorn
Venus	Taurus Libra	Bharani Poorvaphalguni Poorvashadha	Pisces	Virgo
Saturn	Capricorn Aquarius	Pushya Anuradha Uttara-bhadrapada	Libra	Aries
Rahu	Virgo	Ardra Svati Shatabhisha	Taurus	Scorpio
Ketu	Pisces	Asvini Magha Moola	Scorpio	Taurus

Permanent Planetary Relationships

The natural or permanent relationships of planets towards each other is given below:

Planet	Friend	Neutral	Enemy
Sun	Moon, Mars, Jupiter	Mercury	Saturn, Venus, Ketu, Rahu
Mars	Sun, Moon, Jupiter	Venus, Saturn, Ketu, Rahu	Mercury
Mercury	Sun, Venus, Ketu, Rahu	Mars, Jupiter, Saturn	Moon

Planet	Friend	Neutral	Enemy
Jupiter	Sun, Moon, Mars	Saturn, Ketu, Rahu	Mercury, Venus
Venus	Mercury, Saturn, Ketu, Rahu	Mars, Jupiter	Moon, Sun
Saturn	Venus, Mercury, Ketu, Rahu	Jupiter	Sun, Moon, Mars
Rahu	Venus, Saturn, Mercury, Rahu	Mars, Jupiter	Sun, Moon
Ketu	Venus, Saturn, Ketu, Rahu	Mars, Jupiter	Sun, Moon
Moon	Sun, Mercury	Mars, Jupiter, Venus, Saturn	Rahu, Ketu

Temporary Planetary Relationships

Planets are said to become friends and enemies temporarily due to their position from each other in the horoscope. Planets which occupy the 2nd, 3rd, 4th, 10th, 11th, and 12th places from one to the other become friends. Planets in other places from one to another are temporary enemies.

Functional Planetary Relationships

The combined influence of permanent and temporary relationships will determine the functional relationship of planets as follows:

Permanent Friend	+ Temporary Friend	= Best Friend
Permanent Friend	+ Temporary Enemy	= Neutral
Neutral	+ Temporary Enemy	= Enemy
Neutral	+ Temporary Friend	= Friend
Permanent Enemy	+ Temporary Friend	= Neutral
Permanent Enemy	+ Temporary Enemy	= Bitter Enemy

Natural Benefic Planets

Jupiter, Venus, Waxing Moon (from 8th tithi of Shukla Paksha i.e. bright half of lunar month upto 8th tithi of dark half), Mercury alone or when associated with natural benefic planets.

Note: 8th tithi in bright half = longitude of Sun – longitude of Moon is between 84 to 96 degrees (increasing distance).

8th tithi in dark half = decreasing distance between Sun and Moon after Moon reaches 180 degrees from Sun i.e. 96 to 84 degrees.

Natural Malefic Planets
Mars

Saturn, Sun, Waning Moon (from 8th tithi of dark half to 8th tithi of bright half), Mercury when associated with natural malefic planets, Rahu and Ketu.

Lordship Benefic and Malefic Planets for Different Ascendants

Ascendant	Lordship benefic planets	Lordship malefic planets
Aries	Sun, Waning Moon, Mars, Jupiter, Saturn, Venus	Waxing Moon, Saturn, Mercury alone or with natural benefic or malefic, Venus, Rahu, Ketu
Taurus	Sun, Mars, Saturn, Mercury alone or with natural benefic or malefic, Venus, Rahu	Waxing & Waning Moon, Jupiter, Ketu
Gemini	Waxing & Waning Moon, Saturn, Mercury alone or with natural benefic or malefic, Venus, Rahu, Ketu	Sun, Mars, Jupiter, Saturn, Mercury alone or with natural benefic
Cancer	Sun, Waxing & Waning Moon, Mars, Jupiter, Saturn, Ketu	Jupiter, Saturn, Mercury alone or with natural benefic or malefic, Venus, Rahu
Leo	Sun, Mars, Jupiter, Saturn, Mercury alone or with natural benefic or malefic, Ketu	Waxing & Waning Moon, Jupiter, Saturn, Mercury alone or with natural benefic or malefic, Venus, Ketu
Virgo	Saturn, Mercury alone or with natural benefic or malefic, Venus, Rahu, Ketu	Sun, Waxing & Waning Moon, Mars, Jupiter, Satum, Mercury alone or with natural benefic
Libra	Waning Moon, Mars, Satum, Mercury alone or with natural benefic or malefic, Venus	Sun, Waxing Moon, Jupiter, Rahu, Ketu

Ascendant	Lordship benefic planets	Lordship malefic planets
Scorpio	Sun, Waxing & Waning Moon, Mars, Jupiter, Saturn, Ketu	Mercury alone or with natural benefic or malefic, Venus, Rahu
Sagittarius	Sun, Mars, Jupiter, Saturn, Mercury alone or with natural malefic, Rahu, Ketu	Waxing & Waning Moon, Jupiter, Saturn, Mercury alone, Venus
Capricorn	Waning Moon, Mars, Saturn, Mercury alone or with natural benefic or malefic, Venus, Rahu	Sun, Waxing Moon, Mars. Jupiter, Mercury alone or with natural benefic or malefic Ketu
Aquarius	Sun, Mars, Jupiter, Saturn, Mercury alone or with natural benefic or malefic, Venus, Ketu	Waxing & Waning Moon, Mars, Jupiter, Mercury alone or with natural benefic or malefic, Rahu
Pisces	Waxing & Waning Moon, Mars, Jupiter, Mercury alone or with natural malefic, Rahu, Ketu	Sun, Jupiter, Saturn, Mercury alone or with natural benefic, Venus

Note: Some of the planets are both lordship benefic and malefic since one lordship is for a benefic house and the other is for malefic house such as Jupiter for Leo Ascendant is benefic lord for 5th house and malefic lord for 8th house.

Karaka Planets for Different Bhavas

I	bhava	-	Sun
II	bhava	-	Jupiter
III	bhava	-	Mars
IV	bhava	-	Moon, Mercury, Venus, Jupiter, Mars
V	bhava	-	Jupiter
VI	bhava	-	Mars, Saturn
VII	bhava	-	Venus
VIII	bhava	-	Saturn
IX	bhava	-	Sun, Jupiter
X	bhava	-	Sun, Mercury, Jupiter, Saturn
XI	bhava	-	Jupiter
XII	bhava	-	Saturn

Aspects of Planets

All planets aspect the 7th bhava counted from their positions. In addition, Saturn aspects 3rd and 10th bhavas, Mars aspects 4th and 8th bhavas and Jupiter aspects 5th and 9th bhavas counted from their positions.

Deities, Jewels, Colours and Numbers for Planets

The following are the Deities, Jewels, Colours and Numbers which should be used for different planets to strengthen the benefic tendencies or to lessen the malefic tendencies of the planets during their periods:

Planet	Deity	Jewel	Colour	Numbers
Sun	Siva	Ruby	Copper Colour	1 and 4
Moon	Parvati	Pearl	White	2 and 7
Mars	Subrahmanya	Coral	Deep red	9
Rahu	Adishesha	Gomed	Dark	8
Jupiter	Brahma	Topaz	Yellow	3
Saturn	Venkateshwara	Sapphire	Dark	8
Ketu	Ganesha	Cat's eye	Deep red	9
Mercury	Vishnu	Emerald	Green	5
Venus	Lakshmi	Diamond	Variegated colours	6

CHAPTER II

Benefic and Malefic
Analysis of Planets

Planets as per their disposition in a horoscope are subjected to various influences. As given in Chapter I, the planets are identified in various situations in a horoscope. Suitable weightages are given to every particular type of situation. Net weightage and percentage of benefic and malefic tendencies of each planet is calculated.

The following are the various types of benefic and malefic situations and influences that the planets are subjected to in a horoscope. The suggested weightage points are given in brackets for each situation. Aspects and associations of planets are taken from Rasi chart. Positioning of planets in bhavas is taken from Bhava chart.

BENEFIC ANALYSIS

If natural benefic (1)

If lordship benefic (1)

If in own sign (2)

If in exaltation (3)

If debilitated retrograde (3)

If in functional friend's sign (1)

If in lordship benefic's sign (2)

If in natural benefic's sign (1)

If in functional friend's star (1)
If in own star (2)
If in lordship benefic's star (2)
If in natural benefic star (1)
If functional friend of ascendant lord (2)
If in association with functional friend (1)
If in association with lordship benefic (2)
If in association with natural benefic (1)
If aspected by functional friend (1)
If aspected by lordship benefic (2)
If aspected by natural benefic (1)
As natural malefic in 3rd, 6th, 10th or 11th bhavas (1)
As natural benefic not in 12th bhava (1)
As lordship benefic not in 6th, 8th, or 12th bhavas (2)
As Vargottama i.e. same house in Rasi and Navamsa charts (3)
In exaltation in Navamsa chart (3)
In own sign in Navamsa chart (2)
In functional friend's sign in Navamsa chart (1).

MALEFIC ANALYSIS

If natural malefic (1)
If lordship malefic (1)
If in debilitation (2)
If exalted retrograde (2)
If in functional enemy's sign (1)
If in lordship malefic's sign (1)
If in natural malefic's sign (1)
If in functional enemy's star (1)
If in natural malefic's star (1)
If in lordship malefic's star (2)
If functional enemy of ascendant lord (2)
If in association with functional enemy (1)
If in association with lordship malefic (2)

If in association with natural malefic (1)

If aspected by functional enemy (1)

If aspected by lordship malefic (2)

If natural malefic (2)

As natural malefic not in 3rd, 6th, 10th or 11th bhavas (1)

As natural benefic in 12th bhava (1)

As lordship benefic in 6th, 8th or 12th bhavas (2)

As lordship malefic not in 6th, 8th or 12th bhavas (2)

If in debilitation in Navamsa chart (2)

If in functional enemy's sign in Navamsa chart (1)

LORDSHIP BENEFIC AND MALEFIC WEIGHTAGES FOR DIFFERENT ASCENDANTS

The weightages for lordship benefic and malefic planets for different Ascendants are given as follows:

"B" represents the lordship benefic and "M" represents the lordship malefic. Weightages are suggested in the brackets.

Ascendants

	Aries	Taurus	Gemini	Cancer	Leo	Virgo
Sun	5th lord B(1)	4th lord B(1)	3rd lord M(1)	2nd lord B(1)	Ist lord B(2)	12th lord M(1)
Waxing Moon	4th lord M(1)	3rd lord M(1)	2nd lord B(1)	Ist lord B(2)	12th lord M(1)	11th lord M(1)
Waning Moon	4th lord B(1)	3rd lord M(1)	2nd lord B(1)	Ist lord B(2)	12th lord M(1)	11th lord M(1)
Mars	Ist lord B(2)	7th lord B(1)	6th lord M(1)	5th lord B(1)	4th lord B(1)	3rd lord B(1)
	8th lord M(0)	12th lord M(0)	11th lord M(1)	10th lord B(1)	9th lord B(1)	8th lord M(1)
Jupiter	9th lord B(1)	8th lord M(1)	7th lord M(1)	6th lord M(1)	5th lord B(1)	4th lord M(1)
	12th lord M(0)	11th lord M(1)	10th lord M(1)	9th lord B(1)	8th lord M(1)	7th lord M(1)

	Aries	Taurus	Gemini	Cancer	Leo	Virgo
Saturn	10th lord B(1)	9th lord B(1)	8th lord M(1)	7th lord B(1)	6th lord M(1)	5th lord B(1)
	11th lord M(1)	10th lord B(1)	9th lord B(1)	8th lord M(1)	7th lord B(1)	6th lord M(1)
Mercury alone or with	3rd lord M(1)	2nd lord B(1)	Ist lord B(2)	12th lord M(1)	11th lord M(1)	10th lord M(1)
natural benefic	6th lord M(1)	5th lord B(1)	4th lord M(1)	3rd lord M(1)	2nd lord B(1)	Ist lord B(2)
Mercury alone or with	3rd lord M(1)	2nd lord B(1)	Ist lord B(2)	12th lord M(1)	11th lord M(1)	10th lord M(1)
natural malefic	6th lord M(1)	5th lord B(1)	4th lord B(1)	3rd lord M(1)	2nd lord B(1)	Ist lord B(2)
Venus	2nd lord B(1)	Ist lord B(2)	12th lord M(0)	11th lord M(1)	10th lord M(1)	9th lord B(1)
	7th lord M(1)	6th lord M(0)	5th lord B(1)	4th lord M(1)	3rd lord M(1)	2nd lord B(1)
Rahu	6th lord M(1)	5th lord B(1)	4th lord B(1)	3rd lord M(1)	2nd lord B(1)	Ist lord B(2)
Ketu	12th lord M(0)	11th lord M(1)	10th lord B(1)	9th lord B(1)	8th lord M(1)	7th lord B(1)

	Libra	Scorpio	Sagittarius	Capricorn	Aquarius	Pisces
Sun	11th lord M(1)	10th lord B(1)	9th lord B(1)	8th lord M(0)	7th lord B(1)	6th lord M(1)
Waxing Moon	10th lord M(1)	9th lord B(1)	8th lord M(0)	7th lord M(1)	6th lord M(1)	5th lord B(1)
Waning Moon	10th lord B(1)	9th lord B(1)	8th lord M(0)	7th lord B(1)	6th lord M(1)	5th lord B(1)
Mars	2nd lord B(1)	Ist lord B(2)	12th lord M(0)	11th lord M(1)	10th lord B(1)	9th lord B(1)
	7th lord B(1)	6th lord M(0)	5th lord B(1)	4th lord B(1)	3rd lord M(1)	2nd lord B(1)
Jupiter	3rd lord M(1)	2nd lord B(1)	Ist lord B(2)	12th lord M(1)	11th lord M(1)	10th lord M(1)
	6th lord M(1)	5th lord B(1)	4th lord M(1)	3rd lord M(1)	2nd lord B(1)	Ist lord B(2)

	Libra	Scorpio	Sagittarius	Capricorn	Aquarius	Pisces
Saturn	4th lord B(1)	3rd lord B(1)	2nd lord B(1)	Ist lord B(2)	12th lord M(0)	11th lord M(1)
	5th lord B(1)	4th lord B(1)	3rd lord M(1)	2nd lord B(1)	1st lord B(2)	12th lord M(1)
Mercury alone or with natural benefic	9th lord B(1)	8th lord M(1)	7th lord M(1)	6th lord M(1)	5th lord B(1)	4th lord M(1)
	12th lord M(0)	11th lord M(1)	10th lord M(1)	9th lord B(1)	8th lord M(1)	7th lord M(1)
Mercury alone or with natural malefic	9th lord B(1)	8th lord M(1)	7th lord B(1)	6th lord M(1)	5th lord B(1)	4th lord B(1)
	12th lord M(0)	11th lord M(1)	10th lord B(1)	9th lord B(1)	8th lord M(1)	7th lord B(1)
Venus	Ist lord B(2)	12th lord M(1)	11th lord M(1)	10th lord B(1)	9th lord B(1)	8th lord M(1)
	8th lord M(0)	7th lord M(1)	6th lord M(1)	5th lord B(1)	4th lord M(1)	3rd lord M(1)
Rahu	12th lord M(1)	11th lord M(1)	10th lord B(1)	9th lord B(1)	8th lord M(1)	7th lord B(1)
Ketu	6th lord M(1)	5th lord B(1)	4th lord B(1)	3rd lord M(1)	2nd lord B(1)	Ist lord B(2)

CHAPTER III

Benefic and Malefic Analysis of Bhavas

There are twelve bhavas representing various aspects of life. Each bhava is subjected to the influence of different planets. The benefic and malefic percentages of planets are already calculated as given in Chapter II.

The planets influencing the bhavas along with the weightages are as follows:

Planets in the bhava (1)

Lord of the bhava (1)

Planets aspecting the bhava (1/2)

Cusp star lord of the bhava (1/2)

Planets associated with the bhava lord (1/2)

Planets aspecting the bhava lord (1/3)

Karakas of the bhava (1/2).

The net weightages and the final benefic and malefic percentages for each bhava are calculated. The Bhava chart is considered for these purposes.

For example, if two planets aspect the bhava having benefic 4 points and malefic 2 points, the weightage for the condition of "Planets aspecting the bhava" would be benefic 2 points and malefic 1 point because only a weightage of 1/2 is to be taken. Similarly, the weightages for other conditions are found and the net weightages and percentage benefic and malefic are calculated for each bhava.

Knowing the planets which influence each bhava, a list of planets signifying different bhavas can be made.

CHAPTER IV

Broad Life Predictions

Broad life predictions, which may, broadly cover the general pattern on different aspects of life, can be given based on the benefic and malefic analysis of different bhavas. If the benefic percentage of a bhava is 50% or more, it can be taken that the results of that bhava would give benefic results. If the malefic percentage of bhava is 55% or more, results of that particular bhava would be malefic in general. If the malefic percentage of a bhava is between 50% and 55%, the results of that bhava would be moderate. It should be appreciated that even if the benefic percentage of a particular bhava is 70% or so, the effects of that bhava would result in a benefic way only upto 70% (i.e. 70 out of 100 points) and still 30% of malefic results may occur. Similarly, if the malefic percentage of a bhava is 70%, it does not mean that the aspects of that bhava would be totally malefic or bad in life; still 30% benefic results may happen.

For example, if the percentage of the tenth bhava is 70% benefic, it can be taken that the conditions of Profession, Respect etc. pertaining to the significations of the tenth bhava would be definitely very good in life in general. Similarly, if the seventh bhava percentage is 70% malefic, it can be considered that in general the aspects relating to marriage, marital relationship and partnership in life would not go very smooth. Similarly, all other aspects of life are to be understood.

The general characteristics of each Ascendant with respect to the aspects of body, health and temperament and personality and the benefic, malefic and moderate predictions of each bhava are given.

The study of the Model Horoscope given in Chapter VI will throw more light in understanding while giving broad life predictions.

PREDICTIONS OF DIFFERENT ASCENDANTS (LAGNAS)

(I) BODY

(A) Aries Ascendant

You may be of middle stature with round eyes which may be slightly copper coloured. You may have a sharp sight. Your face and neck may be long. Your head may be broad at the temples and narrow at chin. You may have brown or light dark and curly hair. There may be a mark or scar on the head or temples. You may have well set teeth. You are likely to have prominent veins or marks of wound on your body. Your build may be slender. You may generally possess perfect contours. You may have weak knees and nails.

(B) Taurus Ascendant

You may be short, often tending towards corpulence or stoutness. You may have broad beautiful face with large eyes, ears and thick lips. Your body build may be of square type. You may have full forehead. Your hands and thighs may be plump and broad. There may be some mark on the back or sides. You may have an agreeable appearance.

(C) Gemini Ascendant

You may be often tall and straight in stature. You may have a thin and well-developed face. You may have a broad forehead with clear eyes. You may have a prominent but a bit snubbed nose. You may have a depression near the chin. You may be weak. You may have curly hair. You are likely to have fair, handsome and agreeable appearance.

(D) Cancer Ascendant

You may be middle sized and may not be very tall. Your complexion may be white. You may have a full and long face with a nose snubbed to some extent. Your chest may be wide and broad. You are likely to have long arms.

(E) Leo Ascendant

You may have majestic and magnetic appearance probably with an average height. You may have a large and oval face with yellowish eye balls and prominent chin. You may have a thoughtful countenance. Your shoulders may be broad. The upper part of your body may be better formed.

(F) Virgo Ascendant

You may be middle sized with drooping shoulders and arms and prominent chest. You may have a good forehead with straight nose and massive cheek. You may be weak also.

(G) Libra Ascendant

You may have middle sized stature or sometimes tall and lean body. You may have a handsome appearance with broad face and fine eyes. Your features may be regular with broad chest and prominent nose. You may have a youthful appearance.

(H) Scorpio Ascendant

You may have a handsome appearance with tall figure, broad eyes and forehead and curly hair. Your bones will be well-developed. You may have prominent brows. You will have youthful appearance. You may have fierce and big eyes. You may have a broad chest and round thighs, knees and calves. You may have a fish line on the sole of feet.

(I) Sagittarius Ascendant

You may be generally inclined towards corpulence or stoutness. You will be usually good looking with almond eyes, brown hair, well-proportioned teeth and fullness of figure. You may have a large head and neck with prominent nose and ears. You may have bent shoulders. You may have good fleshy arms with bad nails. You are likely to have big teeth and lower lip.

(J) Capricorn Ascendant

You may be tall and lean. You may have stiff hair on the eye brows and the chest. You may have a big head with fairly broad face and large teeth sometimes protruding outside the lips. You may have a big mouth. You are inclined to stoop. Your body may be thin and not fleshy. You may have a prominent nose. You may present an uncouth/awkward appearance. You may have good eyes. The lower part of your body below the waist may be underdeveloped compared to the upper half. You may have a thin waist.

(K) Aquarius Ascendant

You may be generally tall and lean with handsome countenance and attractive appearance and elegant disposition. Your lips may be flushy and cheeks may be broad. You may have prominent temples and buttocks. You may have a weak chest and you may have a tendency to stooping. You may have a large face, neck, back, stomach, waist, thighs and feet. Your ears may be large with hair. Your body may be large with rough hair. You may have prominent veins.

(L) Pisces Ascendant

You may be stout and of middle sized height. You may be inclined towards corpulence or stoutness. You may have a fine body with large head, lustrous face, prominent nose, beautiful eyes and proportionate limbs.

(II) HEALTH

(A) Aries Ascendant

You may have a hot constitution. You may suffer from diseases pertaining to the head. You are likely to have mental affliction and derangement of brain. You may have unpleasant sight seeing. You may be occasionally subjected to hot complaints, piles and the like. You must avoid enterprises obviously involving any serious risks. You may have bad nails and marks of wound on your body.

(B) Taurus Ascendant

Your physical and mental endurances are noteworthy. You may generally suffer from nervous complaints. You will have good memory and powers of imagination. You will be passionate and may fall a prey to sexual diseases. You will have good digestive powers.

(C) Gemini Ascendant

You may have sudden nervous breakdowns. You must be cautious in moving with opposite sex. Your mind will be often conscious of your own depravity.

(D) Cancer Ascendant

You may be nervous. You may have strong emotions and psychic tendencies.

(E) Leo Ascendant

You are likely to suffer from nervous troubles. You may suffer from hunger and thirst or diseases arising therefrom. You may have mental and dental ailments.

(F) Virgo Ascendant

You may be emotional and impulsive. You are liable to suffer from nervous breakdowns or paralysis. You will have a speculative turn of mind.

(G) Libra Ascendant

You will have a sensual disposition. You will suffer in some limb. You may get setbacks in health due to slight causes but you will easily recover.

(H) Scorpio Ascendant

You will be impulsive. You are inclined to sensual things. Your constitution will be hot and you will be liable to suffer from piles. You may be sickly during childhood.

(I) Sagittarius Ascendant

You may be impulsive. You will have phlegmatic temperament. You will exercise strict control over your food and drinks and in regard to your relations with the opposite sex. You must be careful about your lungs. You are liable to suffer from rheumatic pains and the like. You may have bad nails.

(J) Capricorn Ascendant

You may be nervous and weak minded. You will suffer from diseases arising out of 'vata' (wind). You will be allergic to winter and cold. You may have generally good stamina.

(K) Aquarius Ascendant

You may be peevish and liable to suffer from colic pains. You may have chest pain and the like. You should always be kept happy in life by your married partner otherwise your health may suffer. You may have prominent veins. You may indulge in sinful acts for the sake of others' married partners.

(L) Pisces Ascendant

You may be restless.

(III) TEMPERAMENT AND PERSONALITY

(A) Aries Ascendant

You may be proud, heroic, active, aggressive and always on the move or fond of walking. You may have a certain amount of independent thinking, reasoning faculty. You may be ambitious and enterprising. You will be capable and will have the ability to plan. You will not like to be guided by others. You will not be slave to laws of convention or those arbitrarily established. You will be fond of hot food and vegetables and will eat quickly and sparingly. You will be amorous by disposition and fond of opposite sex. You will be intense when interested and vehement when excited. You will be quick tempered. You will have your own ideas of right and wrong. You will be strongly bent upon educational pursuits. You will be rather stubborn but often frank. You will resent imposition and are liable to go to extremes. You will have a practical ideal. You will resort to falsehood in speech. You will be afraid of water. You will be fickleminded sometimes. You will have sudden outbursts of temper but will be easily pleased. You will be courageous and sensitive. You will need a certain amount of cajolery and sycophancy to raise you to action. You will become a pioneer and be martial in spirit. You will love beauty, art and elegance.

(B) Taurus Ascendant

You will be self-reliant and will have a great deal of endurance and latent power and energy. You will generally resemble the bull in your behaviour towards new people if you are not listened to properly. You will have your own principles and ways besides a piercing intellect. You will put your ideas to practice. You will be fond of pleasures, beauty and music. You will be

bound by sentimentality but will appreciate truth. You
will have a magnetic personality. You may be obstinate,
proud and ambitious. You will have a remarkable
ability to commit to memory. You will have business
knack and a surpassing intuition. You may be easily
accessable to adulation. You will be affectionate and
loving. You may be sometimes stubborn, unreasonable
and prejudiced. You will walk sportingly. You will be
fond of women and will have a spirit of sacrifice. You
shall put in hard labour. You will often think that you
are born to exercise authority over others and in a
sense you are right. You are liable to extremes. You
will be jealous. You will be slow to anger but when
provoked you will be furious like a bull.

(C) Gemini Ascendant

You will have sweet speech. You will be learned and
jocular. You will be clever and possess inherent
conversational and literary ability. You will do best in
occupations where there is much activity. You will be
nervous, restless. You will be fond of writing and
reading. You will be ingenious, quickwitted, vivacious
and inconsistent. You will have a wavering mind. You
will be active in motion. You will have to develop a bit
of self-control. You are liable to fraud and deception.
You will have a characteristic nature of trickery and
deceit.

(D) Cancer Ascendant

You will walk swiftly and not in a straightline. You
will be intelligent and fond of astrology or you may be
an astrologer. Your mind will be intuitional, perceptive
and imaginative. You will be bright and extremely
frugal and equally industrious. Your economical nature
will often take the form of miserliness. You may have
sympathy and you may be a coward. You will like
pleasures. Your emotions will be strong and you will
have psychic tendencies. You will be much attached to
children. You will be famous. Your extreme

sensitiveness will render you nervous and queer. You will be receptive to new ideas. You will adapt yourself to any environment. Your mind will be bent upon schemes of trade and manufacture. You will be cautious. You will be desirous of possessions. You can best take up occupations of fluctuating nature. You will be very talkative, self-reliant, honest and unbending. You will be extremely sensitive, inquisitive, nervous and restless. You would like to live near water. You will have many friends and you will be attached to them. You can be brought down by persuasion. You will have reputation as a lover of justice and fairplay.

(E) Leo Ascendant

You will be proud, ambitious as well as avaricious. You will be warm-hearted. You will be of sacrificing spirit. You will be bold and respectful in temperament. You will possess the knack of adapting to any condition of life. You will have a liking for art and music. You will have cheerful and unimpulsive temperament. You will be sensitive. You will have a fixed determination but will get unjustifiably into a bad temper at the slightest provocation but the anger will be quickly pacified. You will have faith and you will be sincere in affection. You will hold a grudge long. You will be an independent thinker. You will stick to orthodoxical principles in religion but be preferably tolerant towards other's precepts and practices. You will be generally misunderstood by your superiors and bosses. You will get on well with women. You will be fond of forests and mountains. You will be courageous and heroic and capable of prevailing upon others. You will be a lover of fine arts and literature and possess a certain amount of philosophical knowledge. You will be a voracious reader. You will lack a natural policy.

(F) Virgo Ascendant

You will speak slowly and truthfully. You will exhibit intelligence and memory when quite young. You will be clever in arts and crafts and you will also exhibit taste in art and literature. You will be fond of female company, You will be discriminating and emotional and will be carried away by impulses. You will be religious, learned and discriminating with intelligence and have a good memory. You can judge things at a glance. You will be careful about your own interests. You will be prudent, economical, diplomatic, and shrewd. You will have a speculative turn of mind. You will love music and fine arts. You will acquire much power and influence over other people.

(G) Libra Ascendant

You will be idealistic, quickwitted, vindictive, forceful and positive. You will be a keen observer of human nature. You will have sensual disposition. You will have keen foresight and reason out things from the standpoint of your own views. You will love justice, peace, order and you will be an agreeable person. You will be intelligent, clean, very active and devoted to gods and brahmins. You will be ambitious. You will be firm in convictions and unmoved by mean motives. You will be somewhat susceptible to feelings of others. You will be more of an idealist than a realist and often contemplate upon schemes like building castles in the air. You will be clever in purchase and sale of goods. You will be skilful and act impartially as arbitrator. You will not be sensitive to what others say about you. You will exert tremendous influence over the masses as political leaders and religious reformers. Sometimes your zeal and enthusiasm may go to such a high pitch that you will force your views upon others of opposite thought, not realising the baneful after-effects of such a practice. You will not hesitate to sacrifice even your living at the altar of freedom and fairplay. You will love excitement. You will not be easily amenable to reason. You will be great a lover of music. You will have special liking for trust and honesty.

(H) Scorpio Ascendant

You may be cruelly inclined. You will be sarcastic and impulsive. You will appreciate luxury but be frugal. You will never speak without weighing each and every word. You will be silent and dignified. You will set at naught conventional habits and customs. You will be extremely fickle-minded. You will love much excitement. You will invite friendship. You will be a good correspondent. You can become an expert musician if you care to practise. You may be proficient in fine arts, dancing and the like. You will vehemently uphold your views but nevertheless will not clash with those holding opposite views. You will be inclined to sensual things but you may control your sensual pleasures. You may be fond of writing. You will often rely too much on your own intelligence. You will have a youthful appearance and a generous disposition. You will be interested in occult forms of study. You will have a subtle mind. You will be influenced with difficulty. You may be often brutal. You will possess gift and enterprise. You will be keenly fond of contest.

(I) Sagittarius Ascendant

You will be active and engaged in work. You will have inclination for philosophy and occult studies and you can acquire great mastery in these subjects. You will be prone to be misunderstood by others unintentionally on account of your haste in conversation. You will never think of schemes to disturb the progress of others. You will hate all external show. You will be god-fearing, honest, humble and free from hypocrisy. You will have strict control over your food and drinks and in regard to your relationship with the opposite sex. You will be brilliant. You will have affable and winning manners. You will be of a pure heart. You will be too conventional and sometimes business-like also. You will be too callous and enthusiastic. You will be prompt and will uphold orthodox views. You will be at times restless and over anxious. You will be humane and somewhat impulsive. You will be enterprising, sympathetic and loving. You will possess good foresight. You will be eloquent in speech. You will be religious and prepared to sacrifice for others. You may be inimical to relations. You cannot be brought round by force but can be prevailed upon by persuasion only. You will overpower your enemies.

(J) Capricorn Ascendant

You will make a big show of being religious though in reality you may not be so religious. You will be self willed, secretive, cunning and determined. You will have the knack to adapt to different circumstances and environments. You will be full of sympathy, generosity and philanthrophy. You will be a chatterbox and will have little or no control over your tongue. You will be noted for your perseverence and strong mindedness. You will be capable of much endeavour. You will be industrious. You will be modest, liberal and sometimes vindictive. You may not easily get on well with your partner. You may be cruel, avaricious, indolent and devoid of shame. You will be fond of walking. You may be an expert in poetry. You may lack confidence and become faulty. You will have great aspirations in life and cannot economise your funds even if you were to be under the influence of adversity. You will take great interest in literature. You will accept advice. You will be gentlemanly in business transactions. You will be stoical to the miseries of life. You may be interested in science and education. You would like to have a lot of show. You will be possessed of an invincible bigotry before which sober counsels will be of no avail. You will be nervous and weak minded. You will dodge your married partner and children.

(K) Aquarius Ascendant

You will be capable of putting hard labour or trying journeys. You may become a teacher, writer or lecturer.

You will be highly intelligent with winning manners and elegant disposition. You will have something subtle in you which will endear you to all you come in contact with. You will be prone to be misunderstood. You will not have sufficient happiness in your family life due to short temper of your married partner. You will betray the interests of even your enemies when trust is placed in you. You will be capable of acquiring very fine education. You will be devoted to your partner. You will soon make friends. You will be clever in attacking others. You should always be kept happy in life by your partner otherwise you may feel very unhappy. You will be peevish and when provoked you will rise like a bull-dog but your anger will be soon subsided. You will be pure in heart and will always be inclined to help others. You may be timid and funky and at times cowardly also. You may indulge in sinful acts for the sake of others' partners. You will be shy to exhibit your talents before a new audience but your conversation will be the most interesting and highly instructive. You may specialise in subjects like astrology. You may be avaricious. You will be fond of scents and flowers. You may be reserved. You will be generous and highly sympathetic, always bent upon helping others. You will have a good memory and will be capable of dealing with facts owing to your humanitarian doctrines. Your literary greatness may come when you are quite young. You will not be able to estimate your capacity well. You will have intuition. You will be a good judge of character. You may have good organising capacity.

(L) Pisces Ascendant

You will be attached to your partner. You will be fond of clothes. You may lack self-confidence. You will be just in your dealings and will be afraid of transgressing laws of truth. You will be under the influence of your married partner. Though generally dependent upon others you will still bear a mark of your own independence. You will be reserved in your manners. You will be rigid in observance of orthodoxical principles and can forego anything but your orthodoxy. You will overcome your enemies. You will be learned and grateful. You will be liable to draw premature conclusions on any matter. You will be god fearing and extremely superstitious and religious. You may drink water frequently and in large quantities. You will be proud of your educational and other attainments. You will be ambitious to exercise authority over others. You may be stubborn, restless and rather timid. You will be physically receptive and stoical. You may be fond of history, antiquarian talks and mythological masterpieces. You will be frugal in spending.

BROAD LIFE PREDICTIONS

(I) FIRST BHAVA
Body, Health, Temperament and Personality

If Benefic:

You may have good body structure. You are likely to maintain good health. Your temperament and personality will be affable.

If Malefic:

Your body structure may not be good. You may suffer from ill health. You may not have a good temperament or a pleasing personality.

If Moderate:

You are likely to have medium body structure. You may not expect very good health. Your temperament and personality may be of moderate nature.

(II) SECOND BHAVA
Wealth, Speech, Family, Face and Eyes, Food

If Benefic:

You are likely to be wealthy. You can speak well. You will have a good family. You may have a fair face with good eyes. You can expect to enjoy good food.

If Malefic:

You may not be wealthy. Your speech may not be good. You may have a troubled family. Your face and eyes may not be attractive. You may not be able to enjoy good food.

If Moderate:

You are not likely to be very wealthy. You may be moderate in your speech. You may have a limited family. Your face and eyes may be alright. You may not enjoy very good food.

(III) THIRD BHAVA
Courage, Younger Brothers and Sisters, Throat, Arms, Shoulders, Communications, Relatives, Friends

If Benefic:

You will be courageous. You may have younger brothers and sisters or your relations with them may be good. You will have good throat, arms and shoulders. You will maintain good communications with others. You may have friends and relatives.

If Malefic:

You may not be courageous. You may not have younger brothers and sisters or your relations with them may not be good. There may be problems in your throat, arms and shoulders. You may not be good at communicating with others. You may not have many friends and relatives.

If Moderate:

You may not be very courageous. You may not have younger brothers and sisters or you may have only moderate relationship with them. Your throat, arms and shoulders may not give you much problems. Your communicating skills may be satisfactory. You may have limited friends and relatives.

(IV) FOURTH BHAVA

Education, Houses, Landed Property, Conveyance, Mother, Chest, Heart, General Happiness

If Benefic:

You will get good education. You will possess houses, landed property and conveyance. You will have a good mother. Your chest and heart will not give problems. You will enjoy good general happiness.

If Malefic:

You may not get good education or there may be breaks in your education. You may not acquire many houses, landed property and conveyance. Your mother may suffer ill health or your relations with her may not be good. Your chest and heart may cause worry to you. You may not have general happiness.

If Moderate:

You may not be highly educated. Your acquisition of houses, landed property and conveyance may be limited. You may maintain moderate relationship with your mother or she may not maintain good health. Your chest may not give you much problem and the functioning of your heart may be satisfactory. You may not expect general happiness.

(V) FIFTH BHAVA
Children, Wisdom, Intelligence, Stomach

If Benefic:

You may have children. You will be endowed with good wisdom and intelligence. Your stomach will function well.

If Malefic:

You may not have children or may have few children. Your wisdom and intelligence may be misdirected. You are likely to have stomach problems.

If Moderate:

You may have limited children. Your wisdom and intelligence may be satisfactory. Your stomach may function in a moderate fashion.

(VI) SIXTH BHAVA
Diseases, Enemies, Debts

If Benefic:

You will not suffer from diseases. You will not have enemies or you will conquer over your enemies. You will not be indebted.

If Malefic:

You may suffer from diseases: Your enemies are likely to have a sway over you. You may incur debts.

If Moderate:

Your diseases may not give you much trouble. You may have limited enemies or you may be able to deal with your enemies. Your debts may be moderate and under control.

(VII) SEVENTH BHAVA
Marriage, Wife/Husband, Marital Relationship, Business Partnership

If Benefic:

You will have a good partner. You will enjoy good marital relationship. Your business partnership will fructify.

If Malefic:

You may not have a very compatible partner and you may suffer from matrimonial happiness. You may lose in your business partnership.

If Moderate:

Your partner may be just normal and your marital relationship may be satisfactory. You may have moderate success in your business partnership.

(VIII) EIGHTH BHAVA
Longevity, Legacies, Secret Organs

If Benefic:

You can expect a long life. You may inherit legacies. You may not have problems with your secret organs.

If Malefic:

You may not expect a very long life. You may not inherit much legacies. Your secret organs may give you problems.

If Moderate:

You may have a normal life span. You may inherit legacies of moderate nature. You may have to guard against diseases of your secret organs.

(IX) NINTH BHAVA
Prosperity, Father, Devotion to Gods and Religious Preceptors, Long Journeys, Hips, Thighs

If Benefic:

You will have good prosperity. Your father will be well-placed. You may be devoted to gods or religious preceptors. You may go on long journeys. Your hips and thighs will be strong.

If Malefic:

You may not expect overall good prosperity. You may not have a highly prosperous father. You may not be interested in gods or religious preceptors. You may not often have long journeys. You may suffer in your hips and thighs.

If Moderate:

You may expect overall good prosperity. Your father may be moderately placed in life. You may take some interest in gods or religious preceptors. You may sometimes go on long journeys. Your hips and thighs may not give problems.

(X) TENTH BHAVA
Profession, Status and Position, Respect, Travels, Life and Activity, Knees, Back

If Benefic:

You will have a good profession. Your status and position will grow. You will be respected. You can expect good travels. Your life and activity will be jubiliant. You will have strong knees and back.

If Malefic:

You may not have a very good profession. You may not expect very good status and position. You may not be respected. You may not expect good travels. Your

life and activity may not be very good. Your knees and
back may be weak.

If Moderate:

Your profession may be satisfactory. You may have
normal status and position. You may command
moderate respect. You may have travels. Your life and
activity may not be very jubiliant. Your knees and back
may not give you much probem.

(XI) ELEVENTH BHAVA
Gains and Income, Elder Brothers and Sisters, Calves of Legs

If Benefic:

You will have good gains and income. You may have
elder brothers and sisters or your relation with them
may be good. You will have strong calves of the legs.

If Malfic:

You may not expect much gains and income. You may
not have elder brothers and sisters or you may not
maintain good relations with them. The calves of your
legs may be weak.

If Moderate:

You can expect moderate gains and income. You may
have elder brothers and sisters or you may maintain
moderate relationship with them. The calves of your
legs may not give problems.

(XII) TWELFTH BHAVA
Losses and Expenditure, Moksha (Enlightenment), Foreign Travels, Sexual Enjoyment, Confinement or Imprisonment, Teeth

If Benefic:

Your expenditure may be for good causes. You may

not have much losses. You can expect to attain Moksha (enlightenment). You will undertake foreign travels. You will have good sexual enjoyment. You may not suffer from confinement or imprisonment. Your teeth will be strong.

If Malefic:

You may incur heavy expenditure and suffer losses or your expenditure may not be for good causes. You may not get Moksha (enlightenment). You may not undertake foreign travels. You may not expect to have very good sexual enjoyment. You may suffer from confinement or imprisonment. Your teeth may give problems.

If Moderate:

You may have tolerable expenditure and losses. You may expect to get Moksha (enlightenment). You may have a chance of foreign travels. Your sexual enjoyment may be normal. There may be a chance of being confined or imprisoned. You may face decay of your teeth.

CHAPTER V

Yearly Predictions

As per the degrees of the positioning of Moon in a particular Rasi Chart at the time of birth, the balance of period of the particular planet ruling at the time of birth can be calculated. As per the Vimsottari Dasa System, the subsequent ruling periods of main planets, periods of sub-planets in the periods of main planets and the inter-periods in the periods of sub-planets can be calculated for the cycle of 120 years.

The significant planets for different bhavas are known from Chapter III and since each bhava represents certain main aspects of life such as body, health, wealth, houses, children, diseases, marriage, prosperity, profession, gains etc., the planets signifying the main aspects of life can be found. Accordingly, the results of the ruling planets can be enumerated on different aspects of life in relation to their positioning in a particular Rasi, Bhava and Lordship of Bhavas.

If the ruling main planet is 50% or more benefic, the benefic results of the planet as per the circumstances of its situation in a horoscope can be taken in general. However, it should be remembered that the extent of the benefic or malefic results would be limited only to the extent of the percentage of benefic or malefic given.

During the sub-period of a planet in the main period of another planet, the net percentage of the sub-period is considered taking the average of the benefic and malefic percentages of the main and sub-period planets. The original benefic and malefic percentage of the sub-period planet should not be taken, since the sub-period planet would be under the influence of the main period planet. Similarly, the inter-period benefic and malefic percentage is worked out taking the average of the benefic and malefic percentages of the main period planet, sub-period planet and the inter-period planet.

The results of the sub-period planets and the inter-period planets are given similar to the results of the main period planets as per their significations of different life aspects.

The predictions can be based broadly only on what all the planets can give under the circumstances in which they are situated in a horoscope depending on the extent of their percentage benefic and malefic influences. The predictions should be picked up judiciously, deligently, cautiously and intelligently pertaining to one's own social, environmental, economical and cultural circumstances.

The different types of predictions, given by all planets, based on their different situations are enumerated under the benefic and malefic categories separately so that the predictions can be picked up easily depending on the benefic or malefic nature of the planets. The Model Horoscope given in Chapter VI would give an indication of the type of predictions.

PREDICTIONS OF DIFFERENT PLANETS INFLUENCING DIFFERENT BHAVAS
(I) DIFFERENT PLANETS INFLUENCING FIRST BHAVA
Body

Sun, if Benefic:

Your body appearance may be expected to be of a stately and dignified stature. You may have good appearance and nobleness of figure. You are likely to improve your complexion.

Sun, if Malefic:

You may not have a stately and dignified body appearance. You may lose lustre of your body. You are likely to lose your hair, tending towards baldness or you may have scanty hair on the head.

Mars, if Benefic:

You are likely to have youthful body figure.

Mars, if Malefic:

You may have scars or eruptions on the body. You may become stout and may not look very tall.

Mercury, if Benefic:

You will be endowed with a good body and complexion.

Mercury, if Malefic:

Your body may become thin with prominent veins.

Jupiter, if Benefic:

You will have magnetic appearance, good body, abundant life force, attractive and adorable face. You will practise exercises that build up your constitution and health. You may improve your complexion.

Jupiter, if Malefic:

You may not have a good body and sufficient life force. Your appearance may not be majestic and attractive. Your body may become fat leading to corpulence. You may also develop a belly.

Venus, if Benefic:

You will have magnetic power and handsome appearance. You may improve complexion.

Venus, if Malefic:

You may not have magnetic personality. There may be some defect in your eyes.

Saturn, if Benefic:

You may be good looking.

Saturn, if Malefic:

You are likely to have a weak emaciated body. You may have defective teeth. You are likely to have hard limbs. Your complexion may be reduced.

Rahu, if Benefic:

You are likely to have a good body.

Rahu, if Malefic:

You may have a weak and thin body and your complexion may not be fair.

Ketu, if Benefic:

You may have a good figure.

Ketu, if Malefic:

You may not have a good figure and your complexion may be reduced.

Moon, if Benefic:

You will have attractive youthful appearance with slender and well-shaped body. You will have good eyes and hair. You may have greater delicay of body. Your complexion will improve.

Moon, if Malefic:

Your body is likely to be a little stout.

Health

Sun, if Benefic:

You will have a good constitution with satisfactory immunity. You will tend to be well-supported by good health and vitality. Your health will also improve.

Sun, if Malefic:

You are likely to have bilious excitement and some ailment in head due to bile. Your body may be of hot constitution and it may be burning sensation. Your blood may become impure and there may be itches and inflammations over the body. You may suffer from eye and skin trouble, heart diseases or fevers. There may be no bodily happiness and you may expect general ill health.

Mars, if Benefic:

You will have good health.

Mars, if Malefic:

You may be prone to cuts, hurts, burns and accidents on your body. You may have heated constitution and there may be eruptions or boils or scars on your body. There may be diseases of stomach, eye, throat or teeth. You may have bilious complaints, impurity of blood, fevers and excessive thirst. There may be fracture of bones or injury to marrow. Abuse of physical resources may lead to your ill health.

Mercury, if Benefic:

You will have good physical activity and your health will be normal.

Mercury, if Malefic:

You may get nervous troubles and a sort of head-ache. You are likely to have eye, throat, skin or mental troubles. Your health may suffer from gastric, bilious or phlegmatic complaints.

Jupiter, if Benefic:

You will have good health. You may practise exercises that build-up your constitution and health. You will have abundant life force.

Jupiter, if Malefic:

Your body may become corpulent and stout leading to health complications. Your self-indulgence especially in regard to gluttony may effect your health. You are likely to suffer from impure blood, intestinal diseases, ear troubles, giddiness, fainting or indigestion. Your composition may be of phlegmatic nature.

Venus, if Benefic:

Your health will improve and your body will get energised.

Venus, if Malefic:

You may suffer from gastric and phlematic complaints. You may have low vitality. You may suffer from anaemia, kidney or urinary distress, eye disease, rickets or diabeties. Your cheeks may get affected.

Saturn, if Benefic:

You will be strong-minded and will maintain good health.

Saturn, if Malefic:

You may be sickly. Your health may be reduced due to cerebral complaints, pains, rheumatism, colic pains, overheat, fatigue, general debility, injury to body, stones in gall bladder or spinal cord troubles. You may suffer from gastric complaints. Your body may be weak and emaciated.

Rahu, if Benefic:

You will have good health.

Rahu, if Malefic:

You may be attacked by contagious diseases. Your body may become emaciated. Your health may be generally unsatisfactory calling for treatment other than normal medical methods. You may suffer from diseases of head or in the upper part of your body. You may be sickly and suffer ill health.

Ketu, if Benefic:

You will maintain good health.

Ketu, if Malefic:

You may suffer from diseases of chronic and acute nature. You may have a emaciated figure and weak constitution. You may get great perspiration. You may suffer from piles or fever. You are likely to get boils on your body due to extreme heat, nervousness which keeps you restless and worried and you may also have ill health due to morbid imaginations.

Moon, if Benefic:

You will have general bodily happiness, good health and strong constitution. You will have tranquility of mind.

Moon, if Malefic:

You are likely to have hysterical tendencies, considerable restlessness, eye diseases, urinary troubles, weak constitution, defect in the ear, mental disease, drowsiness, diseases of lungs, impurity of blood, asthma or skin diseases.

Temperament and Personality

Sun, if Benefic:

You will have a steady and fixed temperament. You will be of Satwika temperament, having pure thoughts and inclined to acts of religious merit. You will be self-reliant, noble, courageous. You will have a strong moral nature. You are likely to be independent, learned and chivalrous. You may be fond of power and daring deeds. You will add respect to your personality and have positive motives. You will have a strong will. You are determined and not easily moved by your own resolve. Your tendency is for an easy going life. You will have satisfactory good relationship with higher officials. You will be fond of reputation, authority, and position. You will have personal magnetism. You would like to be illustrious. You would like to have psychic development.

Sun, if Malefic:

You are likely to be careless of reputation and will neglect personal credit or respect. You are likely to be capricious. You will not be combative. You may not be pioneering. You will be emotional, fiery in nature and of angry temperament. You will be boastful and proud. You may be without mercy with a not forgiving disposition. You are likely to have a cruel nature.

Mars, if Benefic:

You will have independent, persistent, endurant and courageous temperament. You will be self-confident, enterprising, practical, active, ambitious, aspiring and constructive. You are likely to be fond of liberty, journey and wandering. Your personality will be handsome and of youthful appearance so that you will appear younger than your actual age. You will be fond of commanding respect and influence. You are mentally powerful. You will have organising capacity and executive ability and leadership over labourers. You will have zeal and enthusiasm.

Mars, if Malefic:

You are likely to be fiery, hot, impatient, extravagant and violent. You will be of Tamasika temperament, that is, greedy, lustful, and full of anger, intent upon harming others. You may be capricious. You may have pilfering habits. You are likely to be low minded, rash, wicked, destructive and hard hearted. You may indulge in cruel acts. You are likely to be fond of wandering. You may not feel happy.

Mercury, if Benefic:

You will be cheeful, humorous, learned, intellectual, dexterous. You may be fond of fun, imitating others in speech and dress. You will be of Rajasika temperament – fond of pleasures of the senses, decoration, money and a gay life. You will have a refined taste. You will like to have a psychological development. Adaptability is your striking feature. You would like to do virtuous acts and be popular. You are well-informed with studious habits and fertile imagination. You are fond of friends. You will like to support your relatives and you are attached to your partner. You are economical and prudent. Quickness of wit and mental ingenuity will be strongly marked.

Mercury, if Malefic:

You may be cunning and in the habit of speaking with double meaning. You are likely to be nervous.

Jupiter, if Benefic:

You will have a magnetic personality. You will be of Satwika temperament, that is, you will have pure thoughts and will be inclined to acts of religious merit. You will have optimistic spirit, jovial disposition, pleasant manners and a pleasing personality. You would like to execute any work after mature deliberation, that is, after considering pros and cons. You will be wise, mild, knowledgeable, charitable, diplomatic. You will like to command respect.

Jupiter, if Malefic:

You may be sagacious. You may be self-indulgent especially in regard to gluttony.

Venus, if Benefic:

You will be ambitious, bold, practical, affectionate, intelligent, poetical and perseverance. You will have a pleasing and charming personality. Power of attracting others will be an important asset. You will be generally liked, being of cheerful temperament and responsive to emotional side of nature. You will have liking for scents and flowers. You are likely to be fond of dress of various colours. You will be of Rajasika temperament, fond of pleasures of the senses, money and gay life. You will be easy going and accommodating type.

Venus, if Malefic:

You are likely to be lazy, sycophant and you will try for pleasure. You may not be courageous. You may commit sins, not being able to control passions.

Saturn, if Benefic:

Your moral stability is an asset. Your disposition will be .calm. You will be strong-minded, exploring, methodical, industrious and self-confident. You will have much consideration for the welfare of others. You may be thrifty.

Saturn, if Malefic:

You are likely to have a perverted mind with bad thoughts. You may be evil-natured, tyrannical, cunning, unclean, lazy and passionate. You would like to copy and imitate foreign customs and habits. You may quarrel with your friends. You may have a wandering nature. You may be harsh, hard-hearted, despondent, conservative and stubborn. You will have a Tamasika temperament, greedy, lustful and full of anger. You may resort to mean acts and gambling.

Rahu, if Benefic:

You will be obliging, sympathetic, courageous, adventurous and inventive. You will like to be an executive.

Rahu, if Malefic:

You may be cruel, wicked, hypocritical, irreligious, violent and corrupt. You would like to leave the house and travel aimlessly. You may quarrel and develop misunderstanding with relatives and friends.

Ketu, if Benefic:

You will be charming, diplomatic, philosophical and industrious. You are fond of religious resignation. You are likely to have artistic taste, spiritual imitation, sectarian principles. You may have psychic powers.

Ketu, if Malefic:

You will be of a proud temperament. You are likely to be selfish, avaricious and voluptous. You may be quarrelsome. You may have vicious tendencies and secret intrigues. You may be a back-biter.

Moon, if Benefic:

You will have a Satwika temperament, that is, pure thoughts and inclined to acts of religious merit. You will be fanciful, intelligent, soft-spoken and having discrimination. You are likely to be clever, romantic and popular. You will have strength of mind and polite manners. You will have a good personality and attractive appearance. You will be fond of aesthetic pleasures. You will have a fertile imagination. You may be an idealist.

Moon, if Malefic:

You may be warring, shy, stubborn, fickle minded, hysterical. You may never be steady, having considerable restlessness and a worried mind.

(II) DIFFERENT PLANETS INFLUENCING
SECOND BHAVA
Wealth

Sun, if Benefic:

You will get wealth by inheritance, acquisition of landed properties, vehicles and estates. You will have fair chance of gain of wealth from dealing in copper, gold or metals. You may earn from industrious efforts through government service. There is a likelihood of getting wealth from good business through fair means. You may get money from acquisition of a new job. You may gain through government or by holding a responsible position. You will have steady fortune and will be wealthy. You will have patrimony. You can expect to gain in wealth by dealing in fuel, wool, weapons, gold, fire, medicines, forests, mountains and hills, open places, skins, shrines, silk cloth, wheat and by working as goldsmith, money lender, chemist, druggist, doctor and through your courage, will power, self-reliance, political power or positions of authority. You may get wealth from eastern direction.

Sun, if Malefic:

You are liable to financial penalty or confiscation of property by the government. Your losses will occur by offending authorities. You may lose money from prosecutions and through cattle and destruction of property etc. You are inclined to waste your wealth through your extravagant and impulsive expenses.

Mars, if Benefic:

You will increase in your wealth by gains through dealing in iron, steel, timber or chemicals. You may get money from promotion in your profession. You will own houses, conveyance and landed property. You can expect money from your brothers and sisters. You are likely to get wealth by your dealings connected with poisonous gases, fires, military operations, weapons of offence and defence, woollen shawls, blood, deserts, mountains, forests, sulphur, gold, copper, sapphire, corals, burning gases, fire places, engines, cook rooms/ kitchens, chemical laboratories, boilers, mines, minerals and ores, gold fields, armoury, arms and weapons, lands or tobacco. You can expect to earn as warrior, chemist, druggist, engineer or by dealing with cattle or may be connected with dairy products. Your independence, persistence, organising capacity, executive ability, endurance and physical strength will get you good wealth. You can expect to gain wealth from southern direction.

Mars, if Malefic:

You may have loss of wealth by theft and loss of property.

Mercury, if Benefic:

You may get wealthy by dint of your intelligence and gains through teaching, writing or by commissions, advertising, stationery or books. You may become wealthy by dealing in mercantile activity, trade, imports and exports, industries, architecture, weaving, vegetation, base metals, betel leaves, edible oils, nuts, limestone, green grams, emerald, lead, oilseeds or alloys. You may get money by being an accountant, mathematician, orator, bookseller, publisher, broker, poet or through your shrewdness and intellect. You can expect wealth from your maternal uncles, maternal grandfather or paternal relatives. You may gain wealth from commerce, aerial and landed journeys, churches, schools, parks, gambling dens or from the profession of a doctor or tradesman. Your wealth may come from northern direction.

Mercury, if Malefic:

You may not get wealthy by dint of your intelligence and gains through teaching, writing or by commissions, advertising, stationery or books. You may not become wealthy by dealing in mercantile activity, trade, imports and exports, industries, architecture, weaving, vegetation, base metals, betel leaves, edible oils, nuts, limestone, green grams, emerald, lead, oilseeds or alloys. You may not get money by being an accountant, mathematician, orator, bookseller, publisher, broker, poet or through your shrewdness and intellect. You may not expect wealth from your maternal uncles, maternal grandfather or paternal relatives. You may not gain wealth from commerce, aerial and landed journeys, churches, schools, parks, gambling dens or the profession of a doctor or tradesman. Your wealth may not come from northern direction.

Jupiter, If Benefic:

You will get wealth through essence of your knowledge, wisdom, intellect and education. You may acquire silver and topaz. You may get wealth from children, sons, grandsons, learned men, grandfather or through your position as minister or adviser. You may become wealthy by dealing with banks, insurance companies, scriptures, benzoin, quick silver, tin or cardomoms. Your wealth will increase by possessing lands, estates, buildings and vehicles. You will engage in trade, commerce, good business and successful career and become wealthy through your perseverance and vitality. In general your financial position will improve. You can expect wealth from north-eastern direction.

Jupiter, if Malefic:

You will keep your finances at a low ebb. You are inclined to sacrifice your wealth for the good of others.

Venus, if Benefic:

You will get wealth due to favour from ladies, higher officials or artists. You will purchase jewels. You may run hotels and gain from metals (silver, lead) or from other peoples' wealth. You will have inheritance, luxuries, estates, cars, houses. You are likely to become wealthy as a singer, musician, actor, botanist or artist or through marriage and partner in life. You can expect to gain in wealth by dealing in pearls, toilets, meats, intoxicating drinks, vehicles, sugarcane, industry, trade, chemicals, medicines, wool, silk, cotton, luxury articles, perfumes, musical instruments, authorship or through your perseverance and vitality. You may get wealth from south-eastern direction.

Venus, if Malefic:

You may not get wealth due to favour from ladies, higher officials or artists. You may not purchase jewels. You may not run hotels and gain from metals (silver, lead) or from other people's wealth. You may not have inheritance, luxuries, estates, cars, houses. You are not likely to become wealthy being a singer, musician, actor, botanist or artist or through marriage and partner in life. You may not expect to gain in wealth by dealing in pearls, toilets, meats, intoxications drinks, vehicles, sugarcane, industry, trade, chemicals, medicines, wool, silk, cotton, luxury articles, perfumes, musical instruments authorship or through your perseverance and vitality. You may not get wealth from south-eastern direction.

Saturn, if Benefic:

You will gain wealth by success in estate, mines, investment, coal, lead or refrigeration. You may get wealth by dealing in gambling, oils, seeds, pots, woollen fabrics, iron, cereals, atmosphere, air, mountains, hills, forest regions, saphire, elderly people, black grain, barley, astringent, jails, bricklaying, negroes, architecture or vehicles. You can expect gains in wealth from western direction.

Saturn, if Malefic:

You may be bereft of property and conveyance. You may not inherit property and may lose ancestral property. You may land in troubles from houses and vehicles. You may have to put in uphill struggle with maximum labour and minimum wages for getting money. There may be loss of wealth and lack of money.

Rahu, if Benefic:

You will gain in wealth through friends and business. You will try to save money. You may get wealth from foreign travels, maternal grandfather, females, christians or mohammedans. You may gain by dealing in stones, mud, liquid sediments, radio or aerial navigation. You may get wealth as a traveller, inventor, lecturer, goldsmith, aviator, astrologer, scientist or hunter or by dealing in pumps. You can expect to get wealth from south-western direction.

Rahu, if Malefic:

You may suffer loss of ancestral property. You may have financial strain and you may not be very wealthy.

Ketu, if Benefic:

You may accumulate wealth by dealing with fire, flame or mining. You may gain in wealth from friends and through your literary genuis, astrology or artistic taste. You can expect money from paternal grandfather.

Ketu, if Malefic:

You may be deprived of wealth due to loss of ancestral property.

Moon, if Benefic:

You will have access to wealth and good earnings. You will have increase of property and gains in all undertakings. You will obtain money through females and mother. You will gain through social life. You will be endowed with landed property, house, conveyance and vehicles. You will have increase in income and earnings. You will have larger profits. You may get wealth by working as a seaman, travelling agent, navigator or by dealing in cultivation, pearls, gems, milk, juicy articles, vegetation, watery places, bathrooms, blood, liquids or water journeys. You may become wealthy by your intelligence and vital energy. You may expect wealth by dealing in textiles, chemicals (fine chemicals and pharmaceuticals), alcohol, sugarcane, silver, sweet things, barley or wheat. You can expect money from north-eastern direction.

Moon, if Malefic:

You may spend away your wealth. Your financial position may be somewhat variable.

(III) DIFFERENT PLANETS INFLUENCING THIRD BHAVA
Courage

Sun, if Benefic:

You will be courageous due to your self-reliance, powerful vitality, will power and authoritative and fiery nature. You will get victory over enemies. You will indulge in acts of bravery and command respect.

Sun, if Malefic:

You may be timid and anxious.

Mars, if Benefic:

You will be very bold and adventurous due to your endurance, physical strength, mental power and prowess. You will be warlike and manly. You will be victorious over your enemies.

Mars, if Malefic:

You may sometimes suffer from thoughts of suicide due to your timid mentality.

Mercury, if Benefic:

When once a work is undertaken, you will do it to

finish and will never be discouraged. You will be brave and powerful with your power of speech and eloquence.

Mercury, if Malefic:

You may be anxious and not bold.

Jupiter, if Benefic:

You will get gains through your courage having mental calibre and leadership.

Jupiter, if Malefic:

You may not have courage, mental calibre and leadership.

Venus, if Benefic:

You will have courage through your good-mental quality.

Venus, if Malefic:

You may not have courage through your mental quality.

Saturn, if Benefic:

You will be valorous and succeed in litigation and gain victory over your enemies.

Saturn, if Malefic:

You may not be valorous and may not succeed in litigation nor have victory over your enemies.

Rahu, if Benefic:

You will be courageous like a lion due to your violent and adventurous nature.

Rahu, if Malefic:

You will be brave for outward appearance.

Ketu, if Benefic:

You will be adventurous, courageous and will have much fighting stamina.

Ketu, if Malefic:

You may not be adventurous, courageous and may not have much fighting stamina.

Moon, if Benefic:

You will be strong, powerful and more courageous.

Moon, if Malefic:

You may not be strong, powerful and courageous.

(IV) DIFFERENT PLANETS INFLUENCING FOURTH BHAVA
Education

Sun, if Benefic:

You may have interest in occult and philosophical studies, political science or metaphysics. You may have proficiency in mathematics. You are likely to have poetical instincts. You may have education connected with chemistry, drugs, mountains and hills, forests, fuel, skins, wool, weapons, silk cloth, fire or medicine.

Sun, if Malefic:

You may not be successful in your attempts to get education connected with philosophy, political science, metaphysics, mathematics, poetry, chemistry, drugs, mountains and hills, forests, fuel, skins, wool, weapons, silk cloth, fire or medicine.

Mars, if Benefic:

You may get education connected with logic, boilers, mines, minerals and ores, gold field, armoury, army, weapons, lands or organizing and executive capacity. You may also have an inclination to get educated in fields connected with fires, military operations, weapons of offence and defence, chemistry, drugs, gold, copper, surgery, burning gases, dentists, fire places, engineering, engines, iron and steel or chemical laboratories.

Mars, if Malefic:

You may not be successful in education connected with fires, weapons, engineering, chemistry, drugs, mines, surgery, iron and steel or chemical laboratories.

Mercury, if Benefic:

You will be successful in your educational pursuits. You are inclined to pursue literary activities. You may have taste for music and for other fine arts. You may have proficiency in astrology. Your education may lead you to shine well as an educationaist or diplomat. You may be educated in fields connected with science, research, inspection of accounts, atomic energy, mathematics, electrical/electronic engineering, currency, alloys, water reservoirs, poetry, business management, mercantile activity, journalism, commerce, weaving, aerial and land journeys or vegetation.

Mercury, if Malefic:

You may not be successful in your education connected with science, research, accounts, business management, mathematics, engineering, commerce or journalism.

Jupiter, if Benefic:

You will be well-read and educated. You will have acquisition of new knowledge. You will make great philosophical and spiritual advancement. You will have success in education connected with Vedas, Vedantas, legal affairs, diplomacy, proficiency in arts and sciences, law, philosophy, asceticism, bankers, philanthrophists, restaurants, hotels, insurance, travel or research and academic institutions.

Jupiter, if Malefic:

You may not be successful in education connected with arts and sciences, law, banks, insurance, research, travels, restaurants, philosophy or academic institutions.

Venus, if Benefic:

You will be learned and successful in your educational pursuits. You will acquire new knowledge. You are likely to be interested in music. You may be fond of scientific education. You may be successful in education connected with poetical faculty, singers, musicians, dress, fine arts, actors, artists, botanists, authorship, rains, dancings, lakes, sugarcane, trade, medicine, wool, silk or cotton, computers.

Venus, if Malefic:

You may not expect to be successful in education in the fields of fine arts, scientific studies, poetical faculty, botany, medicine, sugarcane or trade.

Saturn, if Benefic:

You may get education connected with mines, oils, woollen fabrics, architectural skill, iron, lead, atmosphere, air, mountains, hills, forests, mass leadership or labour.

Saturn, if Malefic:

You may have interrupted and incomplete education. You may have failure in your educational pursuits. You may not be successful in your attempts to get education connected with mines, oils, architectural skill, iron, lead, mass leadership, labour, atmosphere, mountains, woollen fabrics or forests.

Rahu, if Benefic:

You may be proficient in European languages. You are likely to have good educational pursuits. You may have education connected with lecturers, inventors, aviators, scientists, astrologers, radio, aerial navigation, psychologists or metaphysical studies.

Rahu, if Malefic:

You may not expect to be successful in the fields of education connected with inventors, aviators, scientists, radio, aerial navigation, psychology or metaphysical studies.

Ketu, if Benefic:

You may have artistic taste. You may be a literary genius. You may be good at astrology. You may get education connected with philosophy or mining.

Ketu, if Malefic:

You may have breaks in your educational career. You may not get education connected with artistic taste, literary pursuits, philosophy or mining.

Moon, if Benefic:

You will get high education. You may be interested in political science, psychology or metaphysics. Your education may prepare you to become seamen, travelling agents or navigators. You may be successful in education connected with water, cultivation, pearls, gems, vegetation, watery places, psycho-physiological consciousness, watery substances, lakes, sea, textiles, chemicals, pharmaceuticals, sugarcane or agriculture.

Moon, if Malefic:

You may not get education connected with watery substances, agriculture, textiles, sugarcane, chemicals, pharmaceuticals, travel agents or navigation.

Houses, Landed Property and Conveyance

Sun, if Benefic:

You may purchase landed property, vehicles. You may inherit property. You will gain through estate. You will get patrimony (from father). You may acquire properties from your political power and position and authority.

Sun, if Malefic:

You may have loss of property. You may spend away your paternal property.

Mars, if Benefic:

You will have means of conveyance. You will own houses. You will gain from landed property. You will have interest in acquiring lands.

Mars, if Malefic:

You may get loss of property due to theft, fire etc. You may not be happy on account of houses. You may land in litigation problems about property.

Mercury, if Benefic:

You will gain from landed property and estate.

Mercury, if Malefic:

You may have no fixed abode. You may ever change the car.

Jupiter, if Benefic:

You will have successful estates. You will be in possession of buildings, vehicles etc. You will gain from lands. You will have good conveyance.

Jupiter, if Malefic:

You may not have successful estates. You may not be in possesion of buildings, vehicles etc. You may not have good conveyance.

Venus, if Benefic:

You will easily get inheritance. You will possess estates and own cars. You will have acquisition of house and vehicles.

Venus, if Malefic:

You may not easily get inheritance. You may not possess estates and own cars. You may not have acquisition of house and vehicles.

Saturn, if Benefic:

You will have conveyance.

Saturn, if Malefic:

You may not inherit any property. You may be bereft of property and conveyance. You may have troubles from houses and vehicles. You are likely to lose ancestral property.

Rahu, If Benefic:

You may not have loss of ancestral property.

Rahu, if Malefic:

You may have loss of ancestral property.

Ketu, if Benefic:

You may not be deprived of property and there may not be loss of property.

Ketu, if Malefic:

You may be deprived of property and there may be loss of property.

Moon, if Benefic:

You will inherit. You will gain from wet land. You will possess buildings, vehicles etc.

Moon, if Malefic:

You may not inherit. You may not gain from wet land. You may not possess buildings, vehicles etc.

Happiness

Sun, if Benefic:

You will get reputation and respect from government by getting promotions and acquisition of higher status. You will have access to comforts and rejoicings at home. You will get landed properties and vehicles and gains from estate. You may inherit property also. You will be successful in foreign countries. You will have good entertainment. You will realise your ambitions and fulfilness of deeds. You will go on a pilgrimage. You will get happiness from father. You will have authority and position with political power. You will visit places of worship. You will have good relations with government and officials. You will be happy.

Sun, if Malefic:

You may have obstacles and troubles in life. You may have blood pressure. Your domestic environment may not be good. Your success in political field may be difficult. You may have quarrels with relatives and friends. You may have loss of property. You may get into difficulties. You may have mental worry. You may be bothered about the illness of your mother. You may be devoid of much happiness and may become philosophical.

Mars, if Benefic:

You will have means of conveyance. You will have success in political life. You will get gains from landed property. You will have matrimonial happiness. You will get comforts. You will get happiness from mother, brothers and sisters. You will have organizing and executive ability on account of your commanding, independent leadership qualities. You will have physical strength and mental power. You may acquire gold, sapphire and corals. You will have youthful appearance. You will be happy.

Mars, if Malefic:

You may own houses but will not be happy on that account. You may have a sickly mother. You may lose friends and relatives. You may have disputes in family. You may lose wealth and property due to theft, fire and litigation. There may be danger to your parents and danger to you during journeys. You may be uncomfortable. You may get chest pain. You may have much distress of mind and you may be unhappy.

Mercury, if Benefic:

You will have robust health. You will have success in your educational pursuits. You will be learned and held in great esteem. You will have a good mother and bring happiness to her. You will gain new friends. You will command good conveyance, material comforts and you. will gain from landed properties. You will get promotion in profession or gains in profession. You will have prosperity and happiness in domestic life. You will get happiness from relatives. You will have princely appearance. You will acquire emerald. You will have good education with your intellect, wisdom and shrewdness. You will have power of speech and eloquence. You will have good enjoyments. You will possess or live in palatial buildings. You will have good relations with your maternal uncles, maternal grandfather and paternal relatives and you may gain from them. You will be good at poetry and may become a good poet. You will be happy.

Mercury, if Malefic:

You may be cut off from relations. You may have an unhappy mother.

Jupiter, if Benefic:

You will have good inheritance, conveyance,

buildings, successful estate and gains from lands. You will be wealthy. You will have success in education and you will be well-read. You will be a founder of some charitable institution. You will have a good mother and friends. You will get fame and prosperity. You will lead a comfortable life. You will enjoy favour of the ruling class. You will be a terror to your enemies. You will be religiously inclined. You will be fortunate and respected. You will have a peaceful domestic environment and great spiritual advancement. You will get gains from parents. You will get happiness in respect of mother, friends, servants, partner and agricultural produce. You will have a happy end.

Jupiter, if Malefic:

You may have impediment or delay in birth of children. You may suffer distress due to enemies.

Venus, if Benefic:

You will be learned and successful in educational pursuits. You will have an affectionate mother. You will be loved by relatives and friends. You will aquire, vehicles, property and cattle. You will have perfect domestic harmony. You will get friendship with good people and gain through them. You will have good ornaments and clothes. You will be successful in the fulfilment of desires. You will get good position and become famous and popular. You will lead a comfortable life. You will easily get inheritance. You will get plenty of milk and milky products. You will be respected.

Venus, if Malefic:

You may not be learned and successful in educational pursuits. You may not have an affectionate mother. You may not be loved by relatives and friends. You may not acquire houses, vehicles, property and cattle. You may not have perfect domestic harmony. You may not have friendship with good people and gain through them. You may not have good ornaments and clothes. You may not be successful in the fulfilment of desires. You may not get good position or become famous and popular. You may not lead a comfortable life. You may not easily get inheritance. You may not get plenty of milk and milky products. You may not be respected.

Saturn, if Benefic:

You will have good patrimony. You will succeed in foreign countries. You will have vehicles. You will gain through oilseeds or black grains. You may get treasure.

Saturn, if Malefic:

There may be ill health of your mother or you may be separated from her. You may suffer sudden loss of ancestral property. You may have failure in educational pursuits. You may be bereft of property and conveyance. You may have troubles from houses and vehicles. You may get distress due to partner, children and servants. You may be disliked by relatives. You may develop enmity with politicians. You may get misfortune in own land and voyage to distant places. You may be constantly worried and may have no peace of mind. You may be devoid of happiness. You may have a secluded life.

Rahu, if Benefic:

You may gain through low-born people.

Rahu, if Malefic:

Your educational pursuits may not go smooth. You may be in a subordinate position. You may lose ancestral property. You may quarrel with friends. There may be ill health of your mother. You may have to undertake tedious journeys. There may be no happiness from brothers and friends. You may have adverse effects in respect of happiness from mother, father or partner. You may be subject to fraud or be guilty of fraudulent actions. There may be impediments and you may be constantly worried. You may have little happiness.

Ketu, If Banefic:

There may not be ill health of your mother. You may not have failure in educational career. There may not be domestic quarrels. You may not have loss of ancestral property. You may not be deceived by friends. You may not have misery and unhappiness.

Ketu, if Malefic:

There may be ill health of your mother. You may have failure in educational career. There may be domestic quarrels. You may have loss of ancestral property. You may be deceived by friends. You may have misery and unhappiness.

Moon, if Benefic:

You will inherit landed property and possess buildings and vehicles. You will gain from wet lands. You will have good perfumes and dress. You will get high education. You will be wealthy. You will have good friends and mother. You will derive happiness from relatives. You may become important as a ruler or leader. You will gain through parents. You will have a happy domestic life. You will be successful, popular, cheerful and contented. You will be helped by all. You will enjoy life. You will be endowed with happiness.

Moon, if Malefic:

You may be separated from mother or there may be ill health of your mother. You may have disappointments and difficulties. You may be subjected to theft and fraud. You may be extravagant. You may not be happy mentally.

(V) DIFFERENT PLANETS INFLUENCING
FIFTH BHAVA
Children

Sun, if Benefic:

You will gain through children.

Sun, if Malefic:

You may be deprived of children or may have few children. There may be difficulties during child birth. There may be illness of children. You may have trouble with children.

Mars, if Benefic:

You may have issues or there may not be danger to child birth or surgical aid may not be used during child birth. There may not be danger of injury to the first child. It may not be miserable for your children. You may not have misfortunes through children or disputes with children.

Mars, if Malefic:

You may not have issues or there may be danger to child birth or surgical aid may be used during child birth. There may be danger of injury to first child. Your children may not be comfortable. You may have misfortunes through children or disputes with children.

Mercury, if Benefic:

You will have good and intelligent children. There will be a number of children.

Mercury, if Malefic:

You may not have good and intelligent children. There may not be a number of children.

Jupiter, if Benefic:

There will be a number of children and they will be good. You will be happy with your children.

Jupiter, if Malefic:

You may have grief through partial sterility and you may have few children. You may have limited number of sons and suffer for want of sons. You may have unhappiness in respect of children.

Venus, if Benefic:

You will have beautiful children. You will get happiness through your offspring. There will be prosperity of children.

Venus, if Malefic:

There may be birth of daughters. You may have few sons and more of female children.

Saturn, if Benefic:

You may have children. You may not get a still born child or there might not be premature death of a child. There may not be abortions or ill health of children or their death. You may not adopt a child. You may not suffer for want of sons. You may not have troubles connected with children.

Saturn, if Malefic:

You may not have children. You may get a still born child or there might be premature death of a child. There may be abortions or ill health of children or their death. You may adopt a child. You may suffer for want of sons. You may have troubles connected with children.

Rahu, if Benefic:

You may not lose a number of children. You may not suffer from ill health of children or abortions.

Rahu, if Malefic:

You may lose a number of children. You may suffer from ill health of children or abortions.

Ketu, if Benefic:

There may not be loss of children. You may not suffer from ill health or abortions.

Ketu, if Malefic:

There may be loss of children. You may suffer from ill health or abortions.

Moon, if Benefic:

You will have happiness from children. One of your children may become famous. You will enjoy life in the company of children. You may have sons and daughters.

Moon, if Malefic:

You may have only daughter or many daughters.

(VI) DIFFERENT PLANETS INFLUENCING
SIXTH BHAVA
Diseases

Sun, if Benefic:

You will be strong and healthy. You will have good digestive power. You will enjoy well balanced health.

Sun, if Malefic:

You may have heart trouble or chest pain. You may have weakness and organic troubles. You may have long and troublesome illness. You may suffer from fever, eyesight, accidents due to fire, palpitation, sun stroke, excessive heat, skin diseases, stomach disorders or dislocation of bones. You may have troubles from pitta (bile) and a little of vata (wind). You may have troubles from weapons or danger from poison. There is a likelihood of evil influence of evil spirits.

Mars, if Benefic:

You will have good digestive powers and rich blood.

Mars, if Malefic:

You may have boils and wounds due to impurity of blood. You may have fever, inflammations or injuries. You may also undergo operation. You may have bilious complaints, skin diseases, diseases brought by extreme heat in body, blood pressure, sore eye, disease in stomach, decline of majja in bones or diseases above the neck.

Mercury, if Benefic:

You will study hygiene and may take preventive measures not to get diseases.

Mercury, if Malefic:

You may overwork and get into ill health. You may have mental troubles and chance of nervous breakdown. You may suffer from stomach trouble or disease on tips of fingers. You may get diseases connected with mostly vata (wind), a little of pitta (bile) and stillness of kapha (phelgm). You may have typhoid, shivering fever, diseases in eye, throat and nose, skin diseases or itches. Your liver and digestive organs may be effected. You may suffer from consumption.

Jupiter, if Benefic:

You will maintain good health and may not fall sick. You may gain during unhealthy periods. If indisposed you will be well-attended.

Jupiter, if Malefic:

Your health may suffer through overindulgence. You may have low digestive power. You may lack in vitality and potency. You may have weakness of body and suffer ill health. You may suffer from fever, gulma (disease in

kidney), fainting, ear diseases due to fury of kapha
(phelgm) dosha, diabetes, excessive eating and
drinking, vata (wind) diseases or diseases connected
with inability to think or remember.

Venus, if Benefic:

You will avoid excesses and can maintain good
health.

Venus, if Malefic:

You may suffer from secret ailments or ulcers. Your
health may be affected by too much of indulgence. You
may suffer from skin diseases, diseases connected with
fury of phelgm and 'wind', eye diseases, weakness,
diseases in private organs, fading away of luster in
body, swelling of body, nervous diseases, blood
poisoning, watery diseases (swelling, dropsy, water in
head, indigestion, water in body), extreme heat in body,
fits and swoons, or diseases in face or urinary organs.

Saturn, if Benefic:

You will maintain good digestive power.

Saturn, if Malefic:

You may have sickness through privation or neglect.
You may have illness and operation. You may suffer
from hysteria, ulcers, wounds or diseases arising out of
imbalance of 'wind'. You may suffer from spleen
trouble, diseases caused by vata (wind) and kapha
(phlegm), diseases in legs, weakness due to
overexertion, pains in stomach, mental worry, varicose
veins or more of vata (wind) and little of pitta (bile).
You may worry a great deal and suffer from chronic
melancholia that may sometimes grow into insanity.
Your spinal column may require special care. You may
have more thirst and aversion to eat or drink. You may
have pain in all parts of body. Your diseases may be of
hidden nature and may not be easily diagnosed.

Rahu, if Benefic:

You will have physical and mental stamina.

Rahu, if Malefic:

You may suffer from colic pains, heart trouble or diseases of stomach and abdomen side of belly. You may have health troubles connected with uterus (for females). Your body may become emaciated. You may have difficulty in breathing or extreme heat in body. You may suffer from vishama vyadhi (many diseases coming together) or diseases in feet. Your diseases may be of a hidden type, not susceptible to easy diagnosis.

Ketu, if Benefic:

You will be bestowed with good health.

Ketu, if Malefic:

You may have trouble in eye. Your teeth may become weak. You may have anal diseases. You may suffer from fever and some complaints which cannot be cured by medicines. Your body may become weak and emaciated. There may be boils due to heat. You may suffer physical ailments or nervousness which will keep you restless and worried. You may have stomach ailments. You may have weak constitution.

Moon, if Benefic:

You may not have stomach troubles. You may not have curious and incurable diseases. You may not have stone in the bladder. There may not be any danger from lung troubles. You may not suffer from dysentry, dyspepsia (indigestion, sluggish digestive power), colic pains, general debility and impaired eyesight. You may not have increase in sleep. You may not suffer from watery diseases (swelling, dropsy, water in head), glandular swellings, ulcers, vomiting, diseases in kidneys, diarrhoea, want of blood in body, poisoning of blood and consequent diseases, thirst, sores and boils, diseases connected with more vata (wind) and a little kapha (phelgm) or emaciation.

Moon, if Malefic:

You may have stomach troubles. You may have a curious disease. You may have stone in the bladder. There may be danger from lung troubles. You may suffer from dysentery, dyspepsia (indigestion, sluggish digestive powers), colic pains, general debility or impaired eyesight. You may have increase in sleep. You may suffer from watery diseases (swelling, dropsy, water in head), glandular swellings, ulcers, vomiting, diseases in kidneys, diarrhoea, want of blood in body, poisoning of blood and consequent diseases, thirst, sores and boils, diseases, connected with more vata (wind) and a little kapha (phelgm) or emaciation.

Enemies

Sun, if Benefic:

You will be a terror to enemies due to your courage. You will have victory over your enemies. You may have few enemies.

Sun, if Malefic:

You may have misunderstanding with your father, government and officials. Due to your fiery nature you may develop enmity with others. You may be worried by enemies though you may vanquish them subsequently.

Mars, if Benefic:

You will defeat your enemies and gain victory.

Mars, if Malefic:

You may have constant pinpricks from enemies. You may be much troubled by enemies.

Mercury, if Benefic:

You may be a terror to enemies and there may not be any enemies.

Mercury, if Malefic:

You may have many irksome occasions on account of disputes, petty quarrels and labour troubles.

Jupiter, if Benefic:

You will have success over enemies and overpower them. You will be free from enemies. You will have victory in elections.

Jupiter, if Malefic:

You may be feared and dreaded by enemies.

Venus, if Benefic:

You will overpower enemies and destroy them. You may not have any enemies. You will win in election.

Venus, if Malefic:

You may give rise to enmities with persons of opposite sex. You may have a number of enemies.

Saturn, if Benefic:

You will triumph over enemies and you will get victory over them.

Saturn, if Malefic:

You may be quarrelsome. You may have troubles through subordinates and labour. You may suffer at the hands of enemies.

Rahu, if Benefic:

You will overcome your enemies and get success over them. You may not have any enemies.

Rahu, if Malefic:

You may be oppressed and troubled by enemies.

Ketu, if Benefic:

You will be much liked by relatives.

Ketu, if Malefic:

You may be oppressed by opponents.

Moon, if Benefic:

You may not have many foes. There may not be pressures from enmity and troubles from enemies. You may not suffer from treachery.

Moon, if Malefic:

You may have many foes. There may be pressures from enmity and troubles from enemies. You may suffer from treachery.

Debts

Sun, if Benefic:

You may not lose patrimony and get indebted. You may not expect to obtain debts from government and officials, as in the form of house building loans. You may not also get into debts due to father.

Sun, if Malefic:

You may lose patrimony and get indebted. You may expect to obtain debts from government and officials, may be in the form of house building loans. You may also get into debts due to father.

Mars, if Benefic:

You may not have heavy expenditure of money and loss through animals and poultry and land in debts. You may not be indebted due to brothers and sisters.

You may expect to get money as debt from your brothers and sisters.

Mars, if Malefic:

You may have heavy expenditure of money and loss through animals and poultry and land in debts. You may be indebted due to brothers and sisters. You may not expect to get money as debt from your brothers and sisters.

Mercury, if Benefic:

You may get debt from maternal uncles, maternal grandfather and paternal relatives but you may not be indebted due to them.

Mercury, if Malefic:

You may not get debt from maternal uncles, maternal grandfather and paternal relatives and you may be indebted due to them also.

Jupiter, if Benefic:

You may not get into debt due to children, sons, grandsons and grandfather. You may not expect to get money from learned men as debt.

Jupiter, if Malefic:

You may get into debt due to children, sons, grandsons and grandfather. You may expect to get money from learned men as debt.

Venus, if Benefic:

You may not get indebted due to partner and children. You may not get debt to acquire vehicles.

Venus, if Malefic:

You may get indebted due to partner and children. You may get debt to acquire vehicles.

Saturn, if Benefic:

You may not be indebted due to loss through animals and poultry. You may not incur debt due to servants.

Saturn, if Malefic:

You may be indebted due to loss through animals and poultry. You may not incur debt due to servants.

Rahu, if Benefic:

You may not incur debt due to maternal grandfather and due to intrigues with low class people. Your materialistic tendencies may not lead you into debt.

Rahu, if Malefic:

You may incur debt due to maternal grandfather and due to intrigues with low class people. Your materialistic tendencies may also lead you into debt.

Ketu, if Benefic:

You may not land in debt due to paternal grandfather and due to bankruptcy.

Ketu, if Malefic:

You may land in debt due to paternal grandfather and due to bankruptcy.

Moon, if Benefic:

You may not get pressure from creditors and bank. You may not have loss of money and get into debt. You may not incur debt due to your mother.

Moon, if Malefic:

You may get pressure from creditors and bank. You may have loss of money and get into debt. You may incur debt due to your mother.

(VII) DIFFERENT PLANETS INFLUENCING SEVENTH BHAVA
Marriage and Marital Relationship

Sun, if Benefic:

You will have success after marriage. You will gain through partner.

Sun, if Malefic:

You may have late and delayed marriage with some trouble. You may not have good morals. You may be submissive to your partner. The temperament of your partner may not be good. There may be illness of your partner. Your matrimonial happiness may suffer. You may be henpecked.

Mars, if Benefic:

You may not have two life partners. You may not have trouble with your partner. There may not be ill health of your partner. You may not be henpecked. You may not have an aggressive and combative partner. Your married life may not have clashes and tensions and you may not be disturbed due to matrimonial unhappiness. Your partner may not be fond of change and travel. You may not be submissive to your married partner.

Mars, if Malefic:

You may have two life partners. You may have trouble with your partner. There may be ill health of your partner. You may be henpecked. You may have an aggressive and combative partner. Your married life may have clashes and tensions and you may be disturbed due to matrimonial unhappiness. Your partner may be fond of change and travel. You may be submissive to your married partner.

Mercury, if Benefic:

You may have an early marriage. Your partner may be good looking. You may gain through your partner. Your marriage may be with a wealthy person. Your partner may be more intelligent and shrewd, younger and may be employed. Your marriage may take place through advertisement.

Mercury, if Malefic:

You may have unsettled wedded life.

Jupiter, if Benefic:

You will have a good virtuous, good looking and chaste partner. Your partner will be well-behaved and truthful. You will gain through your partner. You will have a happy partner.

Jupiter, if Malefic:

You may be lustful and inclined to have liaisons.

Venus, if Benefic:

You will have a happy marriage and domestic harmony with a loving and devoted partner. You will get a good beautiful partner. You will have stability in marriage. Both you and your partner will be successful and distinguished in your occupations. You will have good marital relations.

Venus, if Malefic:

You may be passionate. You may be fond of pleasures. Your partner may suffer ill health sometimes.

Saturn, if Benefic:

You will be steady in your affections. You will have a stable marriage.

Saturn, if Malefic:

You may have more than one partner or one marriage or you are likely to have a late marriage. Your partner may not be good looking. Your marriage may be with one, quite advanced in age. There is a probability of a sickly partner. You may be immoral and fond of others. You may be subjected to distress and humiliation on account of persons of opposite sex. You may have an unhappy marriage.

Rahu, if Benefic:

You may not have loss of partner. You may not have troubles from female agency. You may not have separation from partner and relations. You may not suffer in family affairs and your conjugal happiness may not be impaired. Your partner may not suffer from illness. You may not have adverse vitality.

Rahu, if Malefic:

You may face loss or ill health of partner. You may have troubles from female agency. You may have separation from partner and relations. You may suffer in family affairs and your conjugal happiness may be impaired. You may have adverse vitality.

Ketu, if Benefic:

You may not be passionate and may not have connections with unworthy persons. There may not be danger or ill health to your partner. You may not suffer from separation from your partner. Your partner may not be sickly or uneven-tempered. You may not have loss of vitality. You may get a shrewd partner. You may not have an unhappy marriage.

Ketu, if Malefic:

You may be passionate and may have connections with unworthy persons. There may be danger to your partner or your partner may suffer from ill health. You may suffer separation from your partner. Your partner may be sickly or uneven-tempered. You may have loss of vitality. You may not get a shrewd partner. You may have an unhappy marriage.

Moon, if Benefic:

You may have an early marriage. You will have a good looking and handsome partner with good personality. You will have a happy marriage. You will have short journeys and honeymoon.

Moon, if Malefic:

You may be strongly sexed and may run after and be attached to other persons. You may be subservient to your partner's wishes. Your partner may be sickly. Your partner may be fond of change and travel. You may be fond of other persons.

(VIII) DIFFERENT PLANETS INFLUENCING EIGHTH BHAVA
Longevity

Sun, if Benefic:

Your strength of tissues and recuperative power will improve your vitality and contribute to your long life.

Sun, if Malefic:

You may have sickly constitution with complaints in eyes, sores in the face and head, imperfect secretion of bile, dental problems or ailments of private parts. You may have a violent end or you may end by self sacrifice. You may be worried. You may not have a very long span of life.

Mars, if Benefic:

You may not have a bad eyesight. You may not be liable to suffer from piles or fistula. You may not suffer from diseases arising out of impurity of blood, high fever, rupture of veins and arteries, decomposition of marrow, haemorrage or muscular rheumatism. You may have a long life.

Mars, if Malefic:

You may have a bad eyesight. You are liable to suffer from piles or fistula. You may suffer from diseases arising out of impurity of blood, high fever, rupture of veins and arteries, decomposition of marrow, haemorrage or muscular rheumatism. You may not have a very long life-span.

Mercury, if Benefic:

You may be long-lived.

Mercury, if Malefic:

You may have a weak constitution. You may suffer from nervous breakdown and diseases connected with brain, thyroid glands or nervous systems and you may not be very long-lived.

Jupiter, if Benefic:

You will live long.

Jupiter, if Malefic:

You may have colic pains. You may suffer from lever troubles, abscess, undiagnosed or concealed diseases thereby curtailing your length of life.

Venus, if Benefic:

You may not have diseases of urinary tract and you may not have trouble in mind. You may not suffer from muscular rheumatism. You may have a long life.

Venus, if Malefic:

You may have diseases of urinary tract and you may have trouble in mind. You may suffer from muscular rheumatism. You may not have a very long life.

Saturn, if Benefic:

You will have good digestive parts and you will have a long life.

Saturn, if Malefic:

You may be a drunkard. You may have ill health and may suffer from colic pains, danger from poisons, asthma, consumption, stomach diseases, ulcers, lung disorders, spleen troubles or diseases of private parts or piles. You may have chronic and undiagnosed disease. You may have fear of drowning. You may have a slow death eventhough having a very good span of life.

Rahu, if Benefic:

You may not have ill health and suffer from diseases arising out of imbalance of 'wind', ailments of stomach, enlargements of glands and their imperfect functioning, infirmity of limb, undiagnosed diseases of private parts, mental disorders, smallpox, blood poisoning or malaria leading to a life long adversity.

Rahu, if Malefic:

You may have ill health and suffer from diseases arising out of imbalance of 'wind', ailments of stomach, enlargement of glands and their imperfect functioning, infirmity of limb, undiagnosed diseases of private parts, mental disorders, smallpox, blood poisoning or malaria leading to a life long adversity.

Ketu, if Benefic:

You may be long-lived.

Ketu, if Malefic:

You may have ill health and you may suffer from piles and anal complaints, wounds, stomach disorders. You may also suffer from diseases due to disorders in the excretory system, those due to a life of profilgacy and excesses, smallpox, blood poisoning or malaria, becoming an adverse factor of longevity.

Moon, if Benefic:

You will have a good longevity.

Moon, if Malefic:

You may be slender and unhealthy. You may suffer from defective vision, mental torture, physical ailments, respiratory troubles, asthma, diseases connected with nervous system and heart depriving you of a long life.

(IX) DIFFERENT PLANETS INFLUENCING NINTH BHAVA
Prosperity

Sun, if Benefic:

You will be well-read and learned in solar sciences, poetry, music, esoteric or occult subjects. You will be attracted by sublime phenomena and you will be religiously inclined. You will have connections with colleges or legal departments. You will carry out research. You will gain through travels and will be successful overseas. You will do meritorious deeds and be successful in your attempts. You will have dutiful children. You will have self-acquired property and wealth in many lands. You will be a successful agriculturist. You will be respected by superiors. You will have the comfort of servants and means of conveyance. You will have baths in sacred rivers. You will be sincere, self-reliant, devoted, ambitious, enterprising, intelligent and chivalrous. You will construct water tanks, gardens etc. You will get help from patrimonial side. You may have materialistic tendencies. You will be a person of thought and action. You will be charitable, godly, lucky and successful. You will have personal magnetism, vitality, recuperative power, courage, reputation, authority and position. You will have good connections with government and officials. You will get felicitations. You will get prosperity from father. You will acquire gold. You will be benefited from the eastern direction. You will help others. You will have a long life.

Sun, if Malefic:

You may have little patrimony and disagreement with your father. You may lack harmonious relations with your partner. You may do much travelling. Your health may be indifferent. Your father's longevity may not be very good. You may be inimical or hostile towards father or spiritual preceptors. You may change your faith. You may suffer from glandular disease.

Mars, if Benefic:

You will be successful as a trader, naval merchant, leader or commander-in-chief or in fields connected with international trade or requiring organizing and executive capacity. You will get prosperity from brothers. You will have high power and authority. You will get powerful supporters. You will be endowed with children. Your power and prestige will increase. You will do good actions. You will be self-made and enterprising. You will have wealth and happiness. You will be powerful.

Mars, if Malefic:

You may have loss from agriculture. You may have a dependent life. You may perform cruel acts. Your relationship with brothers may not be harmonious. You may be hated by the public. You may have a sickly or short tempered father. There may be ill health of brother. You may acquire corals. You may get prosperity from southern direction.

Mercury, if Benefic:

You will be studious, scientific-minded and highly educated. You will be a lover of music and literature.

You will do virtuous acts. You may be write books or work in diplomatic service. You will have a high position in life. You will be popular, well/known and respected by public. You will be endowed with children and wealth. You will have a fortunate father. You may engage in trade and commerce. You will have success in long journeys and life in foreign places. You will be successful in all kinds of work. You will have happiness and prosperity. You may acquire emerald. You may get property from maternal uncles, maternal grandfather and paternal relations. You will have currency. You may get prosperity from northern direction.

Mercury, if Malefic:

You may be licentious. Your actions may not be commendable.

Jupiter, if Benefic:

You will have good children. You will have a long-lived and fortunate father. You will be successful in your undertakings. You will occupy high position in life as adviser or minister or consultant. You will have association with learned men and worship gods and brahmins. You may have associations with foreigners also. You will be performing religious austerities. You will acquire wealth. You will get reputation and will be famous. You will have correct intuition and clear thought. You will have good travels. You may become a strong leader. You will possess good knowledge and wisdom. You may acquire topaz and silver. You may get properity from sons, grandsons, children or grandfather. You may get prosperity from north-eastern direction.

Jupiter, if Malefic:

You may not have good children. You may not have a long-lived and fortunate father. You may not be successful in your undertakings. You may not occupy high position in life as adviser or minister or consultant. You may not have association with learned men and worship gods and brahmins. You may not have association with foreigners also. You may not be performing religious austerities. You may not gain wealth. You may not get reputation and may not be famous. You may not have correct intuition and clear thought. You may not have good travels. You may not become a strong leader. You may not possess good knowledge and wisdom. You may not aquire topaz and silver. You may not get prosperity from sons, grandsons, children or grandfather. You may not get prosperity from north-eastern direction.

Venus, if Benefic:

You will get prosperity from your partner in life. You will have luxury articles, perfumes, maidservants, pleasant journeys and happiness. You will be endowed with the birth of good children. You will get higher education. You will be good in music and fine arts. You will be successful in foreign lands. You may become head of an infantry army or occupy a high position and honour. You will be hospitable to guests and brahmins. You will have happiness in respect of partner, sons, and friends. You will be wealthy. You will rise in life by dint of your own efforts. You will command respect. You will receive favours from government. You will have popularity and comforts. You will be learned and stick to truth. You will have good reputation and fortune. You may acquire diamonds. You may get your prosperity from southern direction.

Venus, if Malefic:

You may not get prosperity from your partner in life. You may not have luxury articles, perfumes, maidservants, pleasant journeys and happiness. You may not have birth of good children. You may not get higher education. You may not be good in music and fine arts. You may not be successful in foreign lands.

You may not become head of an infantry army or occupy a high position and honour. You may not be hospitable to guests and brahmins. You may not have happiness in respect of partner, sons, and friends. You may not be wealthy. You may not rise life by dint of your own efforts. You may not command respect. You may not receive favours from government. You may not have popularity and comforts. You may not be learned and stick to truth. You may not have good reputation and fortune. You may not acquire diamonds. You may not get your prosperity from southern direction.

Saturn, if Benefic:

You will be a founder of charitable institutions. You will be thrifty in domestic life. You will renovate temples. You will be fond of occult studies. You will get legal success. You will be successful in geology, minerology, occult subjects or metaphysics. You will be rich and happy. You will also get happiness from children. You will have a philosophical turn of mind. You may possess emerald. You may get prosperity from western direction.

Saturn, if Malefic:

You may suffer from misfortunes and loss of wealth. You may have domestic unhappiness. You may suffer in respect of brothers and there may be ill health of brothers. You may be bereft of fortune, wealth and father and you may have no happiness in respect of them. You may have detached attachment. You may cause distress to others. You may be oppressed by enemies. You may live at a place other than your homeland. You may suffer from scandals.

Rahu, if Benefic:

You will be materialistic. You will undertake foreign travels. You may get prosperity from maternal grandfather. You will have increase of self-earned wealth. You will do acts of religious merit. You will have love for your brother. You will get worldly properties, name, fame, wealth and splendour. You will have power, position, political success, fixity of purpose. You will be intelligent and will not abandon work. You may get your prosperity from south-western direction.

Rahu, if Malefic:

You may have loss of ancestral wealth. You may not be fortunate in respect of your children. You may oppose your father. You may not have much happiness. You may be a puppet in the hands of your marriage partner. You may have emaciated waist. You may have an unfortunate father. You may gain from non-Hindus.

Ketu, if Benefic:

You may have prosperity from paternal grandfather. You will have children and good partner. You will be wealthy. You will visit holy places. You will gain from non-Hindus.

Ketu, if Malefic:

You may suffer in respect of your father and there may be danger to father. You may have adverse factor in respect of brothers. You may be involved in cruelty, mean acts and criminal tendencies. You may have malicious inclinations and uneven temper. You may be a religious hypocrite. You may have pain particularly in arms.

Moon, if Benefic:

You may get prosperity from mother. You will have good children. You will gain in wealth and you will have perfect contentment. You will be a builder of charitable institutions. You will get success agriculture and you will be successful in your undertakings. You will be endowed with property, sons, friends, relations. You will do meritorious deeds. You will possess lands and jewels. You are inclined to travel and make long voyages. You may live in foreign lands. You will have romantic and fanciful mind. You will get good dreams and psychic experiences. You will be very popular with ladies. You will be fond of foreign places. You will pay homage to elderly people. You will be a lover of fiction. You will get good reputation. You will be happy. You will have vital energy. You may acquire silver. You may get prosperity from western direction.

Moon, if Malefic:

You may not get property from mother. You may not have several good children. You may not gain wealth and you may not have perfect contentment. You may not be the builder of charitable institutions. You may not get success in agriculture and you may not be successful in your undertakings. You may not be endowed with property, sons, friends, relations. You may not do meritorious deeds. You may not possess lands and jewels. You are not inclined to travel and make long voyages. You may not live in foreign lands. You may not have romantic and fanciful mind. You may not get good dreams and psychic experiences. You may not be very popular with ladies. You may not be fond of foreign places. You may not pay homage to elderly people. You may not be a lover of fiction. You may not get good reputation. You will not be happy. You may not have vital energy. You may not acquire silver. You may not get prosperity from western direction.

(X) DIFFERENT PLANETS INFLUENCING TENTH BHAVA
Profession

Sun, if Benefic:

You will get position of authority and status. You will become head of small society or village. You will have success in political life and business. You will have successful military career. You will found institutions. You may be employed in government service. You will be successful in all that you undertake. You may get promotion. You may acquire a new job. You may be a musician, artist, politician, bankworker, industrialist, millowner, manufacturer, jeweller, financiar or actuary (registrar, accountant). You may be connected with occupations involving children, authority, dignitaries or government. You may be a theatre owner or manager.

Sun, if Malefic:

You may not get position of authority and status. You may not become head of a small society or village. You may not have success in political life and business. You may not have successful military career. You may not found institutions. You may not be employed in government service. You may not be successful in all that you undertake. You may not get promotion. You may not acquire a new job. You may not be a musician, artist, politician, bankworker, industrialist, millowner, manufacturer, jeweller, financiar or actuary (registrar, accountant). You may not be connected with occupations involving children, authority, dignitaries or government. You may be a theatre owner or manager.

Mars, if Benefic:

You will be a good agriculturist. You will gain in profession or business. You will occupy good position in life. You will gain through fine arts. You will own estates. You will have work connected with fires, copper, factories or red things and commodities. You may get promotion. You may be in military or police service. You will be a skilled scientist or technician patronised by rulers or government. You may become head of society, colony or town. You may be a salesman, metallurgist, soldier, politician, bank worker, insurance worker, actuary, industrialist, mill owner, manufacturer, commander-in-chief, logician, organiser, executive, fireman, warrior, military operator, chemist, druggist, surgeon, dentist, or engineer. You will have work connected with boilers, mines, minerals and ores, gold, copper, armoury, army, weapons of defence and offence, lands, burning gases, iron and steel, fire places or chemical laboratories.

Mars, if Malefic:

You may not be a good agriculturist. You may not gain in profession or business. You may not occupy a good position in life. You may not gain through fine arts. You may not own estates. You may have work connected with fires, copper, factories or red things and commodities. You may not get promotion. You may not be in military or police service. You may not be a skilled scientist or technician patronised by rulers or government. You may not become head of society, colony or town. You may not be a salesman, metallurgist, soldier, politician, bank worker, insurance worker, actuary, industrialist, mill owner, manufacturer, commander-in-chief, logician, organiser, executive, fireman, warrior, military operator, chemist, druggist, surgeon, dentist, engineer or cook. You may not have work connected with boilers, mines, and minerals and ores, gold, copper, armoury, army weapons of defence and offence, lands, burning gases, iron and steel, fire places or chemical laboratories.

Mercury, if Benefic:

You will succeed in long journeys. You will take additional charge of duties. You may be engaged in public life. You may work as reporter, electrician or in railways. You will succeed in profession and business. You will get promotion. You will get involved in religious activity and spiritual evolution. You will have success in education. You will be interested in research or antiquities. You may be a copyist or proof reader. Your profession may be connected with currency, alloys, water reservoirs, poetry, authorship, mercantile activity, trade and trading association, commerce, aerial and land journeys, weaving, vegetation, inferior or base metals, accounts, schools, parks, science, research, inspection of accounts, business management, atomic energy, mathematics, electrical/electronic engineering, documentation and recording and all jobs with such work, teaching, writing, radio or communication media. You may be a journalist, accountant, mathematician, orator, public speaker, ambassador, bookseller, merchant, publisher, stationer, grocer, printer, manufacturing representative, architect, correspondent, interpreter, reporter, historian, scientist, philosopher, doctor, astronomer, psychologist, psychoanalyst, judge or lawyer.

Mercury, if Malefic:

You may not succeed in long journeys. You may not get additional charge of duties. You may not be engaged in public life. You may work as reporter, electrician or in railways. You may not succeed in profession and business. You may not get promotion. You may get involved in religious activity and spiritual evolution. You may not have success in education. You may not be interested in research and antiquities. You may not be a copyist or proof reader. Your profession may not be connected with currency, alloys, water reservoirs, poetry, authorship, mercantile activity, trade and trading association, commerce, aerial and land journeys, weaving, vegetation, inferior or base metals, accounts, schools, parks, science, research, inspection of accounts, business management, atomic energy, mathematics, electrical/electronic engineering, documentation and recording and all jobs with such work, teaching, writing, radio or communication media. You may not be a journalist, hawker, accountant, mathematician, orator, public speaker, ambassador, bookseller, merchant, publisher, stationer, grocer, printer, manufacturer's representative, architect, correspondent, interpreter, reporter, historian, scientist, philosopher, doctor, astronomer, psychologist, psychoanalyst, judge or lawyer.

Jupiter, if Benefic:

You will have good relations with higher officials. You will do meritorious deeds. You may become head of a village. You will command many servants. You will get timely promotion. You will be a good agriculturist. You will get success in business. You will be a high official in government. You will head research, academic and educational institution. You will have political life. You will be a sportsperson. Your work will be connected with Vedas, Vedangas, legal affairs, diplomacy, arts and science, philosophy, asceticism, restaurants, hotels, travel, research, law and academic affairs. You may be preceptor, minister, lawyer, banker, philanthrophist, counsellor, lecturer, publisher, writer, astrologer, travel agent, priest and temple trustee, official, cashier, philosopher, literateur, grocer, tobacconist, historian, mathematician, scientist, doctor, astronomer, psychologist, psychoanalyst or judge.

Jupiter, if Malefic:

You may not have good relations with higher officials. You may not do meritorious deeds. You may not become head of a village. You may not command many servants. You may not get timely promotion. You may not be a good agriculturist. You may not get success in business. You may not be a high official in government. You may not head some research, academic or educational institution. You may not have political life. You may not be a sportsperson. Your work may not be connected with Vedas, Vedangas, legal affairs, diplomacy, arts and science, philosophy, asceticism, restaurants, travel, research, law or academic matters. You may not be preceptor, minister, lawyer, banker, philanthropist, counsellor, lecturer, publisher, writer, astrologer, travel agent, priest and temple trustee, official, cashier, philosopher,

literateur,   grocer,   tobacconist,   historian,
mathematician,   scientist,   doctor,   astronomer,
psychologist, psychoanalyst or judge.

Venus, if Benefic:

You may be a lawyer or skilled trader. You will have
healing power. You will profit from cosmetics or
articles used by women. You will act in accordance
with scriptures in your doings. You will not rub on
anybody's wrong side. You will gain through music and
jewellery. You will be popular. You will have work
connected with poetical faculty, dress, fine arts,
authorship, dancing, lakes, water, wind, sugarcane
industry, medicine, silk or cotton. You may be a
botanist, singer, musician, actor, artist, poet, cinema
artist, dancer cosmetician, beautician, dealer in
furnishings and furniture, entertainer of all kinds,
coffee planter, tea estate owner, social secretary,
photographer, engraver, cartoonist, dramatist or
embroiderer. You may be engaged in work connected
with silks and expensive textiles, perfumes, furniture
making, fancy aricles, ladies articles or objects of art
and fashion, computers.

Venus, if Malefic:

You may not be a lawyer or skilled trader. You may
not have healing power. You may not profit from
cosmetics or articles used by women. You may not act
in accordance with scriptures in your doings. You may
rub on wrong side. You may not gain through music or
jewellery. You may not be popular. You may not have
work connected with poetical faculty, dress, fine arts,
authorship, dancings, lakes, water, wind, sugarcane
industry, medicine, silk or cotton. You may not be a
botanist, singer, musician, actor, artist, poet, cinema
artist, dancer, cosmetician, beautician, dealer, in
furnishings and furnitures, entertainer of all kinds,
coffee planter, tea estate . owner, social secretary,
photographer, engraver, connected with silks and

expensive textiles, perfumes, furniture making, fancy articles, ladies articles or objects of art and fashion, computers.

Saturn, if Benefic:

You will be a great worker. You will be a good farmer. You will have professional success and you will get promotions. You will be successful in your undertakings. You will get position of authority. You will have work connected with agriculture or products derived from the bowels of earth such as minerals, oils etc. You will occupy a high position in life. You will be head of an institution or at the helm of affairs in the sphere of your activity. You will get speedy promotion to high level. You will be head of religious institution. You will become a ruler or minister. You will work for down-trodden masses. You will be judicious and work in the capacity of a judge. You will become ascetic in later life. Your work may be connected with oils, woollen fabrics, architecture, iron, lead, atmosphere, air, mountains, hills, forest regions, coal and fuel of every kind, petrol, real estate business, leather goods, farm or factory labour. You may be miner, craftsman, architect, building contractor, philosopher, agriculturist, artisan, mechanic, compositor, mill worker, brick layer or mass leader.

Saturn, if Malefic:

You may not be a great worker. You may not be a good farmer. You may not have professional success and you may not get promotions. You may not be successful in your undertakings. You may not get position of authority. You may have works connected with agriculture or products derived from the bowels of earth such as minerals, oils etc. You may not occupy a high position in life. You may not be head of an institution or at the helm of affairs in the sphere of your activity. You may not get speedy promotion to a high level. You may not head a religious institution. You may not become a ruler or minister. You may not work for down-trodden masses. You may not be judicious and work in the capacity of a judge. You may not become ascetic in later life. Your work may not be connected with oils, woollen fabrics, architecture, iron, lead, atmosphere, air, mountains, hills, forest regions, coal and fuel of every kind, petrol, real estate business, leather goods, farm or factory labour. You may not be a miner, craftman, architect, building contractor, philosopher, agriculturist, artisan, mechanic, compositor, mill worker or mass leader. You may be industrious and yet get financial loss in business. You may have sudden reversals and adversary results. Ultimately you may become sanyasi as you may not own anything.

Rahu, if Benefic:

You will be engaged in work for others. You will have power and position. You will succeed in your undertakings. You will have connections with non-Hindus and gain from them. You will be engaged in music, literature or poetry. You will be skilled as a creative writer or artist. You will have work connected with radio, aerial navigation, metaphysical sciences, water or general staff in offices and government and business organisations. You may become a lecturer, inventor, aviator, scientist, astrologer or psychologist.

Rahu, if Malefic:

You may engage in work for others. You may not have power and position. You may not succeed in your undertakings. You may not have work connected with non-Hindus and gain from them. You may not be engaged in music, literature or poetry. You may not be skilled as a creative writer or artist. You may not have work connected with radio, aerial navigation, metaphysical sciences, waters or general staff in offices and government and business organisations. You may not become a lecturer, inventor, aviator, scientist, astrologer or psychologist.

Ketu, if Benefic:

You will have work connected with scriptures. You will be good in mechanics. You will do highly intelligent work. You will become spiritual and work for poorer classes. You will have power. You may be a philosopher. You may have work connected with mining, astrology, artistic taste, literary genius, water or general staff in offices and government and business organisations.

Ketu, if Malefic:

You may not have work connected with scriptures. You may not be good in mechanics. You may not do highly intelligent work. You may not become spiritual and may not work for poorer classes. You may not have power. You may not be a philosopher. You may not have work connected with mining, astrology, artistic taste, literary genius, water or general staff in offices and government and business organisations.

Moon, if Benefic:

You will have position. You will get promotion in profession or gains in business. You will be successful in your undertakings. You will have work connected with government. You will be skilled in the arts. You will be a trustee of religious or social institutions. You will involve in public life. You will change business or profession. You will become popular. You may have work connected with water, cultivation, pearls, gems, vegetation, watery places, psycho-physiological consciousness, watery substances, lakes, sea, textiles, chemicals, pharmaceuticals, sugarcane, agriculture, travelling and all travelling requisites, plastics or catering. You may become a seaman, travel agent, navigator, sailor, nurse, liquor dealer, laundry owner, confectioner, dairy owner, obstetrician, politician, bank worker, insurance worker, industrialist, mill owner or manufacturer.

Moon, if Malefic:

You may not have any position. You may not get promotion in profession or gains in business. You may not be successful in your undertakings. You may not have work connected with government. You may not be skilled in the arts. You may not be a trustee of religious or social institutions. You may not involve in public life. You may not change business or profession. You may not become popular. You may not have work connected with water, cultivation, pearls, gems, vegetation, watery places, psycho-physiological consciousness, watery substances, lakes, sea, textiles, chemicals, pharmaceuticals, sugarcane, agriculture, travelling and all travelling requisites, plastics, or catering. You may become a seaman, travel agent, navigator, sailor, nurse, liquor dealer, laundry owner, confectioner, dairy owner, obstetrician, politician, bank worker, insurance worker, industrialist, mill owner or manufacturer. You may be unstable.

(XI) DIFFERENT PLANETS INFLUENCING ELEVENTH BHAVA
Gains and Income

Sun, if Benefic:

You will fulfil your ambitions and desires. You will have connection with people in power. You will have permanent friends. You will have social success and good business. You will possess many means of conveyance. You will be wealthy. You will get success without effort. Your wealth will be through fair means. You will get reputation. You will have great success and position. You will gain from several sources and government service. You will attain general prosperity. You will have happy domestic life. You will be endowed with the birth of good children. You will get good servants. Others will be jealous of you. You will have the capacity to befriend and you will have one powerful friend. You will get enjoyment from your

married partner. You will become equivalent to a king.
You will acquire a job. You will do many auspicious
deeds. You will be respectful, loyal, honest, hopeful,
principled, learned, famous, and strong. You will have
profound insight. You will possess permanent friends.
You will be long-lived. You will gain through your
courage, reputation, authority, position, government
officials, father, kings or statesman. You may gain from
dealings in hills, forests, capital towns, fuel, wools,
weapons, silk cloth, gold or medicines. You may gain as
a doctor. You will gain from the eastern direction.

Sun, if Malefic:

You may have many political enemies. You may be
unfriendly with politicians. You may be devoid of
friends. You may have stomach troubles.

Mars, if Benefic:

You will be learned and educated. You will get gains
through agricultural operations and business. You will
have property and wealth. You will have good income.
You will be influential, crafty, commanding,
courageous, religious and pushing. You will have
prosperity and happiness. There will be much inflow of
money. You will get promotion. You will be well-
informed. You will be self-made. You will have a few
reliable friends. Your income will increase. You will
gain from your elder brothers. You will possess
property. You will progress and prosper. You will gain
from brothers. You will gain by dealing in fire places,
mines, minerals or armoury. You may gain by working
in police department or army. You will gain by your
organising and executive capacity, persistence and
leadership. You may expect to gain from the southern
direction.

Mars, if Malefic:

You may have an angry temper and curtail
matrimonial happiness. You may have heavy
expenditure.

Mercury, if Benefic:

You will be wealthy and happy. You will have
mathematical faculty. You may a good astrologer. You
will have many friends among famous men. You will
possess many lands. You will be logical and scientific.
You will succeed in trade. There will be influx of
wealth in large-scale. You will lead a prosperous and
contented life. You will do virtuous deeds and will be
respected. You will be famous. You will be truthful and
you will have a number of obedient servants. You will
be endowed with various worldly comforts. You will get
happiness in respect of children. You will triumph over
enemies. You will own much property. You will have
increased wealth. You will have many acquaintances
but only a few permanent friends. You will associate
with youngsters. You will be generous and charitable.
You will be prosperous and respected. You will be good
in mathematics or astrology. You will gain from
dealings connected with commerce, chemistry, green
grams, emerald, lead, oilseeds, edible oils, intellect,
education, authorship, power of speech and eloquence,
currency or palatial buildings. You may gain as doctor
or tradesperson. You may gain also from maternal
uncles, maternal grandfather and paternal relations.
You may gain from the northern direction.

Mercury, if Malefic:

You may not be wealthy and happy. You may not
have mathematical faculty. You may not be a good
astrologer. You may not have many friends among
famous men. You may not possess many lands. You may
not be logical and scientific. You may not succeed in
trade. There may not be influx of wealth in large scale.
You may not lead a prosperous and contented life. You
may not do virtuous deeds and may not be respected.
You may not be famous. You may not be truthful and
you may not have a number of obedient servants. You
may not be endowed with various worldly comforts. You
may not get happiness in respect of children. You may

not triumph over enemies. You may not own much property. You may not have increased wealth. You may not have many acquaintances. You may not associate with yougsters. You may not be generous and charitable. You may not be prosperous and respected. You may not be good in mathematics or astrology. You may not gain from dealings connected with commerce, chemistry, green grams, emerald, lead, oilseeds, edible oils, intellect, education, authorship, power of speech and eloquence, currency or palatial buildings. You may not gain as doctor or tradesperson. You may not gain from maternal uncles, maternal grandfather and paternal relations. You may not gain from the northern direction.

Jupiter, if Benefic:

You will be a lover of music. You will be wealthy. You will have accumulated funds. You will do good deeds. You will have many friends. You will have gain and accumulation of wealth. You will have birth of good children. You will acquire good house, conveyance etc. You will be respected by people in high position and authority. You will have a large income. You will have servants. You will have good friends. You will gain through social success. You will realise your ambitions. You will learn music and master it. You will enjoy all comforts. You will be well-placed in life. You will be able, statesmanly, god-fearing, charitable, influential, philanthrophic, famous, bold and full of knowledge, intellect and education. You will get topaz and silver. You will gain from children. You may gain as minister and adviser and from insurance companies. You may gain from the north-eastern direction.

Jupiter, if Malefic:

You may have a limited number of children. You may not have high education. You may face obstruction in inflow of wealth.

Venus, if Benefic:

You will have good means of conveyance. You will have many friends. You will get immense riches and great comforts and happiness. You will lead a luxurious life. You will go on a journey to distant places. You will gain through business. You will have good gain of money. You will have the requisites of comforts. You will possess lands and gain in agriculture. You will gain after marriage. You will get good servants. You will get social success. You will be very influential, learned, wealthy, successful, popular and very rich. You will gain from your partner in life. You may gain from your dealings in vehicles, sugarcane, industry, trade, chemicals, medicines, wools, silk or luxury articles, computers. You may gain from the south-eastern direction.

Venus, if Malefic:

You may not have good conveyance. You may not have many friends. You may not get immense riches and great comforts and happiness. You may not lead a luxurious life. You may not go on a journey to distant places. You may not gain through business. You may not have good gain of money. You may not have pleasures of the bed and the requisites of comforts. You may not possess lands and gain in agriculture. You may not gain after marriage. You may not get good servants. You may not get social success. You may not be very influential, learned, wealthy, succcessful, popular and very rich. You may not gain from your partner in life. You may not gain from your dealings in vehicles, sugarcane, industry, trade, chemicals, medicines, wools, silk or luxury articles, computers. You may not gain from the south-eastern direction.

Saturn, if Benefic:

You will be learned, feared and respected. You will be very wealthy. You will have much landed property and conveyance. You will get political respect and success. You will have increased income and gain of wealth. You will attain position of authority. You will succeed in your undertakings. You will lead a prosperous life. You will have happiness all round. You will engage in trade or commerce. You may earn from artisanship. You will have select friends mostly elders. Your hopes will be fulfilled. You will own lands. You will get promotion. You will command authority. You will be influential, strong and industrious. You may gain from servants and elderly people. You may gain from dealing in hills, forest regions, iron, prisons or black grams. You may acquire sapphire. You may gain from the western direction.

Saturn, if Malefic:

You may have interrupted education. You may suffer ill health. You may have an adverse effect in respect of happiness of brothers, sons and your married partner. There may be obstacles in your education. There may be danger to your elder brother.

Rahu, if Benefic:

You will be wealthy. You will be influential among lower castes. You will have children. You will be a good agriculturist. You will gain from business. You will succeed in your profession. You will travel a lot. You will have a large retinue. You will be famous both in your own and opposite camp. You will engage in trade and business or perseveringly apply to the work undertaken. You will gain from non-Hindus. You will gain from good advice tendered from others. You will be heroic in strife and overcome your enemies. You will be happy, respected, intelligent, industrious and courageous. Your health will be generally good. You will gain from materialists, foreign travels and maternal grandfather. You may gain from south-western direction.

Rahu, if Malefic:

You may have a limited number of children. You may have inclination to appropriate other peoples' wealth. You are likely to get diseases of ear.

Ketu, if Benefic:

You will be wealthy. You will gain in all your attempts. You will have increased earnings. You will get success over your enemies. You will perform good deeds and command respect. You will engage perserveringly in work. You will be humorous, witty, intelligent, influential, popular, famous, luxurious, learned, contended and industrious. You will have a excellent position for inflow of money. You may gain from dealings connected with fire, flame or mining. You can expect to gain from your paternal grandfather.

Ketu, if Malefic:

You may not have good children and you may have a limited number of children. You may suffer from ailments of stomach and anal diseases. Your children may be a source of worry to you.

Moon, if Benefic:

You will have many friends. You will possess good lands. You will attain great position. You will be liked and helped by fair sex. You will give donations. You will get gains in business. You will have increased wealth. You will have lucky children. You will have servants. You will be clever in government work. You will gain through social life. You will gain from agriculture. You will realise your ambitions. You will be powerful, philanthrophic, polite, helpful, influential, cultured, charitable, popular, famous, prosperous and well-informed. You will gain through politics. You will have many friends but only a few most reliable permanent friends. You will have literary or artistic taste. You will get great reputation. You will get easy success. You will be a person of principles. You will get general prosperity and happiness. Your mind will be closely and perseveringly devoted to work in hand. You will be wealthy. You will get sons and daughters. You will have yearning (earnest desire) for foreign lands. You will be wide-awake. You will gain from your mother, intelligence and vital energy. You may gain from your dealings connected with watery substances, textiles, chemicals, pharmaceuticals, sugarcane, rice, wheat, agriculture, pearls or silver. You may get your gains from north-western direction.

Moon, if Malefic:

You may not have many children. You may not enjoy. You may not be intelligent. You may suffer in matters of health.

(XII) DIFFERENT PLANETS INFLUENCING TWELFTH BHAVA
Losses and Expenditure

Sun, if Benefic:

You will be ceremonial minded and lover of esoteric and occult knowledge. You will rise in religious matters. You will have a liberal outlook and spend money on benefic objects. You will vanquish your enemies. You will succeed in the fields of medicine, chemistry, occult sciences, association with hospitals, prisons or sanitoriums. You will be self-sacrificing.

Sun, if Malefic:

You may be unsuccessful in work. You may fall in career. You may be poor. You may have disputes with father. There may be loss of wealth. You may have wanderings and tedious journeys. You may have financial strain. You may get loss of energy and vitality. You may be bereft of wealth and happiness in respect of children and also suffer. You may be deviod of strength. You may have sorrows. You may separate from your partner, relatives or brothers. You may land in disputes. You may prefer to lead a secluded life. You may get loss in foreign land. There may be danger to children. You may travel much. You may have impediments in work connected with government. You may be troubled by enemies. You may have disputes with parents. Your wealth may be spent on fines or may be confiscated by the government. There may be loss of wealth through tax raids, government enactments or confiscations. You may not be straight-forward.

Mars, if Benefic:

You will be active. You will have good habits. Good things will happen to brothers.

Mars, if Malefic:

You may be unsuccessful, poor, unpopular, stumbling, dishonest, evil-minded and treacherous. You may have incendiary habits. You may contact diseases. You may be prone to suffering. You are liable to be defrauded and subjected to deception. You may have to face unseen impediments. You may suffer eye disease. You may do cruel acts. You may separate from your partner. You may develop mean tendencies and criminal acts. You may have loss of wealth and consequent grief. You may face destruction of your undertakings. You may fall from grace. You may get indebted and run into an overdraft account. You are liable to criminal case and suffer confinement. You may have adverse matrimonial happiness. You may have loss of money due to dancing girls. You may have expensive litigations and dangerous enemies. Your money may be lost through ransom, cheating and swindlers. You may meet with accidents. You may lose popularity and your career may deteriorate. You may land in danger, injury and scandal. You may visit jails or you are liable to be imprisoned. You may have to face difficulties.

Mercury, if Benefic:

You will become philosophical, intelligent, obliging, gifted, and religiously inclined. You will have a pleasing personality. You will speak sweetly. You will spend on good deeds. You will acquire new skills.

Mercury, if Malefic:

You may have limited progeny. You may be lacking in opportunity. You may have loss of wealth and comforts. You may fall from high position. Your enterprises may end in frustration. You may suffer humiliation. Success may not be achieved. You are likely to invest recklessly in shares, trade and business. Your mother may face danger. You may have losses due to family litigations. Your wealth may dwindle. You may be worried, adulterous, capricious, wayward, narrow-minded, passionate, despondent, devoid of learning, hard-hearted, indolent. You may be fond of occult and secret acts and unusual thoughts. You may enter into petty quarrels and sandals. You may suffer initiality. You may have mental delusions and worries. There may be danger to your maternal uncle. You may be poor.

Jupiter, if Benefic:

You will be honest and pay taxes and tolls properly. You will gain through law, medicines, occult subjects or service in public institutions. You will visit hospitals and asylums. You will have connections with foreigners. You will be pious and in the end of life you will attain Moksha (enlightenment). You will be devoid of attachment. You will be inclined to asceticism in later life. You will have artistic taste. You will travel a lot. You will be elegant in speech. You will get happiness on account of children. You will be religiously inclined to chastity and benevolence. You will accumulate money. You will have good wealth, children and profession.

Jupiter, if Malefic:

You may have a limited number of children or you will be deprived of children. You may have enlargement of spleen. You may have evil tendencies and scandals. You may have a deprived, poor, fallen, struggling and lascivious life. You may be hated by others. You may have loss of wealth. You may be of a wandering nature. People may harbour enmity towards you. You may be sinful in your conduct. You may engage in service of others. You may have hypocritical show of religious fervour. You may be indolent and lazy. Your business may be poor and unlucky. You may suffer loss of children. You may become sadist.

Venus, if Benefic:

You will have increase of wealth. You will get good sexual bliss. You will be economical and save money. You will be well up in amorous arts but indolent and lead a happy-go-lucky life. You will triumph over your enemies. You will have a good partner, marriage and pleasures. You will gain through public and charitable institutions. You will enjoy peaceful life in seclusion. You will have romantic life. You will investigate secret arts.

Venus, if Malefic:

You may not have a good career. You may have unworthy performance. You may have immoral tendencies. You may be low minded, miserly, obscure, licentious, unprincipled, fond of sexual pleasures, liar, unhappy, pretentious and indolent. You may have increased expenses. You may have weak eyes. You may lose relatives. You may suffer in your love affairs. Your health may suffer.

Saturn, if Benefic:

You will be learned in occult science. You will be dexterous. You will be attracted towards yoga in later life. You will have less expenditure and enemies. You will have good longevity.

Saturn, if Malefic:

Your business may fail and your debts may mount. You may land in litigation and loss of prestige. You may have life in a seculded place. You may have to face danger of imprisonment. You may be involved in secret inimical activities. You may have downfall, loss, accidents and injury. You may suffer from secret sorrows. You may have disappointments in love affairs. You may have dissatisfaction in sexual life. You may waste money for nasty purposes. You may have a weak constitution and your vision may be defective. There may be ill health to your children. You may have misery, untold calamity and hardships. You may enter upon a vicious code of conduct. You may commit sins. You may be deformed. You may have many enemies. You may get loss of wealth. You may lose energy. You may be separated from family. You may suffer from criminal prosecutions and displeasure from elders. You may suffer in public estimation due to your low conduct or you may be demoted in career or meet with frustration in business enterprises. You may have heavy expenditure. You may have premature decay of teeth. You may suffer from infirmity of limb. Your maternal uncle may suffer. You may be impudent and indigent. You may be devoid of intelligence. You may be oppressed by enemies.

Rahu, if Benefic:

  You may not be saintly. You will have the
appearance of humility but be courageous. You may not
have loss of wealth. You may not be wandering and may
not be separated from family. You may not be subjected
to criminal prosecutions or punishments. You may not
have unhappiness and misery. You may not have
adverse health. You may not incur heavy-expenditure.
You may not get trouble in the region of heart. You may
not become antagonistic to gentlemen. You may not
wander a great deal. You may not fall from high
position. You may not have unfavourable pleasures of
the bed. You may not suffer loss of limbs through
voilent accidents. You may not have limited progeny.

Rahu, if Malefic:

  You may be saintly. You may have the appearance of
humility but be courageous. You may have loss of
wealth. You may be wandering and may be separated
from your family. You may be subjected to criminal
prosecutions or punishments. You may have
unhappiness and misery. You may have adverse health.
You may incur heavy expenditure. You may get trouble
in the region of heart. You may become antagonistic to
gentlemen. You may wander a great deal. You may fall
from high position. You may have unfavourable
pleasures of the bed. You may suffer loss of limbs
through violent accidents. You may have limited
progeny.

Ketu, if Benefic:

  You may be a traveller. You will perform journey to
distant places. You will be victorious in disputes. You
will get happiness from maternal uncle.

Ketu, if Malefic:

  You may be capricious, licentious and worried. You
may have unsettled mind. You may have foreign

residence. You may be attracted to servile classes. You may have loss of wealth. You may suffer from ill health. You may land in misfortunes, criminal acts and prosecutions, miseries and sorrows. You may indulge secretly in sinful acts. You may incur expenditure on unworthy objects. You may expend away money saved. You may be worried. You may have ailments of feet, in regions of navel and anus and in eye. You may be weak but voluptuous. Your conjugal happiness may be impaired. You may act contrary to advice. You may have mental disturbances and wandering habits. You may reside abroad. You may work amidst servile classes.

Moon, if Benefic:

You will have a good mother. You will go on a journey to distant places. You will speak softly. You will control your senses. You will be merciful. You will be fond of occult subjects. You will gain through hospitals or isolated positions. You will make voyages. You will be romantic.

Moon, if Malefic:

You may have loss of wealth. You may spend much. You may have liberal outlook. You may have ill health, misery, disgrace, defeat, loss of happiness, loss of power, infirmity of some limb, eye sight, undignified position in life, humiliation, ill repute, defective organ, mean behaviour, indiscreet love affairs or an obscure life. Your wealth may be lost through tax raids, government enactments or confiscations. You may have obstacles in all your undertakings. You may be deceived by trusted colleagues. Your mother may have ill health. You may be narrow-minded, solitary, indolent, much worried or proud. Your company may consist of low class persons.

PREDICTIONS OF DIFFERENT PLANETS in Different Rasis
(I) BODY
Sun in Different Rasis

Being in Aries, Sun if Benefic:
You can expect to have strong bones.

Being in Taurus, Sun if Benefic:
Your nose may be prominent.

Being in Cancer, Sun if Benefic:
You may have good appearance.

Being in Leo, Sun if Malefic:
You may have tender, weak and effiminate body.

Being in Sagittarius, Sun if Benefic:
You may have a fully developed body with broad cheeks.

Being in Aquarius, Sun if Benefic:
You may have medium height.

Mars in Different Rasis

Being in Aries, Mars if Malefic:
You may have scars on the body and consequently may not look fair.

Being in Taurus, Mars if Malefic:
Your body may be rough.

Being in Gemini, Mars if Benefic:
You may have a well built middle stature with attractive appearance.

Being in Gemini, Mars if Malefic:
You are likely to be peevish.

Being in Leo, Mars if Benefic:
You may have a strong body.

Being in Leo, Mars if Malefic:
You may have a peevish body.

Being in Libra, Mars if Benefic:
You may have a systematically built tall body with a fair and swarthy complexion and good appearance.

Being in Libra, Mars if Malefic:
You may have a defect in some limb.

Being in Scorpio, Mars if Benefic:
You may have middle stature.

Being in Scorpio, Mars if Malefic:
On your body you may have marks of wounds or those caused by fire.

Being in Aquarius, Mars if Malefic:
You are likely to have rough hair on your body and you may not be pleasing in your appearance.

Being in Pisces, Mars if Benefic:
You may have fair complexion.

Mercury in Different Rasis

Being in Aries, Mercury if Benefic:
You may have middle stature.

Being in Taurus Mercury if Benefic:
You will be well-built.

Being in Gemini, Mercury if Benefic:
    You may be tall.

Being in Leo, Mercury if Benefic:
    You may be tall.

Being in Libra, Mercury if Benefic:
    You may have fair complexion and sanguine disposition.

Being in Scorpio, Mercury if Benefic:
    You may have curly hair.

Being in Sagittarius, Mercury if Benefic:
    You are likely to have tall well-built body structure.

Being in Capricorn, Mercury if Malefic:
    You may have a low status.

Being in Aquarius, Mercury if Benefic:
    Your structure may be of middle nature.

Jupiter in Different Rasis

Being in Aries, Jupiter if Malefic:
    Your body may bear scars of wounds.

Being in Taurus, Jupiter, if Benefic:
    You may be handsome.

Being in Taurus, Jupiter if Malefic:
    You may have stout and large body.

Being in Gemini, Jupiter if Benefic:
    You may have tall well-built body.

Being in Cancer, Jupiter if Malefic:
    You may have swarthy complexion.

Being in Cancer, Jupiter if Benefic:
  You may be handsome.

Being in Leo, Jupiter if Benefic:
  You may have a tall strong and compact body with a commanding appearance.

Being in Virgo, Jupiter if Benefic:
  You are likely to have middle stature.

Being in Libra, Jupiter if Benefic:
  You may be handsome and attractive. You can expect to have a strong body.

Being a Scorpio, Jupiter if Benefic:
  You may have majestic appearance with a tall well-built and strong body.

Being in Scorpio, Jupiter if Malefic:
  You may have a slight hunchback.

Being in Sagittarius, Jupiter if Benefic:
  You may be handsome.

Being in Capricorn, Jupiter if Malefic:
  You may have a weak body.

Being in Pisces, Jupiter if Benefic:
  You may be of medium height.

Being in Pisces, Jupiter if Malefic:
  You may be stout.

Venus in Different Rasis

Being in Taurus, Venus if Benefic:
  You may be strong and well-built with a handsome and pleasing countenance and fair complexion.

Being in Gemini, Venus if Benefic:
You may be handsome.

Being in Cancer, Venus if Benefic:
You may have a strong and good looking body.

Being in Leo, Venus if Benefic:
You may have fair complexion.

Being in Libra, Venus if Benefic:
You may be handsome.

Being in Scorpio, Venus if Benefic:
You may have broad features.

Being in Scorpio, Venus if Malefic:
You may be short-statured.

Being in Sagittarius, Venus if Benefic:
You may have tall and well-developed body with handsome appearance.

Being in Capricorn, Venus if Benefic:
You may be good looking.

Being in Capricorn, Venus if Malefic:
You may have a weak body.

Being in Aquarius, Venus if Benefic:
You may have handsome appearance with middle stature.

Saturn in Different Rasis

Being in Taurus, Saturn if Malefic:
You may not be of fair complexion.

Being in Cancer, Saturn if Benefic:
  You may be cheerful and good looking.

Being in Cancer, Saturn if Malefic:
  There may be space in between your teeth.

Being in Leo, Saturn if Benefic:
  You may be of middle stature.

Being in Virgo, Saturn if Malefic:
  Your complexion may not be fair.

Being in Libra, Saturn if Benefic:
  You may be tall, fair and handsome.

Being in Capricorn, Saturn if Malefic:
  You may have a peevish body.

Being in Aquarius, Saturn if Malefic:
  You are likely to have indolent and inactive eyes.

Moon in Different Rasis

Being in Aries, Moon if Benefic:
  You may have round eyes and good complexion.

Being in Aries, Moon if Malefic:
  Your thighs may be large and your hair may not be good.

Being in Taurus, Moon if Benefic:
  You may have broad chest, plenty of curly hair and adorable looks.

Being in Taurus, Moon if Malefic:
  You may have large thighs and hips. Your waist, feet, shoulders, knees, and face may be broad with thick neck. There may be some mark on one side of the body.

Your eyes may be like that of a bull. You may have a gait like that of a goose.

Being in Gemini, Moon if Benefic:

You may have curly hair, broad limbs and dark eyes.

Being in Gemini, Moon if Malefic:

You may have prominent nose and veins on the body.

Being in Cancer, Moon if Benefic:

You may be of middle stature.

Being in Cancer, Moon if Malefic:

You are likely to be a bit stout with a thick neck.

Being in Leo, Moon if Benefic:

You may have a dignified look. You may be a blonde.

Being in Leo, Moon if Malefic:

You may have large and broad face and cheeks. Your bones may be thick. You are likely to have very light and scanty hair on the body. Your throat may be large. You may have eyes with yellowish tinge and not very large.

Being in Virgo, Moon if Benefic:

You may have soft and adorable body with almond eyes and modest gait and lovely complexion.

Being in Virgo, Moon if Malefic:

You are likely to have sunken shoulders and arms.

Being in Libra, Moon if Benefic:

You may be tall and your eyes may be beautiful.

Being in Libra, Moon if Malefic:

You may have a hard and thin body with raised nose,

small chin and nails, rough thighs and calves and big belly. Your limbs may be deformed and your veins may be prominent.

Being in Scorpio, Moon if Benefic:
You may have broad eyes.

Being in Scorpio, Moon if Malefic:
You may have round shanks and thighs with wide chest. Your complexion may be brown. There may marks of wound or those caused by fire on the body.

Being in Sagittarius, Moon if Benefic:
You may have strong well-built body with round eyes and long arms.

Being in Sagittarius, Moon if Malefic:
You may have a bent body. You are likely to have broad face, large teeth, indistinct shoulders, disfigured nails and arms, broad cheek and waist, high shoulders, large neck and prominent throat.

Being in Capricorn, Moon if Benefic:
Your body may be lean and tall. You may have good eyes and slender waist.

Being in Capricorn, Moon if Malefic:
Your eyes and veins may be prominent. You may have large neck and round calves.

Being in Aquarius, Moon if Benefic:
Your body may be muscular and tall. You may be beautiful minded.

Being in Aquarius, Moon if Malefic:
You may have a large head, face and waist. Your neck may be of camel type. Your skin may be rough with hair. You may have large teeth, big buttocks and

thighs. Your belly may be low. You may have a prominent nose, dry skin, large hands and feet, poor eyes.

Being in Pisces, Moon if Benefic:

You may have a perfect, bright and handsome body.

Being in Pisces, Moon if Malefic:

Your head may be large and your nose may be long.

(II) HEALTH
Sun in Different Rasis

Being in Aries, Sun if Benefic:

You may have strong bones.

Being in Aries, Sun if Malefic:

You may be impulsive and phlegmatic. Your health may cause troubles due to too much heat, excess of bile or blood disorders.

Being in Taurus, Sun if Benefic:

You will be capable of bearing much physical stress and strain like a bull.

Being in Taurus, Sun if Malefic:

You may suffer from diseases of mouth and eyes.

Being in Gemini, Sun if Benefic:

You will be assimilative and maintain good health.

Being in Gemini, Sun if Malefic:

You may have setbacks in health giving rise to mental worries.

Being in Cancer, Sun if Malefic:

You may suffer from imbalance of bile and phlegm in the body. You may not be capable of continuous hard work and easily tired. Constipation may bother you. You may be sickly.

Being in Leo, Sun if Benefic:

You will be strong, deep and will have much stamina.

Being in Virgo, Sun if Malefic:

You may continuously suffer from serious physical diseases. You may not have much physical and mental stamina. Your health may be affected. You may have a tender, weak and effiminate (feminine, delicate) body.

Being in Libra, Sun if Malefic:

Due to your loose morals and being a drunkard, you may spoil your health.

Being in Sagittarius, Sun if Benefic:

You will have much stamina and you will maintain good health.

Being in Capricorn, Sun if Benefic:

Your digestive powers are good.

Being in Capricorn, Sun if Malefic:

You may have much stamina.

Being in Aquarius, Sun if Benefic:

You will have good stamina.

Being in Aquarius, Sun if Malefic:

You may be mentally worried. You are liable to heart diseases.

Being in Pisces, Sun if Malefic:

Your health may be affected due to disease of private parts.

Mars in Different Rasis

Being in Aries, Mars if Benefic:
You will be having much stamina.

Being in Aries, Mars if Malefic:
You may have scars on the body.

Being in Gemini, Mars if Benefic:
You can put up much severe strain due to your bodily vigour and strength.

Being in Gemini, Mars if Malefic:
You may be peevish.

Being in Cancer, Mars if Malefic:
You may get ailments every now and then. In addition you may be worried due to some chronic ailment. You may have defective sight. You will be soft and suffer from ill health.

Being in Leo, Mars if Benefic:
You will be capable of putting up hard labour due to your strong body and great stamina.

Being in Leo, Mars if Malefic:
You may be peevish and worried by mental complaints. You may suffer from stomach troubles.

Being in Virgo, Mars if Malefic:
You are likely to have troubles in digestive organs.

Being in Libra, Mars if Malefic:
You may have some defect in limbs.

Being in Scorpio, Mars if Malefic:
You may suffer from poison (like food poisoning).

You may may have marks of wounds or those caused by fire on your body.

Being in Aquarius, Mars if Malefic:
   You may have danger in water.

Being in Pisces, Mars if Malefic:
   You may have ailments in the body and colic pains (pains in the bowels).

Mercury in Different Rasis

Being in Gemini, Mercury if Malefic:
   You are liable to throat and bronchial troubles.

Being in Cancer, Mercury if Malefic:
   You may be liable to suffer from consumption.

Being in Virgo, Mercury if Benefic:
   You will have undisturbed health.

Being in Virgo, Mercury if Malefic:
   You may suffer from dyspeptic troubles (indigestion) due to your not having self-control. You may develop morbid imaginations and consequently suffer ill health.

Being in Scorpio, Mercury if Malefic:
   You are liable to diseases of generative organs due to your incentive to indulgence.

Being in Capricorn, Mercury if Malefic:
   Your mind feels cramped and you may have ill health.

Being in Pisces, Mercury if Malefic:
   You are liable to suffer from nervous breakdown due to mental derangement. You may suffer from dysentry.

Jupiter in Different Rasis

Being in Aries, Jupiter if Benefic:
You will have much stamina.

Being in Aries, Jupiter if Malefic:
Your body may bear scars of wounds.

Being in Taurus, Jupiter if Benefic:
You will be free from diseases and healthy.

Being in Cancer, Jupiter if Benefic:
You will be strong and will have much stamina having good qualities of head and heart.

Being in Virgo, Jupiter if Malefic:
You may have symptoms of nervous troubles and diseases. You may have bodily ill health.

Being in Libra, Jupiter if Malefic:
You may suffer ill health due to your lust and exhaustion from overactivity.

Being in Scorpio, Jupiter if Benefic:
You will maintain good health being mentally calm and happy.

Being in Scorpio, Jupiter if Malefic:
You may suffer from some chronic ailment.

Being in Sagittarius, Jupiter if Malefic:
You may have weak constitution.

Being in Capricorn, Jupiter if Malefic:
You may have a weak body without having much stamina or virility.

Being in Aquarius, Jupiter if Malefic:

You may suffer from a chronic ailment. You have a tendency for consumption which may lead you to some kind of ill health.

Venus in Different Rasis

Being in Aries, Venus if Malefic:

You may land in many problems with your health due to being too indulgent and having many vices or bad qualities. You may become night blind in your old age.

Being in Taurus, Venus if Malefic:

You may develop symptoms of some ill health troubles.

Being in Cancer, Venus if Benefic:

You will get some mental ease in the end in spite of your ill health problems.

Being in Cancer, Venus if Malefic:

You may not have much stamina or power of resistance and you may suffer from chronic ailments due to excessive indulgence with drinks.

Being in Leo, Venus if Benefic:

You are not much worried and your health may improve.

Being in Leo, Venus if Malefic:

You may have trouble from fires, poisons and hurts. You may suffer from mental disorder, mental disease and sorrow. You are not likely to have much stamina.

Being in Virgo, Venus if Malefic:

You may have mental unrest. You are likely to be liable for troubles relating to nervous breakdown. You may develop symptoms of arthritis.

Being in Scorpio, Venus if Malefic:

Your private parts may be subjected to some diseases. You may have mental affliction and imbalance and suffer from some hidden diseases.

Being in Capricorn, Venus if Malefic:

Your body may be weak and you may have heart disease.

Being in Aquarius, Venus if Malefic:

You may be uneasy due to ailments and agitated in mind.

Being in Pisces, Venus if Malefic:

You may have dyspeptic difficulties (indigestion).

Saturn in Different Rasis

Being in Taurus, Saturn if Malefic:

You are likely to catch contagious disease.

Being in Cancer, Saturn if Malefic:

You may suffer sickness. You are liable to physical diseases and mental afflictions. Your teeth may not be good and you may develop space between the teeth.

Being in Leo, Saturn if Malefic:

Your body may be affected due to hard labour. You may suffer badly from mental worries.

Being in Scorpio, Saturn if Malefic:

You may have some chronic ailment. You may suffer from poison or fire.

Being in Capricorn, Saturn if Malefic:

You may be peevish.

Being in Aquarius, Saturn if Benefic:
You will be strong.

Moon in Different Rasis

Being in Aries, Moon if Benefic:
You will have physical and mental happiness.

Being in Aries, Moon if Malefic:
You may have sores in the head, weak knees, bad nails. Your veins may be prominent. There may be marks of wounds or boils on the body.

Being in Taurus, Moon if Benefic:
You will have mental and physical happiness.

Being in Taurus, Moon if Malefic:
You may suffer from phlegmatic afflictions.

Being in Gemini, Moon if Malefic:
You may have prominent veins on the body.

Being in Leo, Moon if Malefic:
You may have colic troubles, mental anxiety and deformed body. You may suffer from hunger, thirst, stomach troubles and pain in teeth.

Being in Virgo, Moon if Malefic:
You may have soft body with phlegmatic nature. You may suffer from mental and physical restlessness.

Being in Scorpio, Moon if Malefic:
You may suffer from much mental uneasiness. You may have marks of wounds or those caused by fire on your body. You may suffer from poison (like food poisoning).

Being in Sagittarius, Moon if Malefic:
You may have disfigured nails and arms.

Being in Capricorn, Moon if Malefic:
You may be afraid of cold.

(III) TEMPERAMENT AND PERSONALITY

Sun in Different Rasis

Being in Aries, Sun if Benefic:
Your ambitious nature coupled with your intelligence, courage and initiative will make you active and pioneering, leading to a famous and powerful marked personality. You will be fond of travelling generally towards eastern direction.

Being in Aries, Sun if Malefic:
You may not control your senses and behave in a irritable and impulsive fashion. Due to your timid tendencies, you may not be able to act in a reliable way and you may become lazy and inactive.

Being in Taurus, Sun if Benefic:
You will become self-confident and clever in dealing with others due to your originality and intelligence along with your tactful sociable and reflective nature.

Being in Taurus, Sun if Malefic:
You will become sluggish and will not act quickly in attending to an occasion.

Being in Gemini, Sun if Benefic:
Through your critical, assimilative, intelligent and clever tendencies with good memory you will become scholarly and develop good interest in music and other fine arts. Your polite and courteous nature along with your tendency to speak in an agreeable manner will give you liberal outlook in dealing with others and will

also help you in developing friendship with your bosses. You will have a happy and cheerful temperament.

Being in Gemini, Sun if Malefic:

You may not be original in your thinking and actions and you are likely to behave in a shy and reserved fashion.

Being in Cancer, Sun if Benefic:

You will have a gay and happy frame of mind leading to quick actions. You will be fond of taking interest in working with others and you would like to travel.

Being in Cancer, Sun if Malefic:

Due to your sharp and cruel temper you are likely to oppose your own people particularly your father, uncle etc. You may be usually worried, sorrowful and unhappy leading to laziness.

Being in Leo, Sun if Benefic:

Your strong, independent and enthusiastic nature endowed with qualities of leadership and intelligence will give you good organising capacity and talents for propaganda. You will overcome your enemies with your courage. Your humanitarian and generous personality will lead you to a righteous conduct. You will become famous. You are likely to be fond of meat dishes, forests, mountains, cows and cattle.

Being in Leo, Sun if Malefic:

Your proud temperament is likely to make you stubborn, cruel and at times violent. You will be fond of roaming about in solitary places.

Being in Virgo, Sun if Benefic:

Your reasoning faculty and lucid comprehension along with good memory, general intelligence, well-read and scholarly tendencies will help your interests in writing, painting, poetry, mathematics, literature, songs or music. You will be soft and humble with endearing speech. You are likely to pay homage to religious preceptors and engage in serving others and become learned in religious circles.

Being in Virgo, Sun if Malefic:

You may develop misunderstanding with relatives and friends due to your shy and reserved nature and due to your lacking in flattery and adulation. You may have a tender personality.

Being in Libra, Sun if Benefic:

You will be frank and you are likely to be popular.

Being in Libra, Sun if Malefic:

You are likely to resort to all kinds of underhand and low dealings such as smuggling or other unfair practices for earning money due to your base, wicked, pompous nature and loose morals. You may not have the required tactfulness due to your arrogance and lack of enthusiasm and sometimes submissiveness. You may be fond of talking volubly and travelling. You may become a drunkard.

Being in Scorpio, Sun if Benefic:

You will be able to realise many of your ambitions and desires such as starting of new schemes and enterprises, military ability and surgical skill through your adventurous, dexterous, learned and bold approach.

Being in Scorpio, Sun if Malefic:

Your fiery temperament along with your cruel, stubborn, unprincipled, impulsive nature may make you avaricious, quarrelsome and very vindictive to strike your opponent in a subtle and secret manner.

You may become idiotic and inactive. You are likely to be fond of travelling in hilly tracts and countries.

Being in Sagittarius, Sun if Benefic:

Due to your reliable and intelligent tendencies you will be efficient in using arms and executing good deeds. You are likely to be religious and devoted to gods. You may oblige your kith and kin. You will be happy and popular.

Being in Sagittarius, Sun if Malefic:

You may become short-tempered and obstinate.

Being in Capricorn, Sun if Benefic:

You will be pushing and active in executing any work with an obliging and firm commitment. You are likely to be humorous, affable and prudent. You will be fond of walking and travelling.

Being in Capricorn, Sun if Malefic:

You may develop misunderstanding with your own people and friends due to your mean-minded, stubborn, miserly, boring and meddlesome temperament. You will be envious of prosperity of others. You want to get money from others by unfair means and low acts. You may not have mental stability. You may remain ignorant without learning. You may be fond of roaming about near hills and forest regions.

Being in Aquarius, Sun if Benefic:

You may acquire rare faculties and will develop self-esteem.

Being in Aquarius, Sun if Malefic:

You may not expect good friends due to your being stubborn, meanminded, not even-tempered, backbiting, not straight forward and irrelevant talk. You are likely to worry and feel unhappy.

Being in Pisces, Sun if Benefic:

Due to your intelligent, religious and peaceful temperament you will have good friends and affection from relatives and people. You may be loved by persons. You will be famous.

Being in Pisces, Sun if Malefic:

You may be uneventful and prodigal. You are likely to be liable to scandals.

Mars in Different Rasis

Being in Aries, Mars if Benefic:

You may become a leader of a section of an army or head of an institution by being endowed with a heroic spirit and fine martial qualities and because of your organising capacity and commanding active, powerful, pioneering courageous and able personality. You may increase your reputation and respect due to your social, mathematical, statesmanly, frank, generous, truthful and careful nature. You may be fond of walking and travelling.

Being in Aries, Mars if Malefic:

Instead of becoming a hero you may be quarrelsome due to your vague and cruel imaginations and due to your being too sensual. You may not be economical in your domestic dealings.

Being in Taurus, Mars if Benefic:

Your personality will be well-groomed and you will succeed in all struggle by destroying your enemies. You will be good at magic and sports and fond of songs and music. You will be respected by elders and rulers or the government and envied by many.

Being in Taurus, Mars if Malefic:

Due to your sinful, adulterous, loose, unprincipled and animal instinct you may be influenced by others and may be fond of others' partners. You may become antagonistic to your friends because of your stubborn, selfish, cruel, rash, cunning and hard-hearted nature and due to your harsh speech. You may be timid.

Being in Gemini, Mars if Benefic:

You may be good at poetry, dancing, singing and music due to your refined taste and scientific, learned, quick and ingenuous skill. You can be better off in military strategy due to your ambitious, fearless, diplomatic and detective temperament. You may oblige your sons and friends.

Being in Gemini, Mars if Malefic:

You may be without friends because of your rash, tactless and miserly personality. You may be unhappy and subservient.

Being in Virgo, Mars if Benefic:

Your self-confidence, affable and positive approach and pleasing and soft speech will enable you to address meetings and deliver lectures. You may be ceremonial minded and religious. You may be fond of sex and singing due to your clever artisanship. You will be learned and respected by gentlemen. You my be fond of baths and fragrant applications.

Being in Virgo, Mars if Malefic:

You may not be able to discriminate between good and bad being clouded by your revengeful, conceited, boastful, explosive, pretentious and deceptive temperament. Being timid you may fear opponents. You may imitate others.

Being in Libra, Mars if Benefic:

Being kind, gentle and affable, you will love your family. Due to ambition, self confidence, perceptive faculties, foresight and materialistic and hopeful temperament you may become businesslike. You will have a good appearance.

Being in Libra, Mars if Malefic:

You may develop misunderstandings with cousins, brothers and friends due to your boastful, cunning, warlike and easily ruffled temperament. You may be timid and deceived by others. You may waste your money over wine and other vices. You may be fond of flight. You are likely to be talkative.

Being in Scorpio, Mars if Benefic:

You will be respected by government for your clever, diplomatic, positive tendencies and tenacious memory.

Being in Scorpio, Mars if Malefic:

You may indulge in sinful acts and in harming your opponents by your malicious, aggressive, proud, haughty and vindictive nature. You will be fond of giving fights.

Being in Sagittarius, Mars if Benefic:

Being open, frank, statesmanly, exacting and a good citizen you may realise all your hopes and desires and court friendship from political or royal sources. Being fearless, you may a good fighter. You are likely to be pleasure-loving and become famous.

Being in Sagittarius, Mars if Malefic:

You may have many enemies due to your conservative, severe, indifferent, quarrelsome, uncontrolled temperament and because of your harsh speech, liability to extremes and evil intentions. You may depend on others.

Being in Capricorn, Mars if Malefic:

Being brave, industrious, indefatigable, penetrative, independent, wise and tactful you will be victorious in your undertakings. You will be generous, respected, influential, courteous and will patronise your relations. You will be successful and famous. You may succeed in battles and military skill due to your gallant nature.

Being in Aquarius, Mars if Benefic:

Your conventional, meditative and free thinking will give you a forgiving and forgetting temperament. You will be independent and combative.

Being in Aquarius, Mars if Malefic:

You may not get any respect because of your wicked, impulsive, controversial, untruthful and envious nature. You may behave unpleasantly towards mother and servants. You may be fond of drinking and wandering aimlessly. You may be a liar. You may not have a pleasing appearance. You may develop an unhappy mood.

Being in Pisces, Mars if Benefic:

You will be well-known and acquire great reputation and respect as a learned man due to your faithful, exacting, wilful, fearless and sharp-tempered personality.

Being in Pisces, Mars if Malefic:

Being crooked and uncertain in your views and feelings and due to your antogonistic temperament, you may not have many friends and may insult your seniors. Being passionate you may become sterile and restless and suffer from sorrows.

Mercury in Different Rasis

Being in Aries, Mercury if Benefic:

Due to religiousness, intelligence and great endurance and due to diplomatic and clever nature, you will succeed in your social activities. You may be fond of music and dance.

Being in Aries, Mercury if Malefic:

You may develop quarrelsome disposition due to your obstinate, unscrupulous, idiotic, antagonistic, impulsive tendencies. You may have thievish tendencies being a liar and due to greedy, deceitful, untruthful and cunning nature. You may be fond of gambling and may swindle away your money. You may have faith in God. You may be swerving from rectitude.

Being in Taurus, Mercury if Benefic:

You will become famous and learned due to your clever, logical perservering and practical disposition. You will be liberal and generous in giving. Physical exercises, dress, ornaments and flowers will attract you. You will be able to participate in any occasion giving your opinion and accepting advice as well. Your endearing speech and jocular nature will be liked.

Being in Taurus, Mercury if Malefic:

You will be fond of a showy and obstinate type. You may be fond of sensual pleasures.

Being in Gemini, Mercury If Benefic

You will be actively engaged in work through your cultured, tactful, dexterous, inventive, studious habits. You will be good at describing things due to your eloquent and sweet speech. You will be humorous, generous and comfortable and fond of fine arts. You will have winning manners.

Being in Gemini, Mercury if Malefic:

Due to your boastful nature you may become argumentative at times. You may be lazy. Physical labour may attract you.

Being in Cancer, Mercury if Benefic:

You will be able to engage in various works with your diplomatic, discreet, flexible, intelligent, very active nature. You will be witty in your talks. You may develop strong personal love for women/men and songs. You may be religious.

Being in Cancer, Mercury if Malefic:

You will develop enmity with your own people due to your speculative, restless, unchaste and uneven temperament. You may have a low stature.

Being in Leo, Mercury if Benefic:

You will become famous due to your independent thinking, good memory, positive will, good courage. You may be successful as an orator. You would like to confess your deeds. You may show dexterity in fine arts.

Being in Leo, Mercury if Malefic:

You may not be able to do good actions due to idiotic, proud, lazy, boastful, impulsive, unwise and untruthful tendencies. You may be fond of others and would like travelling in hilly and mountainous tracts.

Being in Virgo, Mercury if Benefic:

You will be endowed with many good qualities such as intelligence, learning, ingenuity, intuition, eloquence, forgiveness, virtuous and refined nature, subtlity, cleverness and good manners. You may undertake charitable works due to your religious and sociable temperament. You will be fearless in debates due to good logical or argumentative ability and sweet speech. You will be of a happy disposition.

Being in Virgo, Mercury if Malefic:

You are likely to have morbid imaginations due to your irritable tendency and lack of self-control. Your sexual vigour may not be upto the mark.

Being in Libra, Mercury if Benefic:

You will respect your seniors and will be a good host being of agreeable, courteous, philosophical, faithful, cremonial-minded and sociable nature. Your material tendencies may be marked due to your hopeful disposition and perceptive and discreet faculties. You will be good at speech and may be devotional to gods.

Being in Libra, Mercury if Malefic:

Your love for friends may be pretentious. You may be economical and frugal in your spending. You may be inclined to excesses.

Being in Scorpio, Mercury if Benefic:

You may be fond of good food, drinks and betting because of your materialistic outlook. You may be subtle and bold.

Being in Scorpio, Mercury if Malefic:

You may indulge in unfair practices due to your crafty, malicious, selfish, indiscreet, reckless, untruthful and unwise tendencies. You may be harsh in dealing with others and earn hatred of people and relations. You may not have much faith in God. You may have incentive to indulgence and thievish tendencies.

Being in Sagittarius, Mercury if Benefic:

You will be liked be king or government, respected by polished society and will be well-versed in writing and penmanship because of your being just, learned executive, diplomatic, capable, virtuous, charitable, intelligent, well-informed, generous, courteous, clever in speech and taste in sciences. You are fond of meeting learned and religious people and travelling in eastern regions. You may devote your time to religious affairs or teaching and may worship holy men. Your courage will give you an inclination in martial enterprises and great exhilaration.

Being in Sagittarius, Mercury if Malefic:

You may be cunning, vigorous, superstitious and rash.

Being in Capricorn, Mercury if Benefic:

Being inventive, active, economical and good in crafts you may have business tendencies. You would like to dream about pleasures and enjoyments. You may have business tendencies. Your selfless nature may lead you towards Godly contemplations. You may have patronage of kings or government. Your enemies will be destroyed by you.

Being in Capricorn, Mercury if Malefic:

You may not be endowed with outstanding qualities. Being inconsistent, restless, suspicious, drudging, unintelligent, apprehensive and untruthful you may have to put much physical labour. You may be fond of backbiting and have a cunning and cruel temperament. You may not bother to dress well. Your mind may feel cramped.

Being in Aquarius, Mercury if Benefic:

You may be fond of acquiring all sorts of paraphernalia, indulging in a pleasuresome life and inferior artisanship. You will be frank, sociable and scholarly. You may get good name and fame.

Being in Aquarius, Mercury if Malefic:

You may have little enjoyments in your life and your enemies may trouble you due to your licentious, proud, unfortunate, unclean, not eloquent or intelligent and timid personality.

Being in Pisces, Mercury if Benefic:

Due to your good deeds and clever mental artisanship you may excel your colleagues and may be liked by others.

Being in Pisces, Mercury if Malefic:

You may quarrel with relatives due to your mental derangement, litigation, nervous breakdown and failure in attempts. You may not be very learned in arts and literature. You may not be firm in religious matters.

Jupiter in Different Rasis

Being in Aries, Jupiter if Benefic:

You will be endowed with many qualities such as sympathy, patience, generosity, courteousness, firmness, love of grandeur, and discipline. You will have forgiving, harmonious, prudent and refined temperament. You will be powerful.

Being in Taurus, Jupiter if Benefic:

You will be liked by all and get respect from friends and enemies as well due to stately, elegant, just, diplomatic and creative abilities. Your liberal, sympathetic and courteous nature may promote a sacrificing spirit. You are fond of self-importance and self-gratification. You may do homage to gods, brahmins and cows. You may become popular.

Being in Taurus, Jupiter if Malefic:

You may be despotic (tyrannical, absolute in power).

Being in Gemini, Jupiter if Benefic:

You will deligently engage in work and be respected by seniors as well as relatives due to your benevolent, sagacious, diplomatic, elegant, inventive, religious, very active nature and due to your good memory.

Being in Gemini, Jupiter if Malefic:

You may be afraid of rulers or government.

Being in Cancer, Jupiter if Benefic:

You will oblige people and will be recognised for

your truth and righteous conduct because of your humanitarian work and dignified, faithful, strong and religious and sweet temperament.

Being in Cancer, Jupiter if Malefic:

You are inclined to social gossip.

Being in Leo, Jupiter if Benefic:

You will have a good magnanimous personality and commanding appearance. You will be noted for your good acts and will be respected by rulers or government due to your ambitious, active, prudent, generous, broad-minded, virtuous and harmonious temperament. You are fond of forts, forests and mountainous regions. You will be a loving friend. You may become famous.

Being in Leo, Jupiter if Malefic:

You are likely to get easily offended.

Being in Virgo, Jupiter if Benefic:

You will be good in execution of work due to your endurance, fixed determination and ambitious nature. You will be religious, virtuous, courteous, affectionate and lovable. You may be fond of scents and flowers.

Being in Virgo, Jupiter if Malefic:

You may develop misunderstandings among relatives due to your bombastic and selfish nature. You would like to have stoical resignation and live in foreign countries.

Being in Libra, Jupiter if Benefic:

You will have a pleasing and attractive personality endowed with free, open-minded, courteous, unassuming, religious temperment. You will be strong, able and competent. Your actions will be good and you will be a hospitable host. You may be devoted to gods.

Being in Libra, Jupiter if Malefic:

You may have a tendency to create factions in societies and families due to selfish, lustful active interest in perverted social reforms. You may lead a dissolute and shameful life residing in desolate places or living at a place other than homeland.

Being in Scorpio, Jupiter if Benefic:

You will have a strong and overpowering personality with elegant manners, exalted ideals, forgiving temperament. You will be generous, clever, conventional and ceremonial minded.

Being in Scorpio, Jupiter if Malefic:

You may have to labour hard due to your serious, exacting, selfish, impudent, proud, and jealous nature. You may show pretentions in religious matters. You may be passionate and your moral contact may not be of high order. You may be vindictive at times.

Being in Sagittarius, Jupiter if Benefic:

You will have extreme executive ability due to your influential, noble, noteworthy, trustworthy, open-minded and generous nature. You may be poetic and artistic. You are likely to oblige others. You are fond of visiting holy places.

Being in Sagittarius, Jupiter if Malefic:

You may like to live at many places other than your homeland.

Being in Capricorn, Jupiter if Malefic:

You may have little sense of love for your people due to your tactless, irritable, inconsistent, avaricious acts. Your religious contact may be at its lowest ebb and you may attack sacred institutions due to your irreligious tendencies. You may be disgraceful. You are likely to have low traits of character. You may be timid, melancholic and would like to live at a place other than your native one.

Being in Aquarius, Jupiter if Benefic:

Being compassionate, sympathetic, amenable, prudent, active and humanitarian you will become popular. You may develop meditative and, philosophical temperament. Whatever you do you may be acting intentionally.

Being in Aquarius, Jupiter in Malefic:

Being controversial, speculative, melancholic, dreamy, hard-hearted and avaricious you may not be of a noble temperament. You may be a back-bitter. You may prefer the company of low people and may have liaison with a related person.

Being in Pisces, Jupiter if Benefic:

You will be good in execution of work and in dealing with others having enterprising and political diplomacy, fixed determination and much quiet stamina. You cannot be overpowered by others. You will be respected by friends. You will not be vain.

Venus in Different Rasis

Being in Aries, Venus if Benefic:

You will be praised by friends, as well as by enemies for your active, mutable, artistic, idealist and easy going temperament. You will be fond of picking up acquaintance with noble personages.

Being in Aries, Venus if Malefic:

You may have loose morals, vices, and bad qualities. You may quarrel or enter into litigation due to your extravagant, disgraceful, greedy, licentious, prudent, irreligious, selfish and too indulgent temperament. You may be fickle-minded and sorrowful. You may be fond of having liaisons with others' life partners, forests and mountains. You may not be large-hearted and you are likely to be cruel at heart. You may be voluable in speech but not reliable. You may have thievish mental attitude. You may bring discredit to your family.

Being in Taurus, Venus if Benefic:

You will be noted for your many virtues. You will help and maintain your relations and will be obliging good people through your independent, fearless, elegant and generous nature. You will be sensational and lead a life of great ease and indulgence in company of beautiful persons and joy through association with them. You would be travelling on seas to foreign countries particularly to southern regions. You will have an agreeable appearance. You will be fond of nature, good clothes, scents and flowers.

Being in Taurus, Venus if Malefic:

You are likely to be sensual. You will be fond of the company of a large number of persons. You are liable to show some symptoms of ill health troubles.

Being in Gemini, Venus if Benefic:

You will be loved and respected by others due to your gentle, kind, generous, logical, affectionate and just tendencies. You will control yourself and not indulge in loose life. You may be devoted to gods and brahmins.

Being in Gemini, Venus if Malefic:

You are likely to be over-sexed.

Being in Cancer, Venus if Benefic:

Your personality will be good looking, strong, amorous, tactful and soft. You will be religiously inclined. You may have some mental ease at the end.

Being in Cancer, Venus if Malefic:

You may have disturbance in your good work and discontent with your relations due to your emotional, timid, haughty, inconsistent, sensitive and light character.

Being in Leo, Venus if Benefic:

You are liked by your religious preceptors and brahmins. You will not be of much worried type. You will be fond of relatives and you would like to do good to others and oblige. You may be attracted by fair sex.

Being in Leo, Venus if Malefic:

Being passionate you may be attracted by others and you may derive pleasures and may be subservient to others. You may be premature to conclusions due to your conceited, emotional, jealous, licentious and haughty temperament. You may be wayward and in exile go on aimless wanderings in deserts and avoid detection by law. You may have a stigma on self-respect due to mean fellows and with an inclination to conceal your true identity you may show superior airs and use foul language.

Being in Virgo, Venus if Benefic:

You will be clever and agile. Your temperament will be humble and soft.

Being in Virgo, Venus if Malefic:

You may serve others and indulge in low acts due to your petty minded, licentious and sensitive character. Being unscrupulous and mean you may execute illicit love. You may be talking unnecessarily.

Being in Libra, Venus if Benefic:

You will be liked and respected by society and state due to your statesmanly, generous, philosophical, intuitive faculties. You will be clever in defending and protecting your interest and active in work even in difficult times through your strong and fearless nature. You may be devotional to gods and brahmins. You will get good reputation and become famous. You will have a handsome personality.

Being in Libra, Venus if Malefic:

You may be passionate and extremely sensual and proud. You may be inclined to live at places other than your native land.

Being in Scorpio, Venus if Benefic:

You may be of independent nature. You are likely to be artistic.

Being in Scorpio, Venus if Malefic:

You may bring discredit to your family due to your mean, unjust, proud, haughty, wicked, irreligious and envious nature. You may not be good tempered. You may be intent on damaging the name of others and showing vengeance against relatives.

Being in Sagittarius, Venus if Benefic:

Being religious, philosophical, powerful, generous, chivalrous, frank and clever you will be respected by people and society. You will be fond of recitation of secret writings and you will be fond of dressing up nicely. You will give regard to holy people and ascetics.

Being in Sagittarius, Venus if Malefic:

You may be impertinent, rude and of meddling temperament.

Being in Capricorn, Venus if Benefic:

You will have a good looking personality. Your ambitious nature will lead you to become powerful, industrious and subtle. You will be fond of discussions with learned people. You may be fond of sweating for others.

Being in Capricorn, Venus if Malefic:

Due to your unprincipled, immoral, adulterous nature you may be fond of mean persons. You may be attached to an unworthy or elderly person or you may be under considerable influence of your partner or other person. You may develop perverted ideas of social or religious reforms. You may be rash, unwise. You may be greedy and cunning in deceiving others by speaking lies for monetary gain. You are likely to be boastful. You may not be sexually virile.

Being in Aquarius, Venus if Benefic:

You will be liked by all due to your amusing, handsome, affable, persuasive, witty, chaste and calm personality.

Being in Aquarius, Venus if Malefic:

You may not care for a well-groomed appearance and prefer to remain unclean without bothering to take baths. You may be persistently engaged in work which may not yield the desired results. You may be attracted to any person. You may be timid and effeminate (feminine type).

Being in Pisces, Venus if Benefic:

You will be endowed with many good qualities and will be much respected for being witty, tactful, popular, just, ingenuous, modest, refined and clever. You will do acts of charity and generosity.

Saturn in Different Rasis

Being in Aries, Saturn if Benefic:

You will be fond of travelling.

Being in Aries, Saturn if Malefic:

You may develop misunderstandings among relatives and friends and may not perform good acts but rather commit sinful acts because of being resentful, cruel, fraudulent, immoral, boastful, quarrelsome. You are likely to be gloomy, mischievous, sharp tempered, fiery, impudent, envious and deceitful. You may have to labour hard due to your peevish, ignorant and idiotic nature. Being perverse you may like to wander aimlessly.

Being in Taurus, Saturn if Benefic:

You will be successfully engaged in a variety of works due to your powerful, clever, and persuasive temperament.

Being in Taurus, Saturn if Malefic:

You may have bad friends, and may be attached to an undesirable or elderly person due to your unrighteous conduct and deceitful and irreligious temperament. You may do obscure sinful acts. You may be logical in your arguments.

Being in Gemini, Saturn if Benefic:

You will get respect and reputation from rulers or government and you will exceed your sphere of work due to your great humanitarian work and due to your original, subtle, ingenious, strategic, logical, industrious and active nature. You may be fond of outdoor sports.

Being in Gemini, Saturn if Malefic:

You may not be good tempered due to your narrow minded, wicked, hypocritical, speculative, secretive and mean tendencies. You may be shameless, miserable and not benevolently inclined. You may deceive others and harbour ill feelings. You may receive at times insulting treatment. You may be a liar. You may behave sometimes as a lunatic.

Being in Cancer, Saturn if Benefic:

You will have a good looking and soft personality. You are fond of associating with important people and enjoying luxuries at the cost of others.

Being in Cancer, Saturn if Malefic:

You may not be good-tempered because of your selfish, cunning, deceitful, malicious and stubborn nature. You will be slow and dull and always restless. You may be unsuccessful.

Being in Leo, Saturn if Benefic:

You will be clever in reading and writing.

Being in Leo, Saturn if Malefic:

You will not be good-tempered due to being obstinate, stubborn, conflicting and not noble. You may be engaged in mean acts and be condemned for evil actions due to your menial mentality and full of latent anger.

Being in Virgo, Saturn if Benefic:

You wil oblige others by doing good to others. You will be inclined to enjoy the hospitality of others. You will earn, save and be far sighted and reputed.

Being in Virgo, Saturn if Malefic:

You may not engage in productive work due to your malicious, erratic, unscrupulous nature. You may be shameless, narrow-minded and conservative. You may not be clever as an artisan and you may have bad liaisons without shame.

Being in Libra, Saturn if Benefic:

You will have sound judgement due to your independent, prominent, tactful and powerful temperament and personality. You will be self conceited. You will be respected and will become famous.

Being in Libra, Saturn if Malefic:

You may be fond of associating with persons of loose morals. You may be proud and antagonistic. You may be subservient to others.

Being in Scorpio, Saturn if Benefic:

You will have adventurous and very active temperament. You will get self-respect and fame.

Being in Scorpio, Saturn if Malefic:

You will be disliked and hated due to your rash, indifferent, merciless, mean, self-conceited, reserved, violent, and unscrupulous nature. You are inclined to appropriate other peoples' property. You may suffer many sorrows but outwardly you may appear as if you are enjoying life. You may be vain, cruel, envious, avaricious and of fiery temper. You may be opposed to others.

Being in Sagittarius, Saturn if Benefic:

Being pushful, artful, faithful, courteous, philosophical, religious and due to your righteous conduct you will be clever in dealing with others. You may not be very talkative.

Being in Sagittarius. Saturn if Malefic:

Your personality will be cunning, apparently generous and pretentious.

Being in Capricorn, Saturn if Benefic:

You will have reflective, intellectual and cautious. personality.

Being in Capricorn, Saturn if Malefic:

You may be melancholic, selfish, suspicious, revengeful and greedy. You are likely to be of peevish type.

Being in Aquarius, Saturn if Benefic:

You will be able to imitate variety of works being practical, able, ingenious, and intellectual. You are likely to be reflective and diplomatic. You may be philosophical, strong, and very truthful and prudent (cautious).

Being in Aquarius, Saturn if Malefic:

You may have bad friends being conceited, fiery tempered, deceitful, and addicted to wine and other vices. You may outwardly talk of philosophy and religion.

Being in Pisces, Saturn if Benefic:

You will be endowed with many good qualities. You will be clever, pushful, gifted, good diplomat and have good manners. You will command respect and trust in government.

Being in Pisces, Saturn if Malefic:

You may be indifferent towards sectarian restraints and observations due to your severe, malicious, untrustworthy and scheming nature. You may be sober. You may be of a disguising type.

Moon in Different Rasis

Being in Aries, Moon if Benefic:

Your ambitious nature will make you valiant, enterprising, dexterous, versatile and quick to decide and act,-leading to your popularity, self-respect and perfect contentment. You will be of a loving temperament and fond of travelling. You may like vegetable diet.

Being in Aries, Moon if Malefic:

You may behave idiosyncratically due to your impulsive, irritable, haughty, inflexible, fickle-minded and war like temperament. You are likely to be fond of others and you may be under the influence of your partner. You may be liable to hydrophobia (fear of water). You would like to live in a luxurious, sensual manner.

Being in Taurus, Moon if Benefic:

You will be popular, famous and respected due to your liberal, powerful, ability to command, influential, patient, generous-in-giving qualities and sound judgement. You will be handsome and will have a beautiful gait. You may be a voracious reader. You will be of happy temperament.

Being in Taurus, Moon if Malefic:

You may be influenced by others and be fond of other sex due to your passionate, luxurious and sensual nature. You may have a wavering mind being inconsistent. You are likely to be lazy. You may be a voracious eater.

Being in Gemini, Moon if Benefic:

You will be learned in scriptures and fond of music due to your creative, intelligent, well-read, persuasive and poetic tendencies. Being clever, witty, dexterous, subtle and humorous you will be a powerful speaker. You may be endowed with qualities of a thoughtful reader. You will be fond of enjoying luxuries. You are likely to have adorable and attractive looks.

Being in Gemini, Moon if Malefic:

You may be over-sexed and well up in amorous acts. You may be fond of others and under the influence of your partner.

Being in Cancer, Moon if Benefic:

You will be fond of good dwelling places, tanks, rivers, sea side and flowers and travelling. You may develop a love for astrology due to your piercing, meditative, conventional and wise nature. You are likely to have a kind, good, grateful, cautious and charming personality. You will be of frugal (economical type).

Being in Cancer, Moon if Malefic:

You may be sensitive having too much of imagination. You may be amorous, impetuous (hasty, vehement, passionate).

Being in Leo, Moon if Benefic:

Being bold, ambitious, proud, steady, and sharp temper you will be able to engage in varied work. You will have a dignified look and aristocratic style with your liberal and generous temperament. You may be fond of towns and forests.

Being in Leo, Moon if Malefic:

You are likely to be unhappy due to your irritable, haughty and settled views. You may not get on well with women. You may be influenced by your mother. You may be fond of meat and frequenting forests and hills.

Being in Virgo, Moon if Benefic:

You would like to be engaged in the work of others. You may be attracted towards astrology having clairvoyant (power of seeing things not present to the senses) tendencies. You may be skilled in arts like music and dancing due to your perseverence, intelligent and acute insight. You are likely to have a scheming, attractive and modest life. You will be forgiving, compassionate and learned and would like to stick to truth and purity. You are likely to be a good conversationalist with sweet speech. You may be affluent.

Being in Virgo, Moon if Malefic:

You may be mentally and physically restless because of your being pensive, worried by enemies and swindlers and conceited in self-estimation. You may fond of others.

Being in Libra, Moon if Benefic:

You will be engaged in work and be business-like due to your clever, capable, intelligent, foreseeing, mutable, and aspiring nature. You will have an amicable, just, principled, idealistic and obliging personality. You may develop interest in arts.

Being in Libra, Moon if Malefic:

You may be proud and intoxicated. You may develop inclinations towards acts of cruelty, thievish disposition, probable liaisons with others' partners. You may not have much faith in religion. You may be avaracious and not ambitious.

Being in Scorpio, Moon if Benefic:

You will be clever, frank open-minded, and straight forward.

Being in Scropio, Moon if Malefic:

You may have an intent on harming opponents due to your cruel, malicious, impetuous, obstinate, and vindictive nature. You may be fond of giving a fight. You may indulge in sinful acts due to being immoral. Your liberty and honour may be at a risk. You may be unhappy being agitated due to much mental uneasiness. You may be afraid of political heads.

Being in Sagittarius, Moon if Benefic:

You may be well up in artisan's work and be skilled in finance. You will be courageous and inflexible to threats. You would like to stay near sea coast, river or water. You will have deep and inventive intellect coupled with good speech and upright, ceremonial and reflective mentality. You will be of grateful disposition, affectionate with relations.

Being in Sagittarius, Moon if Malefic:

You would like to be showy. You may have a tendency to yield to praise.

Being in Capricorn, Moon if Benefic:

You may be a connoisseur of singing due to being poetic, clever, sagacious, and quick in perception. You will become famous because of your virtuous, active, crafty, strategic, liberal, cool tempered and religious nature. You will like to stick to truth. You will be attached to partner and children.

Being in Capricorn, Moon if Malefic:

Being selfish you may have a tendency to become a miser. You may be cruel-hearted, base, mean, shameless, inconsistent, unscrupulous, and merciless. You may be fond of wandering and having contact with low persons. You may be afraid of colds.

Being in Aquarius, Moon if Benefic:

You will be fond of arts and you are likely to be clever in artisanship due to your artistic state. You will be beautiful minded with inoffensive, energetic, mystical, grateful, intentional personality.

Being in Aquarius, Moon if Malefic:

You may have misunderstandings among relatives, good people, and enemies due to your adulterous, wicked, indolent, hypocritical and ill-tempered nature. Your emotions may be esoteric (secret) due to your strange brain. You may be liable to fraud and deception. You are likely to be a drunkard. You may be afraid of political authorities. You may be suffering from sorrows.

Being in Pisces, Moon if Benefic:

You will have a good reputation for being learned, steady, simple, adventurous, religious, good-tempered and generous and being a connoisseur of singing. You will be interested in countries and products beyond the sea and inclined to travel by water. You will get authority if engaged in works of arts, artisanship or crafts. You will be fond of reciting religious texts and moral codes. You will have easy access to anything coveted without effort. You will be fond of your partners and children. You will annihilate your enemies. You may be spiritually inclined later in life. You will lead a comfortable life.

Being in Pisces, Moon if Malefic:

You may be under the influence of your partner. You may be subservient to other sex and attached to many young persons due to your loose morals. You may be inclined to get into a bad temper.

(IV) WEALTH

Sun in Different Rasis

Being in Aries, Sun if Benefic:

You will get ornaments. You will be wealthy.

Being in Aries, Sun if Malefic:

You may not be wealthy.

Being in Taurus, Sun if Benefic:

You will get landed property. You will succeed in buying, selling or trading in cloth and scented things. You will improve your wealth.

Being in Gemini, Sun if Benefic:

Though you are liberal in dealing with others your acquisition of wealth is good.

Being in Cancer, Sun if Benefic:

You will have wealth through progress in land, housing and agriculture.

Being in Cancer, Sun if Malefic:

You may not be wealthy.

Being in Leo, Sun if Benefic:

You will have houses, gardens, wells and you will be rich. You may get wealth through dealings connected with forests, mountains, cows and cattle.

Being in Leo, Sun if Malefic:

You may be poor.

Being in Virgo, Sun if Malefic:

You may lose wealth through cattle and houses.

Being in Libra, Sun if Benefic:

You will get wealth through trade connected with liquors, intoxicants, iron etc.

Being in Libra, Sun if Malefic:

You may resort to all kinds of low and underhand dealings such as smuggling of gold or other unfair practices. There may be loss of wealth. You are likely to be reduced to poverty due to heavy expenditure.

Being in Scorpio, Sun if Benefic:

You may get wealth from lands and houses and by dealing in poison or poisonous drugs.

Being in Sagittarius, Sun if Benefic:

You will have accumulation of wealth through good inheritance and unexpected gifts.

Being in Capricorn, Sun if Malefic:

You want to appropriate other people's money by

unfair means. You may try to earn money by means not very commendable. You may lose money through loss of house, cattle and lands. There may be loss of patrimony and loss of wealth.

Being in Aquarius, Sun if Malefic:

There may be loss of land, cattle and property and you may be devoid of wealth.

Being in Pisces, Sun if Benefic:

You will get wealth due to love with persons by whom you will be favoured. You may earn much money by dealing in aqueous products or goods across the water or anything connected with water. You may acquire pearls or may become wealthy by being a pearl merchant.

Mars in Different Rasis

Being in Aries, Mars if Benefic:

You will get success in trade and become wealthy.

Being in Taurus, Mars if Benefic:

You will gain in wealth by good produce from lands.

Being in Taurus, Mars if Malefic:

You may not be wealthy.

Being in Gemini, Mars if Benefic:

You will have access to great wealth of precious stones and metals. You shall become wealthy through agricultural success and success in work and in every respect.

Being in Cancer, Mars if Benefic:

You will be rich and wealthy.

Being in Cancer, Mars if Malefic:

You will not have wealth.

Being in Leo, Mars if Benefic:
You will get wealth through increase in houses and lands,

Being in Leo, Mars if Malefic:
You may be devoid of wealth.

Being in Virgo, Mars if Benefic:
You will be wealthy.

Being in Libra, Mars if Benefic:
You will have self-acquired wealth.

Being in Libra, Mars if Malefic:
You may lose wealth and mortgage your landed property.

Being in Scorpio, Mars if Benefic:
You will have increase in wealth.

Being in Sagittarius, Mars if Benefic:
You are likely to get wealth from political or royal sources.

Being in Capricorn, Mars if Benefic:
There will be increase in your wealth.

Being in Aquarius, Mars if Malefic:
You may have loss of wealth by gambling and speculation because of your own malice and dishonesty.

Being in Pisces, Mars if Benefic:
You can expect wealth through bumper crop in lands and increase in houses.

Being in Pisces, Mars if Malefic:

You may suffer loss of wealth due to your own deceitful conduct.

Mercury in Different Rasis

Being in Aries, Mercury if Benefic:

You may get wealth through cultivation and conveyance.

Being in Aries, Mercury if Malefic:

You may be devoid of wealth.

Being in Taurus, Mercury if Benefic:

You will have plenty of money and you will be wealthy.

Being in Gemini, Mercury if Benefic:

You will be wealthy.

Being in Cancer, Mercury if Malefic:

You may have loss of money due to enmity with partner or other persons. You may lose wealth through loss of land and failure of crops.

Being in Leo, Mercury if Benefic:

You can expect acquisition of wealth from various countries.

Being in Leo, Mercury if Malefic:

You are likely to be poor.

Being in Libra, Mercury if Benefic:

You will gain in wealth by spending discriminately on projects undertaken by you.

Being in Scorpio, Mercury if Benefic:

You are likely to be rich.

Being in Aquarius, Mercury if Benefic:
You will have access to good wealth.

Being in Aquarius, Mercury if Malefic:
You may acquire some wealth by means, not above board.

Jupiter in Different Rasis

Being in Aries, Jupiter if Benefic:
You will be wealthy.

Being in Taurus, Jupiter if Benefic:
You will have acquisition of wealth by gain in agriculture and increase in land. You will have valuable possessions.

Being in Gemini, Jupiter if Benefic:
Being wealthy you will keep part of your money in deposits.

Being in Cancer, Jupiter if Benefic:
You will get wealth from unexpected sources and without effort.

Being in Leo, Jupiter if Benefic:
You will get wealth from gain of lands and much agricultural produce.

Being in Virgo, Jupiter if Benefic:
You will gain in wealth from your connection with theatres, films etc.

Being in Virgo, Jupiter if Malefic:
You may expect loss of wealth.

Being in Libra, Jupiter if Benefic:
You may gain in wealth from your with theatres, films etc.

Being in Scorpio, Jupiter if Benefic:
   You may become wealthy by acquisition of new lands and estates.

Being in Sagittarius, Jupiter if Benefic:
   You will be wealthy due to pretty inheritance.

Being in Capricorn, Jupiter if Malefic:
   You may lose your wealth through loss of property.

Being in Pisces, Jupiter if Benefic:
   You will be very wealthy through good inheritance and acquisition of property.

Venus in Different Rasis

Being in Aries, Venus if Benefic:
   You will become wealthy by your good earnings.

Being in Aries, Venus if Malefic:
   You may lose wealth as a result of quarrels or litigations on account of attachment to a person.

Being in Taurus, Venus if Benefic:
   You will become wealthy due to gains from agriculture.

Being in Gemini, Venus if Benefic:
   You may gain territory and become wealthy.

Being in Cancer, Venus if Malefic:
   You may not be wealthy and you are inclined to seek money from others.

Being in Leo, Venus if Benefic:
   You can expect to get wealth from ladies.

Being in Virgo, Venus if Malefic:
You may lose wealth and mortgage your property.

Being in Libra, Venus if Benefic:
You will have gain of wealth from royal patronage or government or by dealing in vehicles.

Being in Scorpio, Venus if Malefic:
You will have loss of wealth.

Being in Sagittarius, Venus if Benefic:
You will get wealth through your righteous and good conduct.

Being in Capricorn, Venus if Malefic:
You may gain money by deceiving others and by speaking lies.

Being in Pisces, Venus if Benefic:
You will gain money and become wealthy.

Saturn in Different Rasis

Being in Aries, Saturn if Malefic:
You may be poor.

Being in Taurus, Saturn if Benefic:
You may become wealthy through success and gains in your agricultural operations.

Being in Taurus, Saturn if Malefic:
You may be devoid of wealth.

Being in Cancer, Saturn if Malefic:
You may be poor.

Being in Virgo, Saturn if Malefic:
You may not be wealthy.

Being in Libra, Saturn if Benefic:

You will be rich and you can bank upon hoarded (amassed) money.

Being in Scorpio, Saturn if Malefic:

You are inclined to appropriate other peoples' property.

Being in Capricorn, Saturn if Benefic:

You will have gains in wealth.

Being in Aquarius, Saturn if Benefic:

You will be wealthy.

Being in Pisces, Saturn if Benefic:

You will have wealth.

Moon in Different Rasis

Being in Aries, Moon if Benefic:

You will gain wealth and become wealthy.

Being in Taurus, Moon if Benefic:

You will have collection of enormous wealth and you will be rich.

Being in Gemini, Moon if Benefic:

You will acquire much immovable and movable property and become wealthy.

Being in Cancer, Moon if Benefic:

You will have good dwelling. You will get unexpected treasures. You will be rich through immovable property. You will be wealthy.

Being in Leo, Moon if Benefic:

You will get wealth from unexpected sources.

Being in Libra, Moon if Benefic:

You will gain wealth and become wealthy.

Being in Scorpio, Moon if Benefic:

You will become rich and wealthy by being a business person with a flourishing trade of your own and earning money by underhand means.

Being in Scorpio, Moon if Malefic:

You may lose wealth.

Being in Sagittarius, Moon if Benefic:

You will have good inheritance. You will get unexpected gifts and there will be accumulation of wealth. You may gain money through help from women or your married partner.

Being in Capricorn, Moon if Benefic:

You will increase in wealth through lands, houses and success in every new enterprise.

Being in Aquarius, Moon if Malefic:

You may be poor and there may be destruction of property.

Being in Pisces, Moon if Benefic:

You may get sudden wealth from burried treasure or you may inherit. You may get money by dealing with countries and in products beyond sea.

(V) COURAGE
Sun in Different Rasis

Being in Aries, Sun if Benefic:

You will be courageous and powerful. You will be a warrior.

Being in Aries, Sun if Malefic:
  You may be timid.

Being in Gemini, Sun if Malefic:
  You may be shy and reserved.

Being in Leo, Sun if Benefic:
  You will be courageous.

Being in Leo, Sun if Malefic:
  Good effects of your courage will be devalued.

Being in Virgo, Sun if Malefic:
  You may be shy and reserved.

Being in Scorpio, Sun if Benefic:
  You will be bold, adventurous and courageous.

Being in Scorpio, Sun if Malefic:
  Your courage may be devalued.

Being in Capricorn, Sun if Benefic:
  You will be pushful and firm.

Being in Capricorn, Sun if Malefic:
  You may be timid and may not have much stamina.

Mars in Different Rasis

Being in Aries, Mars if Benefic:
  You will be courageous having commanding, powerful and combative tendencies.

Being in Leo, Mars if Benefic:
  You will be combative.

Being in Virgo, Mars if Benefic:
  You may be explosive.

Being in Virgo, Mars if Malefic:
You may not be courageous.

Being in Libra, Mars if Benefic:
You may be warlike.

Being in Sagittarius, Mars if Benefic:
You will be fearless.

Being in Aquarius, Mars if Benefic:
You will be combative.

Mercury in Different Rasis

Being in Scorpio, Mercury if Benefic:
You will be bold.

Being in Sagittarius, Mercury if Benefic:
You will have courage.

Being in Capricorn, Mercury if Malefic:
You may be always apprehensive.

Jupiter in Different Rasis

Being in Aries, Jupiter if Benefic:
You will be powerful and will overcome others with your valour.

Being in Capricorn, Jupiter if Malefic:
You may be timid.

Venus in Different Rasis

Being in Libra, Venus if Benefic:
You will be courageous.

Being in Sagittarius, Venus if Benefic:
You will be powerful.

Being in Capricorn, Venus if Benefic:
You will be powerful.

Being in Capricorn, Venus if Malefic:
You may be always apprehensive.

Being in Aquarius, Venus if Malefic:
You may be timid.

Saturn in Different Rasis

Being in Taurus, Saturn if Benefic:
You will be powerful.

Being in Libra, Saturn if Benefic:
You will be powerful.

Moon in Different Rasis

Being in Aries, Moon if Benefic:
You will be valiant, courageous and warlike.

Being in Cancer, Moon if Benefic:
You will be powerful.

Being in Leo, Moon if Benefic:
You will be bold.

(VI) EDUCATION
Sun in Different Rasis

Being in Taurus, Sun if Benefic:
You may be interested in music and singing.

Being in Gemini, Sun if Benefic:
You may receive good education and you will have an inclination to be interested in music and such other fine arts, astronomy and grammar.

Being in Virgo, Sun if Benefic:

You will be clever in writing, painting, poetry, mathematics. You will be well-read and will receive good education. You will be fond of literature, songs and music.

Being in Sagittarius, Sun if Benefic:

You may be interested in music. You will be clever in using arms. Your education may lead you to become a good physician or artisan or well up in arts and crafts, a pearl merchant.

Being in Pisces, Sun if Benefic:

You may get education which will help you to earn money by dealing in aqueous products or goods across the water or anything connected with water or as a pearl merchant.

Mars in Different Rasis

Being in Aries, Mars if Benefic:

Your education may give you commanding and organising capacity. You may be a mathematician. Your education may be connected with defence department, medical, sanitation, hygiene, surgery or electrical/ electronic engineering.

Being in Taurus, Mars if Benefic:

You will have ability in magic and sports. You will be fond of songs and music. You may get education connected with surgery or highway engineering.

Being in Gemini, Mars if Benefic:

You will be scientific and learned. You may be skilled in music. You may be clever in poetry, dancing, singing, music or be a connoisseur of those requiring mechanical dexerity. You will be clever in military strategy. You may get education leading to become a detective. You may become an aeronautical engineering student.

Being in Cancer, Mars if Benefic:

You may get education for proficiency in agriculture, medicine and surgery. Your education may lead you to work in defence department and in the fields connected with sanitation, hygiene and hydraulic engineering.

Being in Leo, Mars if Benefic:

You will have a tendency to occultism, astrology, astronomy, mathematics. You will have taste in fine arts. Your education may be connected with defence department, medicine, sanitation, hygiene, surgery and electrical/electronic engineering.

Being in Virgo, Mars if Benefic:

You will have successful termination of your educational pursuits. You will have a scientific enterprise. You will be clever in artisanship. You may be learned in highway engineering.

Being in Libra, Mars if Benefic:

You may get education suitable to become business like. You may expect to be educated in aeronautical engineering or surgery.

Being in Scorpio, Mars if Benefic:

You may get education to become a good business person with a flourishing trade of your own. You may be interested in education connected with medicine, surgery, hygiene, sanitation or hydraulic engineering.

Being in Sagittarius, Mars if Benefic:

Your education may be connected with defence department, medicine, surgery, hygiene, sanitation or electrical/electronic engineering.

Being in Capricorn, Mars if Benefic:

Your education may be in highway engineering or for military skills.

Being in Aquarius, Mars if Benefic:

You will be well-versed in dialects. You may be educated in the field connected with aeronautical engineering.

Being in Pisces, Mars if Benefic:

You may get education in medicine, surgery, sanitation, hygiene, defence department, hydraulic engineering.

Mercury in Different Rasis

Being in Aries, Mercury if Benefic:

You will be fond of music and dance. You will be well up in cartography, drawing or painting. Your education may be connected with cattle and cultivation.

Being in Gemini, Mercury if Benefic:

You will have taste for literature, arts and sciences. You may be a musician besides being clever in fine arts.

Being in Cancer, Mercury if Benefic:

Your education may give you gains from water and also products of water or connected with water or goods across seas.

Being in Leo, Mercury if Benefic:

You will have good progress in knowledge.

Being in Virgo, Mercury if Benefic:

You will be proficient in sciences, arts and crafts. Your education may lead you to become a priest, author or literary critic.

Being in Libra, Mercury if Benefic:

You will get education for business, science or literature.

Being in Sagittarius, Mercury if Benefic:

You will have liking for sciences. You will be successful in your education to become well-versed in writing and penmenship and you will devote your time to religious affairs or teaching.

Being in Capricorn, Mercury if Benefic:

You may get education connected with trades in tanneries, leather goods or glassware.

Being in Aquarius, Mercury if Benefic:

You will be proficient in inferior artsmanship. You may be interested in sciences and literature. Your education may lead to a career of employment.

Jupiter in Different Rasis

Being in Aries, Jupiter if Benefic:

Your education may lead you to become head of an army or section of an army.

Being in Taurus, Jupiter if Benefic:

Your education may help you to establish business.

Being in Gemini, Jupiter if Benefic:

You will be clever in arts and sciences. You may become a poet through your educational pursuits.

Being in Cancer, Jupiter if Benefic:

You will be learned. You may study journalism.

Being in Leo, Jupiter if Benefic:

Due to your education you may become head of an army or section of an army or an institution.

Being in Virgo, Jupiter if Benefic:

You may be educated in arts and crafts.

Being in Libra, Jupiter if Benefic:

You will be engaged in the pursuit of learning. You may get education connected with theatres and films.

Being in Scorpio, Jupiter if Benefic:

You may be educated in literature leading to become a scholar and an author.

Being in Sagittarius, Jupiter if Benefic:

Your education may give you extreme executive ability to become a professor or religious preceptor.

Being in Aquarius, Jupiter if Benefic:

You will be learned.

Being in Pisces, Jupiter if Benefic:

You will have great education and gain from exhibition of knowledge. You will be learned and good in dealing with matters of educational and military strategy.

Venus in Different Rasis

Being in Aries, Venus if Benefic:

You will be proficient in music, art and poetry. You may be educated in surgery.

Being in Taurus, Venus if Benefic:

You will have taste in dancing, music, poetry or art.

Being in Gemini, Venus if Benefic:

You will love fine arts, logic, writing, arts and sciences.

Being in Cancer, Venus if Benefic:

You may be educated to become a physician.

Being in Virgo, Venus if Benefic:

You will be a connoisseur of arts.

Being in Libra, Venus if Benefic:

Your interest may be in poetry.

Being in Scorpio, Venus if Benefic:

You may get educated in surgery or art.

Being in Sagittarius, Venus if Benefic:

You will be learned in philosophical studies. You may be interested in recitation of sacred writings.

Being in Capricorn, Venus if Benefic:

You will have progress in general education.

Being in Aquarius, Venus if Benefic:

You will have love for Christian or Islamic literature and its studies.

Saturn in Different Rasis

Being in Taurus, Saturn if Benefic:

You will have education connected with agricultural operations.

Being in Gemini, Saturn if Benefic:

You will have taste for chemical and mechanical sciences and logic.

Being in Leo, Saturn if Benefic:

You will be clever in reading and writing. You may get medical education. Your education may lead you to earn by service.

Being in Virgo, Saturn if Benefic:

Your education may lead you to work as police officer or to work in defence department.

Being in Libra, Saturn if Benefic:

You will get education to do business.

Being in Sagittarius, Saturn if Benefic:

You will have inclination to study philosophical and religious treatises. You will have good knowledge of Shastras (Standard Hindu books).

Being in Capricorn, Saturn if Benefic:

You will be learned.

Being in Pisces, Saturn if Benefic:

Your education may lead you to become a diplomat.

Moon in Different Rasis

Being in Taurus, Moon if Benefic:

You may get education to become a physician.

Being in Gemini, Moon if Benefic:

You will have progress in education of a poetic, scientific and literary type.

Being in Cancer, Moon if Benefic:

You may have love for astrology. You may get education leading to become a scientist.

Being in Virgo, Moon if Benefic:

You may be attracted towards astrology and clairvoyancy. You will be skilled in arts like music and dance.

Being in Libra, Moon if Benefic:

You will have love for arts and social sciences. You

may be scientific. Your education may be in literature and connected with business and also may lead you to become a physician.

Being in Scorpio, Moon if Benefic:

Your education may help you to become a business person.

Being in Sagittarius, Moon if Benefic:

You will be skilled in fine arts and well up in artisan's work.

Being in Capricorn, Moon if Benefic:

You will be a connoisseur of singing.

Being in Aquarius, Moon if Benefic:

You will be fond of art and clever in artisanship, science, and literature.

Being in Pisces, Moon if Benefic:

You will be interested in arts or crafts and literature. You will be reciting religious texts and moral codes. You may be a connoisseur of singing. You may be scientific.

(VII) HOUSES, LANDED PROPERTY AND MEANS OF CONVEYANCE
Sun in Different Rasis

Being in Taurus, Sun if Benefic:

You will have increase in landed property and gains from them.

Being in Cancer, Sun if Benefic:

You will have progress in lands and agriculture and increase in houses.

Being in Leo, Sun if Benefic:
You will have your own house.

Being in Scorpio, Sun if Benefic:
You will gain from land and houses.

Being in Aquarius, Sun if Malefic:
You may have loss of property and lands.

Mars in Different Rasis

Being in Taurus, Mars if Benefic:
You will get good produce from lands.

Being in Gemini, Mars if Benefic:
You will get good agricultural success.

Being in Leo, Mars if Benefic:
There will be increase in houses and lands.

Being in Libra, Mars if Malefic:
You may mortgage your landed property.

Being in Pisces, Mars if Benefic:
You will get bumper crops from lands and you will have increase of houses.

Mercury in Different Rasis

Being in Aries, Mercury if Benefic:
You will get gains from cultivation and you will have means of conveyance.

Being in Cancer, Mercury if Malefic:
You may have loss of lands and failure of crops.

Jupiter in Different Rasis

Being in Taurus, Jupiter if Benefic:
You will get gains in agriculture and you will have

increase in lands. You will get valuable possessions.

Being in Leo, Jupiter if Benefic:
You will have gains of land and much agricultural produce.

Being in Scorpio, Jupiter if Benefic:
You will acquire new lands and estates.

Being in Capricorn, Jupiter if Malefic:
You may get loss of property.

Being in Pisces, Jupiter if Benefic:
You will have requisition of property.

Venus in Different Rasis

Being in Taurus, Venus if Benefic:
You will gain from agriculture.

Being in Gemini, Venus if Benefic:
You will have gain of territory.

Being in Virgo, Venus if Malefic:
You may mortgage your properties.

Being in Libra, Venus if Benefic:
You will possess vehicles.

Saturn in Different Rasis

Being in Taurus, Saturn if Benefic:
You will have success and gains in agricultural operations.

Being in Scorpio, Saturn if Malefic:
You will be inclined to appropriate property of other people.

Moon in Different Rasis

Being in Gemini, Moon if Benefic:
You will be acquiring much immovable and movable properties.

Being in Cancer, Moon if Benefic:
You will be fond of good dwelling.

Being in Aquarius, Moon if Malefic:
You may have destruction of property.

(VIII) HAPPINESS
Sun in Different Rasis

Being in Aries, Sun if Benefic:
You will have pleasure trips and picnics. You will get happiness from partner, children and friends. There will be acquisition of power and position. You will get political success. There will be birth of children. You will be famous.

Being in Aries, Sun if Malefic:
You may suffer disappointments and frustrations in career.

Being in Taurus, Sun if Benefic:
You will be respected by relatives and people. You will have increased landed property. You will get happy meals. You will be famous among relations and friends.

Being in Gemini, Sun if Benefic:
You will be always happy and cheerful. You will receive good education.

Being in Gemini, Sun if Malefic:
You may have mental worries.

Being in Cancer, Sun if Benefic:

You will get increased lands, houses and wealth. You will have many servants. You will get appreciation from bosses. You will perform auspicious events in the house. You will get political success. You will be always happy and gay. You will have happiness of mind.

Being in Cancer, Sun if Malefic:

You may not have very agreeable partner. You may usually have a worried life.

Being in Leo, Sun if Benefic:

You will get respect from bosses. You will have high status and position. You will possess houses and gardens. There will be birth of children. You will be famous.

Being in Virgo, Sun if Benefic:

You will get good education and will be learned in religious lore.

Being in Virgo, Sun if Malefic:

You may have losses in cattle, wealth and houses. You may develop enmity with friends and relatives.

Being in Libra, Sun if Malefic:

You may not get name and fame. You may have frustrations in life. You may incur heavy expenditure. You are likely to suffer at the hands of government. There may be increase of enemies. You may have loss of wealth and brothers. You may face obstructions in your efforts and failures in any undertakings. You may have miserable and complicated life.

Being in Scorpio, Sun if Benefic:

You will gain from lands, house and wealth. You will succeed in fulfilment of mental desires. You will realise many of your ambitious things.

Being in Scorpio, Sun if Malefic:

There may be no achievement of ambitions. You may not have much conjugal happiness.

Being in Sagittarius, Sun if Benefic:

You will be respected by all clans and unions of people and also by government. You will succeed in all your undertakings. You will destory your enemies and get supreme satisfaction everywhere. You will be popular and will enjoy all-round happiness.

Being in Capricorn, Sun if Benefic:

You will get name and self respect.

Being in Capricorn, Sun if Malefic:

You may prove a bad tradesperson. You may be devoid of wealth and support from the relations. There may be loss of house, cattle, lands, and wealth. You may develop enmity with friends. There may be loss of patrimony. You may be unhappy when other people get success and prosper. You may generally lead an unhappy life.

Being in Aquarius, Sun if Benefic:

You will get self-esteem.

Being in Aquarius, Sun if Malefic:

You may be unlucky and unsuccessful. You may not expect happiness from sons. You may be devoid of wealth. You may enter into disputes. You may have separation from your partner. There may be losses in your lands, cattle and property. You may have mental worries.

Being in Pisces, Sun if Benefic:

You will have good friends and you will annihilate your enemies. You will get affection from relatives and people. You will derive happiness from partner, children and friends. You will have good children and servants. There will be auspicious celebrations in your house. You will have smooth sailing in every way. You will be wealthy and peaceful. You will be respected among relations.

Being in Pisces, Sun if Malefic:

You are liable to be involved in scandals.

Mars in Different Rasis

Being in Aries, Mars if Benefic:

You will be rich, commanding and powerful. You will get excessive wealth and gains. You will have increase in reputation and respect. You will get much gains and fame. You will be respected by government. If engaged in trade, you will get success therein.

Being in Taurus, Mars if Benefic:

Your enemies will be destroyed. You will get success in all your struggles and get respected from elders and rulers. You will have good produce from lands.

Being in Taurus, Mars if Malefic:

You may not have a stable position in life. You may be antagonistic of friends.

Being in Gemini, Mars if Benefic:

You will be learned and skilled in music. You will have access to great wealth and precious stones. You will have success in agriculture in every work. You will have children. You will be a connoissuer of poetry, dancing and singing and music.

Being in Gemini, Mars if Malefic:

You may be unhappy.

Being in Cancer, Mars if Benefic:

You will be wealthy. You will have medical and

surgical proficiency. You will gain from agriculture. You may get a government scholarship.

Being in Cancer, Mars if Malefic:

You may have danger from enemies and rulers. You may have litigation problems and loss of honour and reputation. You may suffer from domestic disharmony. You may have misunderstanding among brothers and close relatives.

Being in Leo, Mars if Benefic:

You will be victorious. You may become an author. You will be happy and successful all through. You will get material gains through fine arts. You will have increase in house, grains and lands.

Being in Leo, Mars if Malefic:

You may be extravagant. You may have few children. You may be restless and may have little happiness from your partner. You may be devoid of wealth.

Being in Virgo, Mars if Benefic:

You will undertake scientific enterprises and get beneficial results. You will have successful termination of educational pursuits. You will get happiness from relatives and friends. You will have children. You will be wealthy.

Being in Virgo, Mars if Malefic:

You may get troubles in your marital life. You may fear your opponents. You may incur heavy expenditure.

Being in Libra, Mars if Benefic:

You will have self-earned wealth.

Being in Libra, Mars if Malefic:

You may have miserable life. You may land in misunderstandings with cousins and brothers. There may be ill health of your married partner and children. You may get loss of wealth and gains. You may mortgage your landed property. You may be antagonistic to friends.

Being in Scorpio, Mars if Benefic:

You will have great strides in life. There will be increase in your wealth. You may become head of some department or institution or a business man with a flourishing trade of your own. You will be respected by government. You will have good earnings.

Being in Sagittarius, Mars if Benefic:

You will be famous. You may become a minister. There will be destruction of your enemies. You will realise all your hopes and desires. You will occupy a high position in a large institution.

Being in Sagittarius, Mars if Malefic:

You may have many foes. You may have few children. You may be quarrelsome and enter into litigation problems. Your wealth and happiness may be lessened due to your uncontrolled temper. You may attain happiness and comfort only after hard labour.

Being in Capricorn, Mars if Benefic:

You will be rich. You will attain high political position or become the head of a section of a army or department or institution. You may succeed in battles and get respected for your military skills. You will be victorious in your undertakings. You may have many sons. You will be influential, successful and respected. You will have much paraphernalia. You may gain from quadrupeds. There will be increase in your wealth.

Being in Aquarius, Mars if Benefic:

You will be well-versed in dialects.

Being in Aquarius, Mars if Malefic:

You may be unhappy, miserable and poor. You may face great hardships and difficulties. You may have misunderstandings with rulers and immediate superiors in office. You may get into unpleasantries towards mother and servants. You may be affected with sorrows. There may be loss of money in gambling or speculation. You may be devoid of respect.

Being in Pisces, Mars if Benefic:

You will have much wealth and bumper crops in lands. There will be prosperity and increase in house and business. You will get general success and happiness. You will be respected as a learned man. You will occupy a good position in life with great reputation.

Being in Pisces, Mars if Malefic:

You may land in troubles in love affairs. You may have few children. You may suffer sorrows from many enemies. You may not prosper well in life. You may suffer loss of wealth due to your own deceitful conduct.

Mercury in Different Rasis

Being in Aries, Mercury if Benefic:

You will perform religious and social work. You will get married. You will have the favour of rulers or government. You will gain from cultivation, cattle, precious stones and conveyance. You will be happy.

Being in Aries, Mercury if Malefic:

You may not have a good-married partner. You may labour hard but lose wealth. You may incur debts. You may have to live in confinement. You may be poor.

Being in Taurus, Mercury if Benefic:

You may become a minister. You may have children. You will be wealthy with ornaments. You will be getting titles and names. You will have authority over men. There will be good conjugal happiness. You will enjoy great happiness.

Being in Gemini, Mercury if Benefic:

You will get happiness from your partner and children. There will be marriage ceremonies and recitation of sacred scriptures in your house. You will have successful termination of educational career. There will be acquisition of fame and wealth. You will be comfortable and lead a happy life.

Being in Cancer, Mercury if Benefic:

You will gain from water and also products of water or connected with water or goods across the seas.

Being in Cancer, Mercury if Malefic:

You may suffer from degradation, fines, imprisonments, and penalties. You may have loss of lands and there may be failure of crops. You may enter into enmity with all. You may be disliked by relations. You may antagonise your own people and lose money due to enmity with your married partner. You may be restless.

Being in Leo, Mercury if Benefic:

You will have a remunerative profession. There will be elevation in your position. You will acquire wealth from various countries. You will get progress in knowledge and great reputation. You will be married.

Being in Leo, Mercury if Malefic:

You may have few children. You may be antagonistic to your brother or family. You may not have good partner and happiness thereby. You may be poor.

Being in Virgo, Mercury if Benefic:

You will be favoured by your king or government.

There will be marriage in your house. You will get unexpected gains. You will be learned and proficient in sciences, arts and crafts. You will occupy a senior position. You will lead a happy life.

Being in Libra, Mercury if Malefic:

There will be great works published in your name. You will have the favour of wealthy and educated people without efforts. You will have leadership over men.

Being in Scorpio, Mercury if Malefic:

There may be separation from your married partner and children. You may have mental troubles. You may expect losses from merchandise. You may lose your reputation and power. Your financial returns may not be in proportion to the labour and effort put in. You may not have a good married partner.

Being in Sagittarius, Mercury if Benefic:

You will be respected by polished society. You will get success in eduation. You will be liked by government or king. You may devote your time to religious affairs or teaching. You will be famous.

Being in Capricorn, Mercury if Benefic:

You will be successful in trade and you may start new business also. You will get patronage of kings or government. There will be destruction of your foes and enemies. You will get general success in life.

Being in Capricorn, Mercury if Malefic:

You may be poor and indebted. You may have to put in much physical labour. You may be separated from relations. Various difficulties may oppress you. Your mind may feel cramped.

Being in Aquarius, Mercury if Benefic:

You will have rapid strides in life. There will be acquisition of parapheralia. You will have access to goods and much wealth. You will indulge in a pleasuresome life. You will get good name and become famous.

Being in Aquarius, Mercury if Malefic:

You may not have a congenial married partner. You may incur debts. You may have little enjoyment in life. You may be oppressed by enemies.

Being in Pisces, Mercury if Benefic:

You will have a good-married partner. You will excel your colleagues in rendering service to your boss.

Being in Pisces, Mercury if Malefic:

You may get trouble from thieves. You may quarrel with your relatives and there may be destruction of relations. You may have failure in attempts. You may not be happy in respect of children atleast for sometime.

Jupiter in Different Rasis

Being in Aries, Jupiter if Benefic:

You will acquire landed property and you will be wealthy. You will have a happy marriage. You will succeed in all undertakings and litigations. You will be powerful and elevated to responsible office. You will get great respect from people. You will be blessed with several sons and good servants. You will overcome others with your valour. You will do daring deeds which bring you name and fame.

Being in Aries, Jupiter if Malefic:

You may have heavy expenditure and many enemies.

Being in Taurus, Jupiter if Benefic:

You will have valuable possessions, increase in lands and cattle and acquisition of wealth. You will have access to new territories. You will gain in trade and agriculture. You will be respected by friends as well as enemies. You will have good and dutiful children. You will be well-read. You will be inclined to self-gratification. You will pay homage to gods, brahmins and cows. You will be popular and happy.

Being in Taurus, Jupiter if Malefic:

You may be extravagant.

Being in Gemini, Jupiter if Benefic:

You will be scholarly and learned. You will be respected by seniors as well as relations. You will get good sons and friends. You will have the necessities for comfortable living with good food and clothes. You will keep part of your money in deposits. There will be auspicious celebrations in the family. You may become adviser of a minister.

Being in Gemini, Jupiter if Malefic:

There may be separation from married partner. You may suffer loss of children, brothers and cousins. You may fear from rulers or government. You may have mental uneasiness.

Being in Cancer, Jupiter if Benefic:

You will have political success. You can expect promotions and you may get into exalted positions. You will acquire wealth from unexpected sources and without efforts. You will have journalistic success. There will be perfect harmony in domestic life. You will possess precious jewellery and will be endowed with the comforts of life. You will have a good-married partner and children. You will earn a good name and fame.

Being in Cancer, Jupiter if Malefic:

You may be inclined to social gossip.

Being in Leo, Jupiter if Benefic:

You will have harmonious surroundings. You will get respect from rulers or government. You will gain from agricultural produce and lands. You will be ambitious and realise your own desires. You will be devoted to gods. You will get happiness from partner and children. You will become head of an army or section of army or institution. You will be happy and famous.

Being in Leo, Jupiter if Malefic:

You may incur enmities which may last long.

Being in Virgo, Jupiter if Benefic:

You will have a beautiful married partner and good children and friends. You will gain money from arts, crafts or work connected with them. You will get all comforts of life. You may rise to a high position such as that of a minister. You will be learned.

Being in Virgo, Jupiter if Malefic:

You may develop misunderstandings among relatives. You may expect destruction of your properties. You may have separation from your married partner.

Being in Libra, Jupiter if Benefic:

You will have comfortable living. You will be liked by others. You will get good children and friends. You will attain a high position in life. You will be wealthy and happy.

Being in Libra, Jupiter if Malefic:

You may have a desolate and shameful life. You may reside in desolate places. You may have to face difficulties and troubles.

Being in Scorpio, Jupiter if Benefic:

You will acquire new lands and estates. You will engage yourself in religious worship and philosophical discourses. You will occupy a respectable position. You will be mentally calm. You will have undisturbed progress and happiness.

Being in Scorpio, Jupiter if Malefic:

Your reputation may be at stake. You may not have many children. You may have to labour hard.

Being in Sagittarius, Jupiter if Benefic:

You will have children and much wealth. You will succeed in every undertaking. You will acquire pretty inheritance. You will have great friends. You would occupy a high position. You will visit holy places. You will possess good houses. You will be influential. You will get wide-spread fame and perfect happiness.

Being in Capricorn, Jupiter if Malefic:

You may expect ill health of children and your married partner. You may have loss of property, reputation and self-respect. You may be liable to prosecution and imprisonment. You may have to face numerous enemies. You may have to put in much hard labour for no financial returns. You may have little money and little happiness.

Being in Aquarius, Jupiter if Benefic:

You will become head of your group. You will be much respected.

Being in Aquarius, Jupiter if Malefic:

You may have to face many hardships. You may have to put in much unproductive labour. You may suffer loss of wealth. You may have bad luck.

Being in Pisces, Jupiter if Benefic:

You will get good inheritance. You will have great education. You will gain from your exhibition of knowledge. You will be respected by friends. You cannot be over-powered by others. You will occupy a good position in your life and you will be well off. You will get requisition of property. You will have a general success and happiness. You will get name and fame.

Venus in Different Rasis

Being in Aries, Venus if Benefic:

You will reside in palatial buildings. You will have acquaintance with noble personages. You will wear good clothes. There will be birth of child. You will be praised by friends as well as enemies. You will have good earning and spread of fame.

Being in Aries, Venus if Malefic:

You may be extravagant. You may enter into quarrels and litigations. You may be unhappy.

Being in Taurus, Venus if Benefic:

You will have a life of great ease. You will gain from agriculture. You will be respected by government and your group of people whom you head. You will be wealthy, famous and enjoy much happiness.

Being in Gemini, Venus if Benefic:

You will gain vehicles. You will be loved by others. You will devote your time to gods and brahmins. You will get children. There will be harmony with your married partner. You will have an increase in reputation.

Being in Cancer, Venus if Benefic:

You will be the chief person in your group. You will be religiously inclined. You will get all the desirable necessities for comfort.

Being in Cancer, Venus if Malefic:

There may be destruction of your property. You may develop discontent with your relations. There may be increase of enemies. You may lose wealth.

Being in Leo, Venus if Benefic:

You will get money from women. You will have an excellent partner. You will be married in a high family. You will be liked by religious preceptors and brahmins. You will have unusual happiness.

Being in Leo, Venus if Malefic:

You may have few children. Your better half or child may be sick. You may undertake aimless wanderings.

Being in Virgo, Venus if Benefic:

You will be a scholar.

Being in Virgo, Venus if Malefic:

You may quarrel with your partner and there may be separation. You may mortgage your property. You may expect separation from your relations and friends. You may not have much luxuries. You may be unsuccessful and unhappy.

Being in Libra, Venus if Benefic:

You will gain wealth from royal partronage or government. You will get all comforts and enjoyments in life. You will have a successful marriage and there will be matrimonial felicity. You will be respected. You will get a good name due to devotion to gods and brahmins. You will be well-liked by the society and the state. You will possess vehicles. You will get great reputation. You will be wealthy.

Being in Scorpio, Venus if Benefic:

You will attain good position. You will succeed in defeating your opponents.

Being in Scorpio, Venus if Malefic:

You may be disappointed in love. You may have many miseries and troubles. You may get loss of wealth and property.

Being in Sagittarius, Venus if Benefic:

You will be fond of religious and philosophical studies. You will get success in any undertaking. You will have the necessities and comforts. You will rise to high position. You will be respected. You will acquire wealth. You will have much name and fame.

Being in Capricorn, Venus if Benefic:

You will get freedom from domestic worries. You will have discussions with learned people. There will be progress in general education. You will succeed in all endeavours. You will be powerful.

Being in Capricorn, Venus if Malefic:

You may be always apprehensive. Your efforts may end in frustrations.

Being in Aquarius, Venus if Benefic:

There will be acquisition of fresh property, land and houses. You will get unexpected gains. You will be liked by all. You will attain honours.

Being in Aquarius, Venus if Malefic:

You may be antagonistic to your children and seniors. You may be agitated in mind.

Saturn in Different Rasis

Being in Aries, Saturn if Malefic:

You may get unexpected losses, disappointments in every undertaking. You may be misunderstood among relatives and friends. There may be increase of enemies. You may wander aimlessly.

Being in Taurus, Saturn if Benefic:

You will succeed and gain in agricultural operations. You will have great income. You will be successful and powerful.

Being in Taurus, Saturn if Malefic:

You may have bad friends. You are likely to be insulted. You may be devoid of wealth.

Being in Gemini Saturn if Benefic:

Your services will be recognised. You will profit in speculation and trade. You will get respect from rulers or government. You will occupy a good position with large staff under you. You will attain political success. You will get reputation and fame. You will be endowed with much general happiness.

Being in Gemini, Saturn if Malefic:

You may receive at times insulting treatment. You may incur debts. You may not get much happiness from children.

Being in Cancer, Saturn if Benefic:

You will associate with important people. You will attain a good position in life.

Being in Cancer, Saturn if Malefic:

You may have few children. You may get miseries and calamities. There may be family strife and increase of enemies. You may get trouble from relatives and you may be opposed to your relations. You may not get much happiness from your children. You may be unsuccessful and poor.

Being in Leo, Saturn if Malefic:

You may get disappointments and unrest. You may misappropriate money and consequently you may be prosecuted. You may be hated by all. You may have few children. You may be without relations or you may not be on loving terms with your relations. You may be without partner or you may lack in conjugal happiness. Your children will be a source of trouble to you. You may be unfortunate.

Being in Virgo, Saturn if Benefic:

You may head an institution with a large staff. You will be elevated to an exalted position. You will get favours from royal or governmental source. You will succeed in business. You will have an established fame and reputation. You will make inventions.

Being in Virgo, Saturn if Malefic:

You may not engage in productive work. You may get little happiness from your children. You may not be healthy.

Being in Libra, Saturn if Benefic:

You will be a founder of institutions or the like. You will establish new business concerns. You will occupy a senior position and will be respected in the place where you reside. You will rise in life as age advances. You will be famous and rich.

Being in Scorpio, Saturn if Benefic:

You will get self-respect and fame.

Being in Scorpio, Saturn if Malefic:

You are liable to suffer confinement and sorrows. You may have heavy expenditure. You may be disliked and hated by all. You may lose your prestige. There may be destruction and damage to your property and possessions. You may be unhappy.

Being in Sagittarius, Saturn if Benefic:

You will succeed in philosophical and religious studies. There will be auspicious occasions in house.

You will have illustrious children who will bring credit to you. You may become head or leader of a village or town. You will have mental peace and happiness.

Being in Sagittarius, Saturn if Malefic:

You may enter into troubles with your married partner.

Being in Capricorn, Saturn if Benefic:

There will be harmony and felicity in domestic life. You will gain wealth and business. There will be increase in lands. You will develop friendship with great and illustrious personages. You will be learned.

Being in Aquarius, Saturn if Benefic:

You will succeed in litigations. You will acquire much wealth. You will occupy a good position in life. You will attain mental happiness.

Being in Aquarius, Saturn if Malefic:

You may have bad friends.

Being in Pisces, Saturn if Benefic:

You will have a good-married partner. You will go on pilgrimage to sacred shrines and holy places. You will become chief and get respect from your friends and relatives. You will have good children. You may become the head of an institution, village or town. You will command respect and trust in government. You will be happy.

Being in Pisces, Saturn if Malefic:

You may suffer from sorrows, misery and unrest.

Moon in Different Rasis

Being in Aries, Moon if Benefic:

You will get self-respect. You will gain in wealth. You will have several children. You will have physical

and mental happiness. You will have perfect
contentment.

Being in Aries, Moon if Malefic:

You may have subordinate position. You may be
devoid of happiness from brothers.

Being in Taurus, Moon if Benefic:

You will have great strides in life. You will have
increase in name and fame. You will have physical and
mental happiness. You will be respected. You will be
lucky and popular. You will be happy in the middle and
old age.

Being in Taurus, Moon if Malefic:

You may have love intrigues. You may have more
daughters than sons.

Being in Gemini, Moon if Benefic:

You will be well-read and you will have good
progress in education. You will acquire much
immovable property. You will enjoy luxuries.

Being in Cancer, Moon if Benefic:

You will be wealthy and will have much immovable
property. You will succeed in litigation. You will find
unexpected treasures. You will have a comfortable
house. You may become a minister. You will be
prosperous.

Being in Cancer, Moon if Malefic:

You may undertake unprofitable voyages. You may
go through a cycle of waxing and waning in your career.

Being in Leo, Moon if Benefic:

You will have progress in your education. You will
get much gains from unexpected sources.

Being in Leo, Moon if Malefic:

You may have few children. You may suffer from mental anxiety.

Being in Virgo, Moon if Benefic:

You will be skilled in arts like music and dancing. You will be affluent. You will lead a comfortable and prosperous life.

Being in Virgo, Moon if Malefic:

You may have many daughters. You will get worries from enemies and swindlers. You may suffer from mental and physical restlessness. Your mother may be ill.

Being in Libra, Moon if Benefic:

You will get reverance and respect from learned and holy people. You will be wealthy. You will have increase in friends. You will visit holy places and shrines. There will be destruction of enemies. You will realise your schemes. You will be prosperous.

Being in Libra, Moon if Malefic:

You may be neglected by kinsmen. You may be devoid of relations or you may not have good relations with them. You may suffer financial penalty at the hands of government.

Being in Scorpio, Moon if Benefic:

You will be wealthy. You will be head of some department or institution or a businessman with a flourishing trade of your own. You will be respected by government.

Being in Scorpio, Moon if Malefic:

You may have loss of wealth. Your liberty and honour may be at risk. You may get much mental uneasiness. You may be isolated from parents or preceptors. You may have fear from political heads. There will be destruction of relatives. You will get disappointments in every respect. There may be abortions before the birth of your children. You may be unhappy.

Being in Sagittarius, Moon if Benefic:

You will be skilled in fine arts. You will have a happy marriage and will have many children. You will get good inheritance and unexpected gifts. You may become an author. You will have domestic happiness and felicity. There will be celebration of happy functions. You will accumulate wealth.

Being in Capricorn, Moon if Benefic:

You will go on pilgrimage to holy places. You will succeed in litigations. There will be increase in lands, houses and wealth. You will get success in every new enterprise. You will become famous.

Being in Aquarius, Moon if Malefic:

There may be destruction of your property. You may be afraid of political authority. You may get mental worries from enemies. You may develop misunderstandings among relatives and enemies. You may get sudden elevations and depressions. You may incur enmity with good people. You may suffer from sorrows. You may be poor.

Being in Pisces, Moon if Benefic:

You will take charge of fresh office. You will be annihilating enemies. You will have many children. You will get authority if engaged in works of arts and crafts. You will be connoisseur of singing. You will lead a comfortable life. You will get inheritance or sudden or buried wealth or treasure.

(IX) CHILDREN
Sun in Different Rasis

Being in Aries, Sun if Benefic:
   You may have birth of children.

Being in Leo, Sun if Benefic:
   You may have birth of children and sons. You will get respect among children.

Being in Aquarius, Sun if Malefic:
   You may have no happiness from children.

Being in Pisces, Sun if Benefic:
   You will have good and happy children.

Mars in Different Rasis

Being in Gemini, Mars if Benefic:
   You may have several children and you will oblige children.

Being in Leo, Mars if Malefic:
   You may have few children and only a few sons.

Being in Virgo, Mars if Benefic:
   You may be blessed with many sons.

Being in Sagittarius, Mars if Malefic:
   You may have few children.

Being in Capricorn, Mars if Benefic:
   You may get children.

Mercury in Different Rasis

Being in Taurus, Mercury if Benefic:
   You may have children.

Being in Gemini, Mercury if Benefic:
   You may have twin children.

Being in Leo, Mercury if Malefic:
   You may have few children. You may have adverse factor in respect of issues.

Being in Libra, Mercury if Benefic:
   You will be attached to children.

Being in Pisces, Mercury if Malefic:
   You will be happy in respect of children at least for sometime.

Jupiter in Different Rasis

Being in Leo, Jupiter if Benefic:
   You will have happiness from children.

Being in Virgo, Jupiter if Benefic:
   You will have good children.

Venus in Different Rasis

Being in Aries, Venus if Benefic:
   There may be birth of a child.

Being in Cancer, Venus if Benefic:
   You may have children.

Being in Leo, Venus if Malefic:
   You may have few children.

Being in Gemini, Venus if Malefic:
   You may not get much happiness from children.

Being in Virgo, Venus if Malefic:
   You may have little happiness from children.

Being in Sagittarius, Venus if Benefic:
You will have illustrious children who will bring credit to you.

Being in Aries, Venus if Benefic:
You may have children.

Being in Virgo, Venus if Malefic:
You are likely to have more daughters than sons.

Being in Pisces, Venus if Benefic:
You will be fond of children.

(X) DISEASES
Sun in Different Rasis

Being in Aries, Sun if Malefic:
You may be phlegmatic. You may have too much of heat. You may have excess of bile and blood disorders.

Being in Aries, Sun if Benefic:
You will have strong bones.

Being in Taurus, Sun if Malefic:
You may suffer from diseases of mouth and eyes.

Being in Virgo, Sun if Malefic:
You may suffer from physical diseases. Your health may be affected, yet you may have much physical and mental stamina.

Being in Capricorn, Sun if Benefic:
Your digestive powers will be good.

Being in Aquarius, Sun if Benefic:
You will have great stamina.

Being in Aquarius, Sun if Malefic:

You will not have much stamina. You are liable to heart troubles.

Being in Pisces, Sun if Malefic:

You may get diseases of private parts.

Mars in Different Rasis

Being in Aries, Mars if Benefic:

You will have much stamina.

Being in Gemini, Mars if Benefic:

You will have much bodily vigour and strength.

Being in Cancer, Mars if Benefic:

You will have good health.

Being in Cancer, Mars if Malefic:

You may have ill health and defective sight. You may be worried due to chronic ailments.

Being in Leo, Mars if Benefic:

You will have a strong body.

Being in Leo, Mars if Malefic:

You may have stomach troubles.

Being in Virgo, Mars if Malefic:

You may get troubles of digestive organs.

Being in Libra, Mars if Malefic:

You may have some defect in limbs.

Being in Scorpio, Mars if Malefic:

You may have marks of wound or those caused by fire

on body. You may suffer from poison (like blood poisoning).

Being in Sagittarius, Mars if Malefic:
    You may have marks of wounds on body.

Being in Pisces, Mars if Malefic:
    You may suffer from ailments of body.

Mercury in Different Rasis

Being in Virgo, Mercury if Benefic:
    You will have undisturbed health.

Being in Virgo, Mercury if Malefic:
    You may have dyspeptic difficulties (indigestion).

Being in Pisces, Mercury if Malefic:
    You may have dysentery, nervous breakdown or mental derangement.

Jupiter in Different Rasis

Being in Aries, Jupiter if Benefic:
    You will have much stamina.

Being in Aries, Jupiter if Malefic:
    Your body may bear scars of wounds.

Being in Taurus, Jupiter if Benefic:
    You will be free from diseases. You will have good health.

Being in Virgo, Jupiter if Malefic:
    You may have bodily ill health. You may have symptoms of nervous troubles and diseases.

Being in Sagittarius. Jupiter if Malefic:
    You may have a weak constitution.

Being in Capricorn, Jupiter if Malefic:
You may not have much stamina or virility.

Venus in Different Rasis

Being in Aries, Venus if Malefic:
You may become night blind in old age.

Being in Cancer, Venus if Malefic:
You will have power of resistance and much stamina.

Being in Leo, Venus if Malefic:
You may suffer from mental diseases and sorrows.

Being in Virgo, Venus if Malefic:
You may have troubles in generative organs often leading to surgical operation. You may have symptoms of arthritis. You may have troubles related to nervous breakdown.

Being in Scorpio, Venus if Malefic:
You may suffer from diseases of hidden parts or hidden diseases.

Being in Pisces, Venus if Malefic:
You may have dyspeptic difficulties (indigestion).

Saturn in Different Rasis

Being in Cancer, Saturn if Malefic:
You may have physical diseases and mental afflictions.

Being in Scorpio, Saturn if Malefic:
You may suffer from poison or fire (like burns or food poisoning). You may have depletion of energy arising out of chronic ailment.

Moon in Different Rasis

Being in Aries, Moon if Malefic:

You may have sores in head. You may have weak knees and bad nails. Your hair may not be good. You may have prominent veins. You may have marks of wound or boils on the body.

Being in Taurus, Moon if Malefic:

You may have phlegmatic afflictions.

Being in Leo, Moon if Malefic:

You may suffer from hunger, thirst and stomach troubles. You may have pain in teeth.

Being in Virgo, Moon if Malefic:

You may be phlegmatic.

Being in Libra, Moon if Malefic:

You may have sickly constitution with prominent veins.

Being in Scorpio, Moon if Malefic:

You may have on your body marks of wound or those connected by fire.

(XI) ENEMIES
Sun in Different Rasis

Being in Aries, Sun if Malefic:

You may have quarrels among friends and relatives.

Being in Taurus, Sun if Benefic:

You may not have many enemies. You will have friendship with bosses.

Being in Taurus, Sun if Malefic:

You may have enmity or hatred of women.

Being in Cancer, Sun if Malefic:
  You may oppose your own people, particularly your father or uncle.

Being in Leo, Sun if Benefic:
  You will annihilate your enemies.

Being in Libra, Sun if Malefic:
  You may always be troubled by enemies.

Being in Scorpio, Sun if Benefic:
  You will strike your enemy in a subtle and secret manner like a scorpion.

Being in Scorpio, Sun if Malefic:
  You may be quarrelsome and develop enemies.

Being in Sagittarius, Sun if Benefic:
  You will destroy your enemies.

Being in Capricorn, Sun if Malefic:
  You may develop misunderstandings among your own people.

Being in Aquarius, Sun if Malefic:
  You may have disputes.

Being in Pisces, Sun if Benefic:
  You will annihilate a host of your enemies.

Mars in Different Rasis

Being in Aries, Mars if Malefic:
  You may be quarrelsome and may have enemies.

Being in Taurus, Mars if Benefic:
  You will destroy your enemies.

Being in Taurus, Mars if Malefic:
You may be antagonistic to friends.

Being in Gemini, Mars if Malefic:
You may be without friends.

Being in Cancer, Mars if Malefic:
You may have danger from enemies and rulers. You may have litigation problems. You may develop misunderstandings among brothers and close relatives. You may be without friends.

Being in Virgo, Mars if Malefic:
You may fear your opponents.

Being in Libra, Mars if Malefic:
You may be antagonistic to friends.

Being in Scorpio, Mars if Benefic:
You may be intent on harming your opponents.

Being in Sagittarius, Mars if Benefic:
There will be destruction of your enemies.

Being in Sagittarius, Mars if Malefic:
You may have many foes. You may get into litigation problems.

Being in Aquarius, Mars if Malefic:
You may have misunderstandings with rulers and immediate superiors in your office.

Being in Pisces, Mars if Malefic:
You may have many enemies.

Mercury in Different Rasis

Being in Aries, Mercury if Malefic:

You may have a quarrelsome disposition which may develop enemies.

Being in Taurus, Mercury if Benefic:

You will have friends among women of eminence.

Being in Cancer, Mercury if Malefic:

You may be disliked by relations. You may be antagonistic to your own people.

Being in Aquarius, Mercury if Malefic:

You may be oppressed by your enemies.

Being in Pisces, Mercury if Malefic:

You may have fear from thieves. There may be destruction of relations and you may have quarrels with relatives. You may enter into litigation problems.

Jupiter in Different Rasis

Being in Aries, Jupiter if Benefic:

You will have success in all litigations.

Being in Taurus, Jupiter if Benefic:

You will get respect from friends as well as foes.

Being in Leo, Jupiter if Malefic:

Your enmities may last long.

Being in Virgo, Jupiter if Malefic:

You may have misunderstandings with relatives.

Being in Capricorn, Jupter if Malefic:

There may be springing up of numerous enemies. You are liable to prosecution and incarceration (imprisonment).

Venus in Different Rasis

Being in Cancer, Venus if Malefic:
There may be increase in number of enemies.

Being in Virgo, Venus if Malefic:
You may have quarrels with partner.

Being in Scorpio, Venus if Benefic:
You will succeed in defeating your opponents.

Being in Scorpio, Venus if Malefic:
You may have vengeance against relatives. You may, by favouring a lady, oppose or enter into litigation with another party and thereby damage your property.

Being in Aquarius, Venus if Malefic:
You may be antagonistic to your children and seniors (father etc.).

Saturn in Different Rasis

Being in Aries, Saturn if Malefic:
You may have misunderstandings among relatives and friends. There may be increase in number of enemies. You may be quarrelsome. You may have no friends.

Being in Cancer, Saturn if Malefic:
There may be increase of enemies. You may have trouble from relatives.

Being in Leo, Saturn if Malefic:
You may be hated by all. You may be without relatives or you may not be on loving terms with them. You may have trouble from your sons.

Being in Libra, Saturn if Malefic:
You may be antagonistic and develop enemies.

Being in Scorpio, Saturn if Malefic:
   You may be disliked and hated by all.

Being in Sagittarius, Saturn if Malefic:
   You may have troubles with your married partner.

Being in Aquarius, Saturn if Malefic:
   You may have bad friends.

Moon in Different Rasis

Being in Cancer, Moon if Benefic:
   You will have success in litigation.

Being in Leo, Moon if Malefic:
   You may not get on well with women.

Being in Virgo, Moon if Malefic:
   You may have worries from enemies.

Being in Libra, Moon if Benefic:
   You will have increase of friends. There will be destruction of enemies.

Being in Libra, Moon if Malefic:
   You may not be on good terms with relations.

Being in Scorpio, Moon if Benefic:
   You will be intent on harming opponents.

Being in Sagittarius, Moon if Benefic:
   You will be inflexible to threats.

Being in Aquarius, Moon if Malefic:
   You may have fear from political authority. You may have mental worries from enemies. You may have misunderstandings among relations and enemies. You

may be liable to fraud and deception. You may incur. enmity of good people.

Being in Pisces, Moon if Benefic:
You will annihilate enemies.

(XII) DEBTS
Mercury in Different Rasis

Being in Scorpio, Mercury if Malefic:
You may be indebted.

Mars in Different Rasis

Being in Virgo, Mars if Malefic:
You may incur heavy expenditure.

Jupiter in Different Rasis

Being in Aries, Jupiter if Malefic:
You may have much expenditure.

Being in Taurus, Jupiter if Malefic:
You may be extravagant.

Venus in Different Rasis

Being in Virgo, Venus if Malefic:
You may mortgage your property.

Being in Scorpio, Venus if Malefic:
You may get into debts.

Saturn in Different Rasis

Being in Gemini, Saturn if Malefic:
You may incur debts.

Being in Scorpio, Saturn if Malefic:
You may suffer heavy expenditure.

(XIII) MARRIAGE AND MARITAL RELATIONSHIP
Sun in Different Rasis

Being in Aries, Sun if Benefic:

You will have happiness due to your married partner. You will have company of beautiful and lovely women.

Being in Taurus, Sun if Malefic:

You may not be an ardent lover of your married partner.

Being in Cancer, Sun if Malefic:

You may not have a very agreeable married partner.

Being in Scorpio, Sun if Malefic:

You may not have much conjugal happiness.

Being in Aquarius, Sun if Malefic:

You may have separation from your married partner.

Being in Pisces, Sun if Benefic:

You will have happiness from your married partner.

Mars in Different Rasis

Being in Taurus, Mars if Malefic:

You may be under the influence of women. You may not be attached to your life partner.

Being in Leo, Mars if Malefic:

You may have little happiness from your married partner.

Being in Virgo, Mars if Benefic:

You may have general love for the opposite sex.

Being in Libra, Mars if Benefic:
You will love your family.

Being in Libra, Mars if Malefic:
You may have contacts with persons of other sex or may be under their influence.

Mercury in Different Rasis

Being in Taurus, Mercury if Malefic:
You are likely to have contact with handsome young persons.

Being in Gemini, Mercury if Benefic:
You will get happiness from your married partner.

Being in Gemini, Mercury if Malefic:
You may not have marital happiness.

Being in Cancer, Mercury if Malefic:
You may lose money due to enmity of your married partner.

Being in Leo, Mercury if Benefic:
You are likely to have early marriage.

Being in Leo, Mercury if Malefic:
You may be subservient to women. You may be fond of other persons. You may not have a good married partner or you may not have happiness through your married partner. You may be desirous of company of opposite sex.

Being in Virgo, Mercury if Malefic:
You sexual vigour may be less than normal.

Being in Libra, Mercury if Benefic:
You will be attached to your married partner.

Jupiter in Different Rasis

Being in Gemini, Jupiter if Malefic:

There may be separation from your married partner.

Being in Cancer, Jupiter if Benefic:

You will have a good-married partner.

Being in Virgo, Jupiter if Benefic:

You will have a beautiful married partner.

Being in Scorpio, Jupiter if Malefic:

You may have sensual passions and you may be subservient to persons of opposite sex.

Being in Aquarius, Jupiter if Malefic:

You may have illicit contact with a relation.

Venus in Different Rasis

Being in Aries, Venus if Benefic:

You will have happy marital relations.

Being in Aries, Venus if Malefic:

You may have relation with others. You may be confined due to a woman. You may enter into quarrels or litigations on account of attachment to a woman and lose wealth as a result thereof.

Being in Taurus, Venus if Malefic:

You will have company of beautiful persons and you will get joy through association with them. You may have company of a large number of persons.

Being in Gemini, Venus if Benefic:

You will have good harmony with your partner. You will have a check over your inclination to indulge in loose life.

Being in Geimni, Venus if Malefic:
You may be over-sensual.

Being in Cancer, Venus if Malefic:
You may not have good-marital relationship.

Being in Leo, Venus if Benefic:
You will have an excellent partner and you will be married in high family.

Being in Leo, Venus if Malefic:
You may be attracted by fair sex. Your better-half may be sick. You may adore ladies and derive pleasures.

Being in Virgo, Venus if Malefic:
You may long for love affairs.

Being in Libra, Venus if Benefic:
You will have a successful marriage and matrimonial felicity.

Being in Libra, Venus if Malefic:
You will have a period of extreme sensuality and you will be passionate.

Being in Scorpio, Venus if Malefic:
You will get disappointments in love. You may enter into enmity with a woman of loose character. You may favour a lady.

Being in Capricorn, Venus if Malefic:
You will be under considerable influence of your married partner or other woman.

Being in Aquarius, Venus if Malefic:
You may be attached to another person. You may

have stray connections with servile persons. You may
be attached to an unworthy person or you may be under
considerable influence of your married partner or
other person.

Saturn in Different Rasis

Being in Taurus, Saturn if Malefic:

You may be constantly attached to other person. You
may be a favourite of undesirable or elderly person.

Being in Leo, Saturn if Malefic:

You may not have a partner or you may be lacking
conjugal happiness.

Being in Libra, Saturn if Malefic:

You will be fond of association with persons of loose
morals and you may be subservient to others.

Being in Sagittarius, Saturn if Malefic:

You may land into trouble with your partner.

Being in Aquarius, Saturn if Malefic:

You may be addicted to other persons. You may enter
into adultery with others.

Being in Pisces, Saturn if Malefic:

You will have a good partner.

Moon in Different Rasis

Being in Aries, Moon if Malefic:

You will be under the influence of your married
partner.

Being in Gemini, Moon if Malefic:

You may be oversexed and under the influence of
your partner.

Being in Libra, Moon if Malefic:

You will love other persons and may have probable illicit connections with others.

Being in Sagittarius, Moon if Benefic:

You will have a happy marriage. You will receive happiness from your married partner.

Being in Capricorn, Moon if Malefic:

You may have probable connections with other person.

Being in Aquarius, Moon if Malefic:

You may not have good conduct.

Being in Pisces, Moon if Malefic:

You may be attached to many young persons. You may be subservient to fair sex. You may have loose morals. You may be under the influence of your partner.

(XIV) LONGEVITY
Sun in Different Rasis

Being in Aries, Sun if Benefic:

You will have strong bones.

Being in Aries, Sun if Malefic:

Your health may be in trouble due to too much heat, excess of bile or blood disorders.

Being in Taurus, Sun if Benefic:

You will be capable of bearing much physical stress and strain like a bull.

Being in Taurus, Sun if Malefic:

You may suffer from disease of mouth and eyes.

Being in Gemini, Sun if Malefic:

You may have set-backs in health giving rise to mental worries.

Being in Cancer, Sun if Benefic:

You will have happiness of mind.

Being in Cancer, Sun if Malefic:

You may be sickly and suffer from constipation, imbalance of bile and phlegm in the body.

Being in Leo, Sun if Benefic:

You will be strong and will have much stamina.

Being in Virgo, Sun if Malefic:

You may have a tender, weak, and effeminate body. You may not have much physical and mental stamina. Your health may be affected. You may continuously suffer from some physical disease.

Being in Libra, Sun if Malefic:

You may be a drunkard and may have loose morals affecting your longevity.

Being in Sagittarius, Sun if Benefic:

You will have a fully developed body, much stamina and good health, leading to good longevity.

Being in Capricorn, Sun if Benefic:

Your digestive powers will be good and will give you good longevity.

Being in Capricorn, Sun if Malefic:

You may not have much stamina and may suffer from diseases leading to some kind of troubles and you may not have very long life.

Being in Aquarius, Sun if Benefic:
You will have great stamina.

Being in Aquarius, Sun if Malefic:
You are liable to heart troubles and mental worries.

Being in Pisces, Sun if Malefic:
You may have disease of private parts.

Mars in Different Rasis

Being in Aries, Mars if Benefic:
You will have much stamina.

Being in Gemini, Mars if Benefic:
You will have good bodily vigour and strength. You can put up with severe strain.

Being in Cancer, Mars if Benefic:
You will have good health.

Being in Cancer, Mars if Malefic:
You may have ill health with defective sight. You may be worried due to some chronic ailment.

Being in Leo, Mars if Benefic:
You will have strong body and great stamina.

Being in Leo, Mars if Malefic:
You may have stomach troubles and you may be worried by mental complaints.

Being in Aquarius, Mars if Malefic:
You may face danger in water.

Being in Pisces, Mars if Malefic:
You may have ailments of body.

Mercury in Different Rasis

Being in Gemini, Mercury if Malefic:
You are liable to throat and bronchial troubles.

Being in Cancer, Mercury if Malefic:
You are liable to consumption and you may be restless.

Being in Virgo, Mercury if Benefic:
You will have undisturbed health.

Being in Virgo, Mercury if Malefic:
You may get into indigestion problem.

Being in Libra, Mercury if Malefic:
You may have inclination to excesses.

Being in Scorpio, Mercury if Malefic:
You are liable to disease of generative organs. You may have general debility.

Being in Pisces, Mercury if Malefic:
You may suffer from dysentery, mental derailment or nervous breakdown.

Jupiter in Different Rasis

Being in Aries, Jupiter if Malefic:
You may have wounds on body.

Being in Taurus, Jupiter if Benefic:
You will be free from diseases.

Being in Gemini, Jupiter if Benefic:
You will be well-built.

Being in Gemini, Jupiter if Malefic:
You may have mental uneasiness.

Being in Leo, Jupiter if Benefic:
You will have strong and compact body with much stamina.

Being in Virgo, Jupiter if Malefic:
You may have bodily ill health and symptoms of nervous troubles.

Being in Libra, Jupiter if Benefic:
You will be having a strong health.

Being in Scorpio, Jupiter if Benefic:
You will be well-built and mentally calm and happy.

Being in Scorpio, Jupiter if Malefic:
You may suffer from some chronic ailment.

Being in Sagittarius, Jupiter if Malefic:
You may have weak constitution.

Being in Capricorn, Jupiter if Malefic:
You may have a weak body and may not have much stamina and virility.

Venus in Different Rasis

Being in Taurus, Venus if Benefic:
You will have a well-built and strong body.

Being in Taurus, Venus if Malefic:
You may have symptoms of some troubles due to ill health.

Being in Cancer, Venus if Malefic:
You may suffer from chronic ailments, caused by

excessive indulgence in drinks. You may not have much stamina and power of resistance.

Being in Leo, Venus if Malefic:
   You may not have much stamina.

Being in Virgo, Venus if Malefic:
   You may often get troubles in generative organs, leading to surgical operations. You may develop symptoms of arthritis. You may have troubles relating to nervous breakdown and mental unrest.

Being in Scorpio, Venus if Malefic:
   You may suffer from diseases of private parts or from some hidden diseases.

Being in Capricorn, Venus if Malefic:
   You may have a weak body and you may suffer from heart disease.

Being in Pisces, Venus if Malefic:
   You may have dyspeptic difficulties (indigestion).

Saturn in Different Rasis

Being in Taurus, Saturn if Malefic:
   You may get into contagious disease.

Being in Cancer, Saturn if Malefic:
   You may have physical disease and mental afflictions. You may always be restless.

Being in Scorpio, Saturn if Malefic:
   You may suffer from fire or poison (such as burn or food poisoning). You may have depletion of energies arising out of a chronic ailment.

Being in Pisces, Saturn if Benefic:
   You will have a good end to life and peaceful death.

Moon in Different Rasis

Being in Aries, Moon if Malefic:
You may have sores in head, weak knees, bad nails and boils on body.

Being in Taurus, Moon if Malefic:
You may have phlegmatic afflictions.

Being in Leo, Moon if Malefic:
You may have deformed body and pain in teeth.

Being in Virgo, Moon if Malefic:
You may have soft body with phlematic composition and mental physical restlessness.

Being in Libra, Moon if Malefic:
You may be thin with deformed limbs and sickly constitution.

Being in Scorpio, Moon if Malefic:
You may have wounds caused by fire on body. You may suffer from poison (like food poisoning).

Being in Sagittarius, Moon if Benefic:
You will have well-built and strong body.

Being in Capricorn, Moon if Malefic:
You may have a lean body.

Being in Aquarius, Moon if Malefic:
You may be inclined to drink wine.

Being in Pisces, Moon if Benefic:
You will have a perfect build and bright body.

(XV) PROSPERITY
Sun in Different Rasis

Being in Aries, Sun if Benefic:

You will be wealthy and famous. You will be capable of rising to the highest pinnacle of leadership. You will gain from cattle and gold. You will progress in your career. You will acquire ornaments. You will have happiness due to partner, children and friends. You will have pleasure trips and picnic parties. You will get birth of children. You will have much respect from high personages. You will get power and political success.

Being in Aries, Sun if Malefic:

You may not be rich. You may suffer from disappointments and frustrations in career. You may quarrel with friends and relatives.

Being in Taurus, Sun if Benefic:

You will have happy meals and delicious drinks. You will gain from landed property and wealth. You will get respect from relatives and people. You will succeed in buying, selling and trading in cloth or scented things. You will be an expert of music or singing. You will be capable of bearing much physical stress and strain. You will be clever in dealing with others. You will not have many enemies. You will improve your landed properties. You will be famous among relations and friends.

Being in Taurus, Sun if Malefic:

You may have enmity or hatred of other persons. The good effects regarding your prosperity will be devalued.

Being in Gemini, Sun if Benefic:

You will be scholarly. You will be always happy and cheerful. You will receive good education. You will be learned and fond of astrology. You will be wealthy. You will get respect from educationists. You will develop friendship with superiors.

Being in Cancer, Sun if Benefic:

You will have many servants. You will get appreciation from bosses. You will have happiness of mind. You will perform auspicious events in the house. You will progress in your lands and agriculture. You will get political success. You will be always gay and happy.

Being in Cancer, Sun if Malefic:

You may usually have a worried life. You may not be rich. Your married partner may not be an agreeable person.

Being in Leo, Sun if Benefic:

You will have organising capacity and talent for propaganda. You will get respect from bosses. You will attain high status and position. You will possess houses, gardens and wells. There will be birth of children. You will have favourable relatives. You will be endowed with intelligence. You will be rich. You will annihilate your enemies. You will be respected by your children.

Being in Leo, Sun if Malefic:

You may frequent solitary places. You may not be very rich.

Being in Virgo, Sun if Benefic:

You will be well-read, scholarly and will receive good education. You will be intelligent. You will pay homage to religious preceptors and you will be efficient in serving others. You will be learned in religious lore.

Being in Virgo, Sun if Malefic:

You may have losses in cattle and wealth. You may develop enmity with relatives and friends. You may

have misunderstandings with the nearest and dearest
people.

Being in Libra, Sun if Benefic:

You will engage in trade pertaining to liquor or
intoxicants and you will get money.

Being in Libra, Sun if Malefic:

You may not get name and fame. You may meet with
many frustrations in life. Your expenditure may be
heavy. You may suffer at the hands of government. You
may have loss of wealth. There may be increase of
enemies. You may lose your brothers. There may be
destruction of all efforts and failure in any
undertakings. You may have a miserable and
complicated life. You may be always troubled by
enemies and reduced to poverty.

Being in Scorpio, Sun if Benefic:

You will have success in the later half of life. You
will be very learned. You may earn from poison or
poisonous drugs. You will gain from lands, houses and
wealth. You will fulfil your mental desires. You will
start new schemes and enterprises and realise many of
your ambitions.

Being in Scorpio, Sun if Malefic:

There may be no achievement of your ambitions in
your first half when the pace of progress may be very
slow. You may not have much conjugal happiness.

Being in Sagittarius, Sun if Benefic:

You will be rich and respected by all clans, unions of
people and also by government. You will be happy,
popular and intelligent. You will be clever in the use of
arms. You may be a good physician or artisan or well up
in arts and crafts. You will succeed in all your
undertakings. You will have supreme satisfaction in
every way and all-round happiness.

Being in Capricorn, Sun if Benefic:

You will get self-respect and name.

Being in Capricorn, Sun if Malefic:

You may prove a bad tradesman. You may not be very learned. You may be devoid of help and support from your relatives. You may engage in a variety of work and earn by means, not very commendable. You may have loss of house, cattle, lands and wealth. You may develop enmity with friends. You may have loss of patrimony. You may have misunderstandings with your own people. You may not be very rich.

Being in Aquarius, Sun if Benefic:

You will have self-esteem and great stamina with rare faculties.

Being in Aquarius, Sun if Malefic:

You may have no happiness from children. You may be devoid of wealth. You may always get mentally worried. You may have loss of married partner, wealth, lands, cattle and property. You may be unsuccessful, poor, unlucky and unhappy.

Being in Pisces, Sun if Benefic:

You may become a pearl merchant. You will be peaceful and wealthy. You will have good friends and you will be loyal to them. You will gain money and comforts due to love with ladies by whom you will be favoured. You will be intelligent and annihilate your enemies. You will earn name and fame. You will have good children and servants. You may earn much money by dealing in aqueous products or goods across the water or anything connected with water. You will get affection from relatives and people. You will have happiness of partner, children and friends. You will conduct auspicious celebrations. You will be respected by relations. There will be smooth sailing in every sphere of your activity.

Being in Pisces, Sun if Malefic:

You are liable to scandals. You may lead an uneventful life.

Mars in Different Rasis

Being in Aries, Mars if Benefic:

You will have organising capacity. You will gain in wealth. You will have increase of reputation and respect. You will own cattle. You will succeed in trade. You will be commanding, powerful and rich. You will have much gain and fame.

Being in Taurus, Mars if Benefic:

You will succeed in all your struggles. You will be respected by elders and rulers. You will get good produce from lands. You will be envied by many.

Being in Taurus, Mars if Malefic:

You may not have a stable position in life. You may not have several children. You may be antagonistic to friends. You may not be wealthy.

Being in Gemini, Mars if Benefic:

You will have a loving family. You will be learned. You will have access to great wealth and precious stones. You will get agricultural success. You will get success in work and in every respect. You will have children.

Being in Gemini, Mars if Malefic:

You may be without friends and you may be unhappy.

Being in Cancer, Mars if Benefic:

You will be intelligent and wealthy. You will have medical and surgical proficiency. You will gain from agriculture. You may get a government sholarship in your childhood or be supported by someone other than your family.

Being in Cancer, Mars if Malefic:

You may get danger from enemies and rulers. You may land in litigation problems. You may lose honour and reputation. There may be domestic disharmony. You may have misunderstandings among brothers and close relatives. You may be without friends.

Being in Leo, Mars if Benefic:

You will be happy and successful all through. You will get material gains through fine arts. You will have increase in houses, grains and lands.

Being in Leo, Mars if Malefic:

You may be extravagent. You may have few children. You may be restless. You may be devoid of wealth. You may get little happiness from your married partner.

Being in Virgo, Mars if Benefic:

You will be self-confident. You will undertake scientific enterprise and get beneficial results. You will have successful educational pursuits. You will be learned and be respected by others. You will have children. You will be wealthy.

Being in Virgo, Mars if Malefic:

You may incur heavy expenditure. You may fear your opponents.

Being in Libra, Mars if Benefic:

You will have self-earned wealth.

Being in Libra, Mars if Malefic:

You may have loss of wealth and grains and you may mortgage your landed property. Your married partner or children may have ill health. You may lead a miserable life. You may develop misunderstandings with your cousins and brothers. You may waste money over wine and other vices.

Being in Scorpio, Mars if Benefic:

You will become head of some department or institution or a businessman with a flourishing trade of your own. You will be respected by government. You will be rich.

Being in Sagittarius, Mars if Benefic:

You may become a minister. You will have earnings from political success. You will be famous. You will destroy your enemies. You will realise all your hopes and desires. You will occupy a high position in government or large institution. You will attain happiness.

Being in Sagittarius, Mars if Malefic:

You may have many foes. You may have litigation problems. You may have few children. Your wealth and happiness may be lessened due to your uncontrolled temper.

Being in Capricorn, Mars if Benefic:

You will be rich, you will attain high political position. You will have many sons. You will be successful and respected. You will get success in battles and be respected for your military skill. You will gain from quadrapeds. You will have increase in wealth. You will be equal to a king. You may become head of a section of an army or department or institution. You will be victorious in all your undertakings. You will have much paraphernalia.

Being in Aquarius, Mars if Malefic:

You may be unhappy, miserable, poor and afflicted with sorrows and great hardships and difficulties. You may have misunderstanding with rulers and immediate superiors in office. You may not be wealthy. You may lose money by gambling or speculation due to your own malice and dishonesty.

Being in Pisces, Mars if Benefic:

You will have general success and happiness. You will have wealth. You will get bumper crops in your lands. There will be prosperity and increase of business. You will get great reputation. You will occupy a good position in life. You will be well-known.

Being in Pisces, Mars if Malefic:

You may have few children. You may be restless. You may have many enemies. You may suffer deep sorrows. You may suffer loss of wealth due to your own deceitful conduct. You may have few sons who may not be intelligent. You may not progress well in life.

Mercury in Different Rasis

Being in Aries, Mercury if Benefic:

You will have marriage, if not married. You will get favours from rulers or government. You will gain from cultivation, cattle, precious stones, conveyances and you will get happiness through them.

Being in Aries, Mercury if Malefic:

You may not have a good married partner. You may have loss of wealth. You may incur debts. You may have to live in confinement.

Being in Taurus, Mercury if Benefic:

You may become a minister. You will have children. You will be well-read. You will get titles and names. You will have great happiness. You will acquire ornaments. You will have authority over men. You may have sons. You will get plenty of money. You will have good conjugal happiness.

Being in Gemini, Mercury if Benefic:

You will get happiness from your partner and children. There will be marriage ceremonies in your house. You will be comfortable. You will have access to treasures. You will have acquisition of fame and wealth. You will lead a happy and comfortable life.

Being in Cancer, Mercury if Benefic:

You will do trade in pearls. You will gain from water and also from products of water or connected with water or goods across seas.

Being in Cancer, Mercury if Malefic:

You may suffer fines, imprisonments and penalties. You may have loss of lands and failure of crops. You may develop enmity with all. You may be restless. You may lose money due to enmity with your partner or other persons.

Being in Leo, Mercury if Benefic:

You will have remunerative profession. You will get elevation in your career. You will acquire wealth from various sources. You will get married, if not married, You will get great reputation and fame.

Being in Leo, Mercury if Malefic:

You may be poor. You may have few children. You may not have good-married partner or happiness through your partner. You may not have issues.

Being in Virgo, Mercury if Benefic:

You will have most auspicious and happy period of life. You will get favour from kings or the government. You will be admired. There will be marriage in the house. You will have increase in intelligence. You will get unexpected gains. You will be learned. You will occupy a senior position.

Being in Libra, Mercury if Benefic:

There will be great works published in your name. You will get favour of wealthy and educated people without efforts. You will have leadership over men. You will be inclined to have business at various places and in different directions. You will be attached to your married partner and children.

Being in Scorpio, Mercury if Malefic:

You may have separation from your married partner and children. You may have mental troubles. You may have loss from merchandise. You may have loss of reputation and power. You may not have a good partner or you may be attached to another unworthy person. Your financial returns may not be in proportion to labour and effort put in. You may not get approbation of good people.

Being in Sagittarius, Mercury if Benefic:

You will be respected by polished society. You will be learned and succeed in education. You will be famous. You may occupy an eminent position. You may become a minister or priest. You will be well-versed in writing and penmanship. You will be liked by king or government.

Being in Capricorn, Mercury if Benefic:

You will get success in trade. You will start new businesslike enterprises in tanneries, leather goods, glassware etc. You will get patronage of kings or government. You will be able to destroy your foes and enemies. You will have general success in life.

Being in Capricorn, Mercury if Malefic:

You may be a debtor. You may be restless, poor and oppressed by various difficulties. You may be separated from relations.

Being in Aquarius, Mercury if Benefic:

You will be famous. You will make great strides in life. You will be a scholar. You will have acquisition of paraphernalia. You will have access to good food and much wealth. You will get good name and fame.

Being in Aquarius, Mercury if Malefic:

You may not have a congenial married partner. You may incur debts. You may be oppressed by enemies. You may have little enjoyment in life.

Being in Pisces, Mercury if Benefic:

You will excel your colleagues in rendering service to your master. You will have a good married partner. You will do good deeds liked by all.

Being in Pisces, Mercury if Malefic:

You may land in litigations. You may have quarrels with your relations. You may have mental derangement due to your failure in attempts. You may not be happy in respect of children at least for sometime.

Jupiter in Different Rasis

Being in Aries, Jupiter if Benefic:

You will be powerful and wealthy. You will have many children. You will have happy marriage. You will acquire landed property. You will have general prosperity and success in all undertakings. You will be elevated to a responsible office or you will be appointed as a trustee. You will get great respect from your people. You may become the head of an army or section of an army. You will be blessed with a partner and children. You will have good servants. You will be daring in deeds which will bring you name and fame. You will overcome others with your valour. If not in army, you may command a dominating position in an institution.

Being in Aries, Jupiter if Malefic:

You may have heavy expenditure. You may have many enemies.

Being in Taurus, Jupiter if Benefic:

You will have acquisition of wealth. You will

establish your business on a firm foundation. You will gain in trade and agriculture. You will have increase in lands and cattle. You will have dutiful sons. You will be intelligent and popular. You will have valuable possessions.

Being in Taurus, Jupiter if Malefic:

You may be extravagant.

Being in Gemini, Jupiter if Benefic:

You will be scholarly and learned. You will be comfortable. You will be respected by seniors as well as relatives. You will be very intelligent and happy. You will have sons and friends. You will have good food and good clothes and have the necessities for comfortable living. You will keep part of your money in deposit. You will celebrate many occasions in your family. You may become a minister, or adviser or counsellor.

Being in Gemini, Jupiter if Malefic:

Your partner or sweet heart may have ill health. You may have loss of children, brothers and cousins. You may have mental uneasiness.

Being in Cancer, Jupiter if Benefic:

You will have much political success. You will get promotion and rise to an exalted position. You may be engaged in national service. You may expect wealth from unexpected sources and without efforts. You will get journalistic success. You may become minister of education or lands. You will have perfect harmony in domestic life. You will be well-read and intelligent. You will have a good-married partner and sons. You will be endowed with comforts of life. You will earn a good name and fame for your magnificient deeds.

Being in Cancer, Jupiter if Malefic:

You may be inclined to social gossip.

Being in Leo, Jupiter if Benefic:

You will be intelligent and respected by rulers or the government. You will gain in lands and much agricultural produce. You will realise your desires and ambitions. You will be learned and famous. You will get happiness from your married partner and children. You may become head of an army, section of an army or institution.

Being in Leo, Jupiter if Malefic:

Your enmities may last long.

Being in Virgo, Jupiter if Benefic:

You will be fortunate. You will have a beautiful married partner. You will be learned. You will have all the comforts of life. You will get good sons and friends. You will gain money from your erudition, arts and crafts or work connected with them. You may rise to a high position such as that of a minister or counsellor.

Being in Virgo, Jupiter if Malefic:

There may be destruction of your properties. You may have loss of wealth. You may land in misunderstandings with relatives.

Being in Libra, Jupiter if Benefic:

You will have comfortable living. You will be wealthy and happy. You will liked by others. You will have several good sons and friends. You may gain money in work connected with theatres or films. You will attain high position in life.

Being in Libra, Jupiter if Malefic:

You may reside in desolate places. You may lead a dissolute and shameful life. You may have to face difficulties and troubles.

Being in Scorpio, Jupiter if Benefic:

You will have mental calmness and happiness. You will have acquisition of new lands and estates. You will get undisturbed progress. You will get happiness from your married partner. You will occupy a respectable position. If following a literary line you would be a scholar and an author.

Being in Scorpio, Jupiter if Malefic:

Your reputation may be at stake. You may not have many children.

Being in Sagittarius, Jupiter if Benefic:

You will have much wealth. You will get many sons. You will succeed in every undertaking. You will get widespread fame and perfect happiness. You will get pretty inheritance. You will be rich and influential. You may be a big zamindar. You will have good houses. You will occupy a high position such as that of a chieftan or minister. You may become a professor or religious preceptor.

Being in Capricorn, Jupiter if Malefic:

You may be disgraceful and unhappy. You may have illness of children. Your partner may be sick. You may have loss of property, reputation and self-respect. You may be liable to prosecutions and imprisonment. You may have upspringing of numerous enemies.

Being in Aquarius, Jupiter if Benefic:

You will be learned. You will become head of your group. You will get much respect.

Being in Aquarius, Jupiter if Malefic:

You may have bad luck. You may have to face many hardships. You may have loss of wealth. You may not be intelligent. You may destroy your wealth or lessen your wealth by your speech.

Being in Pisces, Jupiter if Benefic:

You will get good inheritance. You will get great
name and great education. You will gain from
exhibition of your knowledge. You will have requisition
of property and general success and happiness. You
will be learned and respected by your friends. You will
earn praise, name and fame for your work and conduct.
You will be very wealthy. You may become a minister
or head of a section of an army. In other words, you will
occupy a good position in life and will be well off.

Venus in Different Rasis

Being in Aries, Venus if Benefic:

You will reside in palatial buildings. You will be
wear good clothes. You will spread your fame. You will
be much respected. There will be birth of a child. You
will be praised by friends as well as enemies. You will
occupy a good position in life.

Being in Aries, Venus if Malefic:

You may be extravagant. You may have quarrels or
you will enter into litigations on account of attachment
to a woman and lose wealth as a part thereof. You may
bring discredit to your family.

Being in Taurus Venus if Benefic:

You will have a life of great ease and indulgence.
You will have enjoyment of much happiness. You will
realise all ambitions of material life. You will get
redemption from debts. You will earn from agriculture,
cows and you will be wealthy. You will be learned and
famous. You will be respected by the king or the
government or your group of people whom you head.

Being in Gemini Venus if Benefic:

You will be rich and respected. You will be learned
and intelligent. You will gain territory and vehicles.
You will have increase of reputation. You will get

mental peace. There will be harmony with your married partner. You will be loved by others. You will be well up in arts and sciences. You will become wealthy.

Being in Cancer, Venus if Benefic:

You may have children. You will be strong and become the chief person in your group. You will be having all the desirable necessities for comforts. You will have some mental ease in the end.

Being in Cancer, Venus if Malefic:

You may suffer from grief and terror. Your property may be destroyed. You may have loss of wealth. You may by sorrowful and unhappy.

Being in Leo, Venus if Benefic:

You will get money through women. You will have excellent married partner. You will get unusual happiness. You will not have much worries. You will have happiness and money from ladies. You will be married in high family.

Being in Leo, Venus if Malefic:

You may have few children. You will have troubles from fires, poisons and hurts. There may be sickness of your better half or a child. You may get sorrows.

Being in Virgo, Venus if Benefic:

You will be good at arts. You will be respected as a scholar in religious congress at holy places.

Being in Virgo, Venus if Malefic:

You may be unhappy and unsuccessful. You may have quarrels with your married partner or separation from your partner. You may mortgage your property and may not have mental rest. You may be separated from your relatives and friends. You may have much grief and sorrow. You may be poor and may not have much happiness or luxuries.

Being in Libra, Venus if Benefic:

You will get great reputation. You will gain wealth from royal patronage or the government. You will have matrimonial felicity. You will be respected, strong, learned and very wealthy. You will get good name due to your devotion to gods and brahmins. You will be liked by society and the state and become famous. You will possess vehicles.

Being in Scorpio, Venus if Benefic:

You will attain good position. You will succeed in defeating your opponents.

Being in Scorpio, Venus if Malefic:

You may have many miseries and troubles. You may get loss of wealth and property. You may be poor and indebted. You may, by favouring a lady, oppose or enter into litigation with another party and thereby damage your own property and you may bring discredit to your family.

Being in Sagittarius, Venus if Benefic:

You will have much name and fame. You will get success in your undertakings. You will have general prosperity. You will be powerful and respected. You will earn wealth. You will have the necessities for comforts due to your righteous and good actions. You will rise to high position such as that of a minister. You will possess cows. You will be respected by people and society.

Being in Capricorn, Venus if Benefic:

You will be powerful. You will have progress in general education and you will be learned. You will have freedom from domestic worries. You will succeed in all your endeavours.

Being in Capricorn, Venus if Malefic:

You may be very sorrowful. Your efforts may end in frustrations.

Being in Aquarius, Venus if Benefic:

You will have acquisition of fresh property, lands and houses. You will get honours and unexpected gains. You will be liked by all.

Being in Aquarius, Venus if Malefic:

You may be antagonistic to your children and seniors (father etc.). You may be agitated in mind. You may be persistently engaged in work which may not yield the desired results.

Being in Pisces, Venus if Benefic:

You will be learned and popular. You will be powerful and much respected. You will be exalted to high political power and have great success. You will get promotion to a responsible office. You will have perfect happiness in domestic life and there will be smooth sailing in every respect. You will be very famous. You will be engaged in big projects. You will be very wealthy. You will defeat your enemies. You will be favourite of the king or the government. You will occupy an eminent position.

Saturn in Different Rasis

Being in Aries, Saturn if Malefic:

You may have unexpected losses. You may have disappointments in every undertaking. You may develop misunderstandings among relatives and friends. There may be increase of enemies. You may not perform good acts but rather commit sinful acts. You may be unfortunate and sorrowful.

Being in Taurus, Saturn if Benefic:

You will follow a career of service. You will be

engaged in a variety of work and will be successful. You will gain in agricultural operations. You will have great income and access to things desired. You will be powerful.

Being in Taurus, Saturn if Malefic:

You may be devoid of wealth. You may have bad friends. You may be insulted.

Being in Gemini, Saturn if Benefic:

Your services will be recognised. You will get profits in speculation and trade. You will be respected from rulers or the government. You will have political success and reputation. You will have much general happiness. You will occupy a good position with a large staff under you.

Being in Gemini, Saturn if Malefic:

You may be miserable. You may be accused in a criminal act. You may incur debts. You may not get much happiness from children.

Being in Cancer, Saturn if Benefic:

You will be intelligent and attain a good position in life. You will enjoy luxuries at the cost of others. The middle part of your life will be better than the first one third or last one third.

Being in Cancer, Saturn if Malefic:

You may be poor. You may have few children. You may have miseries and calamities. There may be family strife and increase of enemies. You may get troubles from relatives. You may always be restless. You may not get much happiness from children.

Being in Leo, Saturn if Malefic:

You may have a period of uneasiness. You may have disappointments and unrest. You may be hated by all.

You may be without relatives. You may be without your partner or you may be lacking conjugal happiness. Your children may be a source of trouble to you.

Being in Virgo, Saturn if Benefic:

You will head an institution with a large staff such as a police officer or work in defence department. You will be elevated to an exalted position. You will get royal favour. You will have business success. You will have establishment of fame and success.

Being in Virgo, Saturn if Malefic:

You may not be wealthy. You may not engage in productive work. You may get little happiness from children.

Being in Libra, Saturn if Benefic:

You will be rich and famous. You will be powerful and respected. You will establish fresh branches of your business concern. You will get great honour and respect. You will occupy a senior position among people and will be respected in a village or town where you reside. You will be very rich-equal to a king. You will earn money and respect by touring or contacts with foreign countries. You will rise in life as age advances.

Being in Libra, Saturn if Malefic:

You may be antagonistic and develop enemies. You may be fond of association with persons of loose morals.

Being in Scorpio, Saturn if Malefic:

You may suffer from poison or fire (burns or food poisoning). You may have many sorrows. You may have heavy expenditure. You may suffer from confinement. You may be disliked and hated by all. You may get loss of prestige, self-respect and fame. There may be destruction or damage to property and possessions.

Being in Sagittarius, Saturn if Benefic:

You will succeed in philosophical and religious studies. There will be auspicious occasions like marriage ceremonies at home. You will get happiness and mental peace throughout. You will have illustrious children who will bring credit to you. You will enjoy wealth particularly in the last one third part of life. You may become head or leader of a village or town, section of an army or have many employees under you.

Being in Sagittarius, Saturn if Malefic:

You may have trouble with your partner.

Being in Capricorn, Saturn if Benefic:

You will be intelligent. You will have harmony and felicity in your domestic life. You will have increase in lands and wealth and business. You will develop friendship with great and illustrious personages.

Being in Aquarius, Saturn if Benefic:

You will succeed in litigation. You will have mental happiness and acquisition of wealth. You will be strong and happy. You will initiate a variety of works. You will be wealthy. You will occupy a good position in life.

Being in Aquarius, Saturn if Malefic:

You may be addicted to wine and other vices. You may have bad friends.

Being in Pisces, Saturn if Benefic:

You will be happy. You will have a good married partner. You may be a good jeweller or diplomat. You will be a chief among friends and relatives. You will have good children. You may become head of an institution, village or town. You will command respect and trust in government. You will be wealthy.

Moon in Different Rasis

Being in Aries, Moon if Benefic:

You will have self-respect. You will have physical and mental happiness. You will gain in wealth. You may have several children. You will have perfect contentment.

Being in Aries, Moon if Malefic:

You may be in a subordinate position. You may be devoid of happiness from brother.

Being in Taurus, Moon if Benefic:

You will be happy in middle age and old age. You will make great strides in life. You will be rich, respected, lucky and popular. You will have increase of fame and name. You will have collection of enormous wealth. You will get mental and physical happiness. You will enjoy well.

Being in Taurus, Moon if Malefic:

You may have a wavering mind. You may have love intrigues.

Being in Gemini, Moon if Benefic:

You will be well-read and will progress in education. You will acquire much immovable and movable properties. You will enjoy luxuries. You will be intelligent.

Being in Cancer, Moon if Benefic:

You will be wealthy and powerful. You will have much immovable property. You may become a scientist. You will succeed in litigation. You will get unexpected findings of treasure. You will be prosperous. You will have a comfortable house. You may become minister.

Being in Cancer, Moon if Malefic:

There may be a cycle of waxing and waning in your career. You may undertake unprofitable voyages.

Being in Leo, Moon if Benefic:

You will have progress in education. You will get much gains from unexpected sources.

Being in Leo, Moon if Malefic:

You may be inclined to be unhappy. You may have a few children. You may have mental anxiety.

Being in Virgo, Moon if Benefic:

You will be intelligent and comfortable.

Being in Virgo, Moon if Malefic:

You may have worries from enemies and swindlers. You may suffer from mental and physical restlessness. You may have more daughters than sons.

Being in Libra, Moon if Benefic:

You will get reverence and respect from learned and holy people. You will be wealthy. You will have increase in friends. You will gain wealth.

Being in Libra, Moon if Malefic:

You may suffer from financial penalty at the hands of government. You will be devoid of relatives or you may not have good terms with them.

Being in Scorpio, Moon if Benefic:

You will be head of some department or institution. You may be a business person with a flourishing trade of your own. You will be rich and respected by government.

Being in Scorpio, Moon if Malefic:

You may have loss of wealth. Your honour may be at risk and you may have much mental uneasiness. You may have to face disappointments in every respect. You may gain money by underhand means.

Being in Sagittarius, Moon if Benefic:

You will have a happy marriage. You will have many children. You will get good inheritance and unexpected gifts. You will get help from your married partner and women. You will have domestic happiness and felicity. There will be celebrations of happy functions. You will have accumulation of wealth and there will be undisturbed progress of normal private affairs.

Being in Capricorn, Moon if Benefic:

You will succeed in litigation. There will be increase in lands and houses. You will be ever attached to your married partner and children. You will get success in every new enterprise.

Being in Aquarius, Moon if Malefic:

There may be destruction of property. You may have mental worries from enemies. You may have misunderstandings with relations and friends. You may suffer sorrows and you may be poor.

Being in Pisces, Moon if Benefic:

You will take charge of a fresh office. You will have easy access to anything coveted without effort. You may be a dealer in pearls. You will annihilate your enemies. You will get good reputation. You will have many children. You will get authority if engaged in works of arts, artisanship or crafts. You will be learned. You will lead a comfortable life. You will be happy. You may inherit or get all of a sudden buried wealth or treasure.

(XVI) PROFESSION
Sun in Different Rasis

Being in Aries, Sun if Benefic:

You may be a warrior or connected with manufacture of or trade in arms. You will be capable of rising to the highest pinnacle of leadership. You will have progress in career.

Being in Aries, Sun if Malefic:

You may have frustrations in career.

Being in Taurus, Sun if Benefic:

You will succeed in buying, selling or trade in cloth and scented things. You will be a connoisseur of music and singing.

Being in Gemini, Sun if Benefic:

You may be an astronomer, grammarian, musician or fine art expert.

Being in Cancer, Sun if Benefic:

You will be engaged in work of others. You may a politician.

Being in Leo, Sun if Benefic:

You will be a organiser or propagandist. You may be fond of work connected with forests, mountains and cows and cattle.

Being in Virgo, Sun if Benefic:

You may be a writer, painter, poet, mathematician. You may be fond of literature, songs and music.

Being in Libra, Sun if Benefic:

You may be engaged in trade pertaining to liquor or intoxicants and you will get money from them.,

Being in Libra, Sun if Malefic:

You may be a smuggler. You may earn by dealing in base metals such as iron.

Being in Scorpio, Sun if Benefic:

You may be a surgeon. You may work in military department. You may earn from dealings with poison and poisonous drugs.

Being in Sagittarius, Sun if Benefic:

You may be a musician. You may a good artisan or well up in arts and crafts. You may become a good physician.

Being in Capricorn, Sun if Malefic:

You may prove a bad tradesperson.

Being in Pisces, Sun if Benefic:

You may be a pearl merchant. You can earn much money by dealing in aqueous products or goods across water or anything connected with water.

Mars in Different Rasis

Being in Aries, Mars if Benefic:

You will be an organiser and commander. You may be mathematician. You may become a leader of a section of army or head of an institution.

Being in Taurus, Mars if Benefic:

You may be a singer or musician.

Being in Gemini, Mars if Benefic:

You may be a scientist, musician, diplomat, detective or agriculturist. You will succeed in every respect. You will deal in work connected with precious stones and metals. You may become an artisan requiring mechanical dexterity. You may be a military strategist.

Being in Cancer, Mars if Benefic:

You may be agriculturist, surgeon or doctor.

Being in Leo, Mars if Benefic:

You may be occulist, astrologer or astronomer or mathematician. Your work may be connected with fine arts. You will be persevering in work.

Being in Virgo, Mars if Benefic:

You may be scientist or your work may be connected with a scientific enterprise.

Being in Sagittarius, Mars if Benefic:

You may occupy a high position in government or large institution.

Being in Capricorn, Mars if Benefic:

You may work in military. You may be head of an army department or institution.

Being in Aquarius, Mars if Malefic:

You may have misunderstandings with your immediate superiors in office or rulers or government.

Being in Pisces, Mars if Benefic:

Your business will increase.

Mercury in Different Rasis

Being in Aries, Mercury if Benefic:

You will have work connected with agriculture, cattle or precious stones. You may be a musician or dancer.

Being in Taurus, Mercury if Benefic:

You may a minister or musician. You may have work connected with physical exercises, dresses, ornaments or flowers.

Being in Gemini, Mercury if Benefic:

You will have work connected with literature, arts or sciences. You may be a musician or a good grammarian.

Being in Cancer, Mercury if Benefic:

You may be a singer. You will be engaged in various works. You will have work connected with water and also products of water or connected with goods across the sea.

Being in Leo, Mercury if Benefic:

You will have a remunerative profession. You may have work connected with various countries. You may be a mountaineer.

Being in Virgo, Mercury if Benefic:

You may an author, priest, astronomer or literary critic. You may work with your proficiency in sciences, arts or crafts. You will occupy a senior position.

Being in Libra, Mercury if Benefic:

You will have business in various places in different directions.

Being in Scorpio, Mercury if Benefic:

You will have work connected with sciences. You may be an executive. You may occupy an eminent position. You may become a priest or a minister or a writer or religious teacher.

Being in Capricorn, Mercury if Benefic:

You will earn in trade. You may have inception of new businesslike enterprises in tanneries, leather goods or glassware. You will have business tendencies.

Being in Aquarius, Mercury if Benefic:

You will **have a** career of employment. You may be an artisan.

Being in Pisces, Mercury if Benefic:

You may be martial artsman.

Jupiter in Different Rasis

Being in Aries, Jupiter if Benefic:

You will have success in your undertakings. You will be elevated to a responsible position or office or be appointed as a trustee. You may be head of army or section of an army. If not in army, you may command a dominating position in an institution.

Being in Taurus, Jupiter if Benefic:

You will establish business on a firm foundation. You will gain in trade. You may be an agriculturist.

Being in Gemini, Jupiter if Benefic:

You will deligently engage in work. You may be an artist or scientist.

Being in Cancer, Jupiter if Benefic:

You may be a politician or you will have political success. You will get promotions. You will go to an exalted position. You may be a journalist. You may become a minister of education or lands.

Being in Leo, Jupiter if Benefic:

You may be musician or head of an army or section of an army or an institution. You may have work connected with forts, forests or mountain regions.

Being in Virgo, Jupiter if Benefic:

You will be clever in execution of works. You will have work connected with scents, flowers, arts or crafts. You will get high position in life. You may become minister or counsellor.

Being in Libra, Jupiter if Benefic:

You will have work connected with theatres or films. You will attain high position in life.

Being in Scorpio, Jupiter if Benefic:

You will occupy a respectable position. If following a literary line, you will be a scholar or author.

Being in Sagittarius, Jupiter if Benefic:

You may be minister. You may become a poet, professor or religious preceptor.

Being in Aquarius, Jupiter if Benefic:

You may be philosopher. You may become head of your group.

Being in Aquarius, Jupiter if Malefic:

You will put in much unproductive labour connected with water or artisanship.

Being in Pisces, Jupiter if Benefic:

You will have determination in execution of work. You may be minister or head of a section of an army. You will have good position in life. You may have educational service or you may become a military strategist.

Venus in Different Rasis

Being in Aries, Venus if Benefic:

You will occupy a good position in life.

Being in Taurus, Venus if Benefic:

You will have work connected with agriculture, cows, cattle, scents or flowers. You may be the head of a group.

Being in Gemini, Venus if Benefic:

You will work in arts, sciences, music, dancing, writing or painting.

Being in Virgo, Venus if Benefic:

You will be an expert in arts and a scholar in religious congress.

Being in Libra, Venus if Benefic:

You may be statesman, poet or philosopher.

Being in Sagittarius, Venus if Benefic:

You may be a philosopher. You will have success in your undertakings. You will rise to high position such as that of a minister.

Being in Capricorn, Venus if Benefic:

You will get success in all endeavours.

Being in Aquarius, Venus if Benefic:

You will have work connected with Christian or Islamic literature.

Being in Pisces, Venus if Benefic:

You will have high political power. You will get promotion to responsible office.

Saturn in Different Rasis

Being in Aries, Saturn if Malefic:

You may have to labour hard.

Being in Taurus, Saturn if Benefic:

You will be engaged in a variety of work. You will have work connected with agricultural operations.

Being in Gemini, Saturn if Benefic:

Your services will be recognised. You will get profits

in speculation or trade. You will have political success. You will have work connected with chemical and mechanical sciences. You may a logician. You will occupy a good position with a large staff under you.

Being in Cancer, Saturn if Benefic:
You will attain a good position in life.

Being in Leo, Saturn if Benefic:
You may be a writer. You may have work connected with water.

Being in Virgo, Saturn if Benefic:
You may be the head of an institution with a large staff such as police officer or work in defence department. You will have public life. You will be elevated to an exalted position. You will become an inventor.

Being in Virgo, Saturn if Malefic:
You may engage in unproductive work.

Being in Libra, Saturn if Benefic:
If proprietor of a business concern, you will establish fresh branches. You will occupy a senior position among people and will be respected in your village or town.

Being in Scorpio, Saturn if Malefic:
You may be hated by your superiors.

Being in Sagittarius, Saturn if Benefic:
You may be a philosopher. You may become head of village or town or section of army or have many employees under you.

Being in Capricorn, Saturn if Benefic:
You will have gains from business.

Being in Aquarius, Saturn if Benefic:

You will initiate a variety of work. You will occupy a good position in life.

Being in Pisces, Saturn if Benefic:

You will be a good diplomat.

Moon in Different Rasis

Being in Aries, Moon if Malefic:

You may have a subordinate position.

Being in Cancer, Moon if Benefic:

You may be a scientist or minister.

Being in Leo, Moon if Benefic:

You will engage in varied work.

Being in Virgo, Moon if Benefic:

You may be an astrologer, clairvoyant, musician or dancer. You may be engaged in other people's work.

Being in Libra, Moon if Benefic:

You will have work connected with arts.

Being in Scorpio, Moon if Benefic:

You will be head of some department or institution. You may be a businessman with a flourishing trade of your own.

Being in Sagittarius, Moon if Benefic:

You will have work connected with fine arts and literature. You may be an author. You may be well versed in artisan work.

Being in Capricorn, Moon if Benefic:

You will have success in every new enterprise.

Being in Aquarius, Moon if Benefic:

You may be an artist or artisan.

Being in Pisces, Moon if Benefic:

You will take charge of a fresh office. You may a singer. You will serve the government. You may get authority if engaged in works of arts, artisanship or crafts. You may deal with countries and in products beyond the seas.

(XVII) GAINS AND INCOME
Sun in Different Rasis

Being in Aries, Sun if Benefic:

You will gain due to cattle and gold.

Being in Aries, Sun if Malefic:

You may not be rich.

Being in Taurus, Sun if Benefic:

You will gain from landed property and wealth. You will succeed in buying, selling or trading in cloth or scented things. You will have increase in landed properties.

Being in Gemini, Sun if Benefic:

You will be wealthy and liberal in dealings with others.

Being in Cancer, Sun if Benefic:

You will have increase in lands, houses and wealth. There will be progress in lands and agriculture.

Being in Cancer, Sun if Malefic:

You may not be rich.

Being in Leo, Sun if Benefic:

You will have house, gardens and wells. You will be

rich. You will be fond of forests, mountains and cows and cattle.

Being in Leo, Sun if Malefic:
   You may be poor.

Being in Virgo, Sun if Malefic:
   You may lose in cattle, wealth and house.

Being in Libra, Sun if Benefic:
   You will gain in trade pertaining to liquors or intoxicants. You will earn living by dealing in iron, steel etc.

Being in Libra, Sun if Malefic:
   You may resort to all kinds of underhand dealings such as smuggling of gold or other unfair practices for earning money. You may have heavy expenditure. You may be reduced to poverty.

Being in Scorpio, Sun if Benefic:
   You may earn from poison or poisonous drugs. You will gain from lands, houses and wealth.

Being in Sagittarius, Sun if Benefic:
   You will become rich.

Being in Capricorn, Sun if Malefic:
   You may prove to be a bad tradesman. You may not be rich. You want to appropriate other people's money by unfair means. You may earn by means not very commendable. You may have loss of house, cattle, lands, wealth and patrimony.

Being in Aquarius, Sun If Banefic:
   You may gain by being a pearl merchant. You may gain money and comforts due to love with persons by whom you will be favoured. You can earn money by

dealing in aqueous products or goods across the water or anything connected with water.

Being in Aquarius, Sun if Malefic:

You may be poor and devoid of wealth. You may have loss of married partner, wealth, land, cattle and property.

Mars in Different Rasis

Being in Aries, Mars if Benefic:

You will gain wealth. You will be owner of cattle. If engaged in trade you will gain therein. There will be much gains in general.

Being in Taurus, Mars if Benefic:

You will gain from good produce from lands.

Being in Taurus, Mars if Malefic:

You may not be wealthy.

Being in Gemini, Mars if Benefic:

You will have access to great wealth, precious stones, metals and agricultural success. You will succeed in work in every respect.

Being in Cancer, Mars if Benefic:

You will be wealthy. You will gain from agriculture. You will earn through boats, ships, and goods transported by them. You may get government scholarship.

Being in Cancer, Mars if Malefic:

There may be lack of wealth.

Being in Leo, Mars if Benefic:

You will gain through your taste in fine arts and materials. You will have increase in lands, grains and lands.

Being in Leo, Mars if Malefic:
   You may be devoid of wealth.

Being in Virgo, Mars if Benefic:
   You will be wealthy and will have children.

Being in Virgo, Mars if Malefic:
   You may have heavy expenditure.

Being in Libra, Mars if Benefic:
   You will have self-earned wealth.

Being in Libra, Mars if Malefic:
   You may have loss of wealth and grains and you may
mortgage your landed property. You may waste money
over wine and women/men and you will be under their
influence.

Being in Scorpio, Mars if Benefic:
   You will have increase in wealth and good earnings.
You will have a business with a flourishing trade of
your own. You will be rich.

Being in Sagittarius, Mars if Malefic:
   Your wealth may be reduced due to your
uncontrolled temper.

Being in Capricorn, Mars if Benefic:
   You will be rich. You will gain from quadrapeds. You
will have increase in wealth. You will have much
paraphernalia.

Being in Aquarius, Mars if Malefic:
   You may lose money in gambling or speculation due
to your own malice and dishonesty.

Being in Pisces, Mars if Benefic:
   You will have much wealth. You will have prosperity

and increase of house and business.

Mercury in Different Rasis

Being in Aries, Mercury if Benefic:
　You will gain from cultivation, cattle, precious stones and means of conveyance.

Being in Aries, Mercury if Malefic:
　You may be devoid of wealth. You may labour hard but lose wealth.

Being in Taurus, Mercury if Benefic:
　You will have plenty of money and you will be wealthy.

Being in Gemini, Mercury if Benefic:
　You will be wealthy.

Being in Cancer, Mercury if Benefic:
　You will gain from water and also products of water or connected with water or goods across seas.

Being in Cancer, Mercury if Malefic:
　You may have loss of land and failure of crops. You may be speculative and may lose money. You will have loss of money due to enmity with your married partner or other persons.

Being in Leo, Mercury if Benefic:
　You will be wealthy.

Being in Leo, Mercury if Malefic:
　You may be poor.

Being in Libra, Mercury if Benefic:
　You will be intent upon earning money.

Being in Scorpio, Mercury if Benefic:
You will have riches.

Being in Scorpio, Mercury if Malefic:
You may lose from merchandise. You may be without wealth and be indebted.

Being in Capricorn, Mercury if Benefic:
You will have success in trade.

Being in Capricorn, Mercury if Malefic:
You may be poor and indebted.

Being in Aquarius, Mercury if Benefic:
You will have access to good and much wealth.

Being in Aquarius, Mercury if Malefic:
You may acquire some wealth by means not above board, but incur debts.

Jupiter in Different Rasis

Being in Aries, Jupiter if Benefic:
You will have acquisition of landed property. You will succeed in all undertakings.

Being in Aries, Jupiter if Malefic:
You may incur heavy expenditure.

Being in Taurus, Jupiter if Benefic:
You will have acquisition of wealth. You will gain in trade and agriculture. You will have increase in lands and cattle. You will be wealthy. You will have valuable possessions.

Being in Taurus, Jupiter if Malefic:
You may be extravagant.

Being in Gemini, Jupiter if Benefic:

You will have the necessities for comfortable living. You will keep part of your money in your deposits.

Being in Cancer, Jupiter if Benefic:

You will have much political success. You will get promotion. You will have acquisition of wealth from unexpected sources and without effort. You will be wealthy.

Being in Leo, Jupiter if Benefic:

You will have much agricultural produce and gain of lands.

Being in Virgo, Jupiter if Benefic:

You will gain by your arts, crafts or works connected with them.

Being in Virgo, Jupiter if Malefic:

You may have loss of wealth.

Being in Libra, Jupiter if Benefic:

You may gain money connected with theatre or films.

Being in Scorpio, Jupiter if Benefic:

You will have acquisition of new lands and estates.

Being in Sagittarius, Jupiter if Benefic:

You will have much wealth. You will succeed in your undertakings. You will get inheritance. You will be rich and wealthy.

Being in Capricorn, Jupiter if Malefic:

You may have low financial returns and you may have little money.

Being in Aquarius, Jupiter if Malefic:

You may destroy your wealth or lessen your income by your speech.

Being in Pisces, Jupiter if Benefic:

You will have good inheritance. You will gain from exhibition of knowledge. You will have requisition of property.

Venus in Different Rasis

Being in Aries, Venus if Benefic:

You will have good earnings.

Being in Aries, Venus if Malefic:

You may lose wealth on account of attachment to a woman.

Being in Taurus, Venus if Benefic:

You will gain from agriculture and cows.

Being in Gemini, Venus if Benefic:

You will have gain of territory and vehicles. You will be wealthy.

Being in Leo, Venus if Benefic:

You will gain money from ladies.

Being in Virgo, Venus if Malefic:

You may be poor.

Being in Libra, Venus if Benefic:

You will have gain of wealth from royal patronage or government. You will have comforts and conveyances. You will be wealthy.

Being in Scorpio, Venus if Malefic:

You may have loss of wealth and property by

favouring a lady and opposing another party thereby.

Being in Sagittarius, Venus if Benefic:

You will have success in your undertakings. You will be wealthy.

Being in Capricorn, Venus if Benefic:

You will succeed in all your endeavours.

Being in Aquarius, Venus if Benefic:

You will have acquisition of fresh property, lands and houses. You will get unexpected gains.

Being in Pisces, Venus if Benefic:

You will get promotion to responsible office. You will have high political power and great success. You will be wealthy. You will gain money and respect from good folk.

Saturn in Different Rasis

Being in Taurus, Saturn if Benefic:

You will get success and gain in agricultural operations. You will have much prospects from the cattle and other domestic animals. You will have great income and access to things desired.

Being in Taurus, Saturn if Malefic:

You may be devoid of wealth.

Being in Gemini, Saturn if Benefic:

You will make profits in speculation and trade.

Being in Gemini, Saturn if Malefic:

You may incur debts.

Being in Virgo, Saturn if Malefic:

You may not engage in productive work.

Being in Libra, Saturn if Benefic:

You will be rich. You will establish fresh branches of business.

Being in Scorpio, Saturn if Malefic:

You may suffer heavy expenditure.

Being in Sagittarius, Saturn if Benefic:

You will enjoy wealth particularly in the last one third part of life, when you will be much respected.

Being in Capricorn, Saturn if Benefic:

You will gain in wealth and business.

Being in Aquarius, Saturn if Benefic:

You will succeed in litigation. You will have acquisition of wealth.

Moon in Different Rasis

Being in Aries, Moon if Benefic:

You will gain wealth.

Being in Taurus, Moon if Benefic:

You will collect enormous wealth and you will be rich.

Being in Gemini, Moon if Benefic:

You will acquire much immovable and movable properties.

Being in Cancer, Moon if Benefic:

You will have much immovable property. You will get unexpected finding of treasure. You will be wealthy.

Being in Leo, Moon if Benefic:

You will get gain much from unexpected sources.

Being in Libra, Moon if Benefic:

You will gain in wealth.

Being in Libra, Moon if Malefic:

You may lose through women. You may suffer financial penalty at the hands of government.

Being in Scorpio, Moon if Benefic:

You will be rich and wealthy. You will be a business person with a flourishing trade of your own.

Being in Scorpio, Moon if Malefic:

You may gain money by underhand means. You may have loss of wealth.

Being in Sagittarius, Moon if Benefic:

You will get good inheritance and unexpected gifts. You will get help from women and your married partner. You will have accumulation of wealth.

Being in Capricorn, Moon if Benefic:

You will have increase in lands, houses and wealth. You will succeed in every respect from a new enterprise.

Being in Aquarius, Moon if Malefic:

There may be destruction of property and you may be poor.

Being in Pisces, Moon if Benefic:

You may inherit or get sudden buried wealth or treasure. You will gain from your interest in countries and products beyond sea.

(XVIII) LOSSES AND EXPENDITURE
Sun in Different Rasis

Being in Aries, Sun if Malefic:

You may suffer disappointments and frustrations in your career. You may quarrel with friends and relations. You may have enmity of or be hated by other persons. You may reside in foreign countries.

Being in Taurus, Sun if Malefic:

You may have enmity of or be hated by women.

Being in Gemini, Sun if Malefic:

You may have set-backs in health which may give rise to mental worries.

Being in Cancer, Sun if Malefic:

You may oppose your own people particularly your father and uncle. You may be frequenting solitary places. You may be travelling to foreign countries.

Being in Virgo, Sun if Malefic:

You may have losses in cattle, wealth and houses. You may develop enmity with relatives and friends. You may have misunderstandings with the nearest and dearest people.

Being in Libra, Sun if Malefic:

You may not get name and fame. You may meet with many frustrations in life. Your expenditure may be heavy. You may be hostile and may suffer at the hands of government. You will lose wealth. There may be increase of enemies and loss of brothers and fame. There may be destruction of all your affairs and failure in any undertaking. You may expect illness of brothers and friends. You may lead a miserable and complicated life. You may be always troubled by enemies. You may be reduced to poverty.

Being in Scorpio, Sun if Malefic:

You may not achieve your ambitions. Mostly in the first half of your life your progress may be very slow. You may not have much conjugal happiness. You are likely to be hurt by fire, weapons or poison. You may be travelling through hilly tracks and countries.

Being in Capricorn, Sun if Malefic:

You may prove to be a bad tradesman. You may be devoid of help and support from your relations. You may be always roaming about near mountains and forests. You may suffer loss of house, cattle, lands and wealth. You may develop enmity with friends and misunderstandings among your own people. There may be loss of patrimony.

Being in Aquarius, Sun if Malefic:

You may not have happiness from children. You may be devoid of wealth. You may land in disputes and may be always having mental worries. You may expect loss of your married partner, land, cattle and property.

Being in Pisces, Sun if Malefic:

You are liable to scandals.

Mars in Different Rasis

Being in Aries, Mars if Benefic:

You may gain in wealth and you will be economical in domestic dealings.

Being in Gemini, Mars if Benefic:

You will have access to wealth.

Being in Gemini, Mars if Malefic:

You may be miserly.

Being in Cancer, Mars if Benefic:
 You will be wealthy. You will have travel and voyages.

Being in Cancer, Mars if Malefic:
 There may be a cycle of good wealth and lack of wealth. You may have alternate sufferings from ailments.

Being in Leo, Mars if Benefic:
 You will be generous and fond of roaming in forest regions. You will get material gains.

Being in Leo, Mars if Malefic:
 You may be miserly and devoid of wealth.

Being in Virgo, Mars if Benefic:
 You will be wealthy.

Being in Virgo, Mars if Malefic:
 You may incur heavy expenditure.

Being in Libra, Mars if Benefic:
 You will be wealthy and fond of travelling by air.

Being in Libra, Mars if Malefic:
 You may have loss of wealth and you may mortgage your landed property. You may waste money over wine and vices and may be under their influence.

Being in Scorpio, Mars if Benefic:
 You will get good earnings.

Being in Sagittarius, Mars if Benefic:
 You will be earning from political sources.

Being in Sagittarius, Mars if Malefic:

Your wealth and happiness may be reduced due to your uncontrolled temper.

Being in Capricorn, Mars if Benefic:

You will have increase in wealth.

Being in Aquarius, Mars if Malefic:

You may be poor and lose money by gambling or speculation due to own malice and dishonesty. You may be fond of wandering.

Being in Pisces, Mars if Benefic:

You will have much wealth.

Being in Pisces, Mars if Malefic:

You may live at a place other than your own land. You may suffer loss of wealth due to your own deceitful conduct.

Mercury in Different Rasis

Being in Aries, Mercury if Benefic:

You will get gains.

Being in Aries, Mercury if Malefic:

You may be devoid of wealth and may incur debts. You may have to live in confinement.

Being in Gemini, Mercury if Benefic:

You will have acquisition of wealth.

Being in Gemini, Mercury if Malefic:

You may have loss of lands and money due to enmity with your partner. You may live at a place other than your homeland.

Being in Leo, Mercury if Benefic:
   You will acquire wealth from various countries.

Being in Leo, Mercury if Malefic:
   You may be travelling in hilly and mountainous tracts.

Being in Libra, Mercury if Benefic:
   You will be frugal and economical. You will spend discriminately on projects for gain of wealth.

Being in Scorpio, Mercury if Malefic:
   You may get losses from merchandise. You may have loss of reputation and power.

Being in Capricorn, Mercury if Benefic:
   You will be economical.

Being in Capricorn, Mercury if Malefic:
   You may be poor and indebted.

Being in Aquarius, Mercury if Benefic:
   You will have access to wealth.

Being in Aquarius, Mercury if Malefic:
   You may incur debts.

Jupiter in Different Rasis

Being in Aries, Jupiter if Benefic:
   You will be generous and succeed in all your undertakings and litigations. You will acquire landed property.

Being in Aries, Jupiter if Malefic:
   You may have heavy expenditure.

Being in Taurus, Jupiter if Benefic:

You will have acquisition of wealth and gains in trade and agriculture. You will get income from lands. You will be liberal. You will possess valuable things.

Being in Taurus, Jupiter if Malefic:

You may be extravagant.

Being in Gemini, Jupiter if Benefic:

You will keep part of your money in safe deposits.

Being in Cancer, Jupiter if Benefic:

You will acquire wealth without efforts from unexpected sources.

Being in Leo, Jupiter if Benefic:

You will be generous and prudent. You will gain lands. You will be fond of forts, forests and mountain regions.

Being in Virgo, Jupiter if Benefic:

You will gain money from arts, crafts or work connected with them.

Being in Virgo, Jupiter if Malefic:

You may have residence in foreign countries. You may expect destruction of your properties and loss of wealth.

Being in Libra, Jupiter if Benefic:

You will be wealthy and may gain money by dealing in theatres, films etc.

Being in Libra, Jupiter if Malefic:

You may reside in desolate places and at a place other than your homeland. You may land in great difficulties and troubles.

Being in Scorpio, Jupiter if Benefic:

You may acquire new lands and estates. You will be generous.

Being in Sagittarius, Jupiter if Benefic:

You will get a pretty inheritance and will become rich.

Being in Sagittarius, Jupiter if Malefic:

You may live at places other than your homeland.

Being in Capricorn, Jupiter if Malefic:

You may have loss of property, reputation and self-respect. You are liable to prosecutions and imprisonment. You may have to put in much hard labour for low financial returns. You may live at a place other than your native land.

Being in Acquarius, Jupiter if Malefic:

You may have loss of wealth and many hardships. You are likely to destroy your wealth or reduce your income by your speech.

Being in Pisces, Jupiter if Benefic:

You will acquire property and you will become wealthy.

Venus in Different Rasis

Being in Aries, Venus if Benefic:

You will get good earnings.

Being in Aries, Venus if Malefic:

You may be extravagant.

Being in Taurus, Venus if Benefic:

You will travel on seas to foreign countries particularly southern side. You will get redemption of debts and you will become wealthy.

Being in Gemini, Venus if Benefic:
   You will become wealthy.

Being in Cancer, Venus if Malefic:
   You may be inclined to seek money from others and you may have loss of wealth.

Being in Virgo, Venus if Malefic:
   You may mortgage your property and you may become poor.

Being in Libra, Venus if Benefic:
   You will be generous.

Being in Libra, Venus if Malefic:
   You may be inclined to live at a place other than your native land.

Being in Scorpio, Venus if Malefic:
   You may have loss of wealth and property. You may oppose or enter into litigation with another party and thereby damage your own property.

Being in Sagittarius, Venus if Benefic:
   You will become wealthy.

Being in Capricorn, Venus if Benefic:
   You will succeed in all your undertakings and endeavours.

Being in Capricorn, Venus if Malefic:
   Your efforts may end in frustrations.

Being in Aquarius, Venus if Benefic:
   You will acquire fresh property.

Being in Pisces, Venus if Benefic:
You will do acts of charity and generosity and you will be wealthy.

Saturn in Different Rasis

Being in Aries, Saturn if Benefic:
You will be fond of travelling.

Being in Aries, Saturn if Malefic:
You may be wandering aimlessly.

Being in Taurus, Saturn if Benefic:
You will get good income.

Being in Taurus, Saturn if Malefic:
You may be devoid of wealth.

Being in Gemini, Saturn if Malefic:
You may not be benevolently inclined and you may be accused in criminal case. You may incur debts.

Being in Cancer, Saturn if Malefic:
You may be poor and may have to take recourse to begging.

Being in Virgo, Saturn if Malefic:
You may not engage yourself in productive work and will not become wealthy.

Being in Libra, Saturn if Benefic:
You will be travelling in countries inhabited by Christians and Muslims.

Being in Scorpio, Saturn if Malefic:
You are liable to suffer confinement or physical chastisement or reprimands. You may suffer heavy expenditure.

Being in Sagittarius, Saturn if Malefic:
   You may be apparently generous.

Being in Capricorn, Saturn if Benefic:
   You will gain wealth.

Being in Capricorn, Saturn if Malefic:
   You may be prudent.

Being in Aquarius, Saturn if Benefic:
   You will have acquisition of wealth.

Being in Aquarius, Saturn if Malefic:
   You may be addicted to wine and vices and lose your wealth.

Moon in Different Rasis

Being in Aries, Moon if Benefic:
   You will be fond of travelling. You will gain in wealth.

Being in Taurus, Moon if Benefic:
   You will be liberal, rich and wealthy.

Being in Gemini, Moon if Benefic:
   You will acquire property.

Being in Cancer, Moon if Benefic:
   You will be fond of travelling. You will be frugal and you will add to your wealth.

Being in Cancer, Moon if Malefic:
   You may undertake unprofitable voyages. You may live at a place other than your native home land.

Being in Leo, Moon if Benefic:
You will be liberal and generous in giving. You will get much gains.

Being in Leo, Moon if Malefic:
You may be frequenting forests and hills.

Being in Libra, Moon if Benefic:
You may gain in wealth.

Being in Libra, Moon if Malefic:
You may lose through women. You may suffer financial penalty at the hands of government.

Being in Scorpio, Moon if Benefic:
You may gain money by underhand means and become wealthy.

Being in Scorpio, Moon if Malefic:
You may lose your wealth.

Being in Sagittarius, Moon if Benefic:
You will have accumulation of wealth.

Being in Capricorn, Moon if Benefic:
You will be liberal.

Being in Capricorn, Moon if Malefic:
You may be wandering aimlessly.

Being in Aquarius, Moon if Malefic:
There may be destruction of your property and you may become poor.

Being in Pisces, Moon if Benefic:
You may get sudden wealth. You will be inclined to travel by water. You will be interested in countries and

products beyond sea. You will be generous in giving. You may be spiritually inclined later in life.

PREDICTIONS OF DIFFERENT BHAVA LORDS
IN DIFFERENT BHAVAS

(I) AS FIRST BHAVA LORD IN DIFFERENT BHAVAS
Temperament and Personality

As first lord in first bhava: If Benefic

You may live by your own exertions and independent spirit.

As first lord in first bhava: If Malefic

You may not live by your own exertions and independent spirit.

As first lord in second bhava: If Benefic

You will have good character. You will be respectable and generous hearted and well-disposed. You will gladly discharge your duties towards kith and kin. You will be ambitious and blessed with forethought. You may have prominent eyes.

As first lord in second bhava: If Malefic

You may not have good temperament. You may not be respectable and generous hearted and well-disposed. You may not gladly discharge your duties towards kith and kin. You may not be ambitious and blessed with forethought. You may not have prominent eyes.

As first lord in third bhava: If Benefic

You are highly courageous, respectable, intelligent and happy. You may be famous as a physician or mathematician.

As first lord in third bhava: If Malefic

You may not be highly courageous, respectable, intelligent and happy. You may not be famous as a physician or mathematician.

As first lord in fourth bhava: If Benefic

You will be materialistic. You will behave well and become famous. You may have a fair looking and well-built personality.

As first lord in fourth bhava: If Malefic

You may not be materialistic. You may not behave well and become famous. You may not have a fair looking and well-built personality.

As first lord in fifth bhava: If Benefic

You will be in the good grace of rulers and political parties. You may propitiate deities.

As first lord in fifth bhava: If Malefic

You may be of sharp temperament. You may be subservient and serving others.

As first lord in sixth bhava: If Benefic

You are courageous, respectable, intelligent and happy.

As first lord in sixth bhava: If Malefic

You may not be courageous, respectable, intelligent and happy.

As first lord in seventh bhava: If Benefic

You may spend most of your time in travelling in foreign countries. You may lead a licentious life. Later in life you may become detached from worldly affairs and try to lead an ascetic life.

As first lord in seventh bhava: If Malefic

You may not spend most of your time in travelling in foreign countries. You may not lead a licentious life. Later in life you may not become detached from worldly affairs or try to lead an ascetic life.

As first lord in eighth bhava: If Benefic

You will be learned and interested in occultism. You will take pride in helping others. You will have a number of friends. You are religiously inclined.

As first lord in eighth bhava: If Malefic

You are likely to have gambling tendencies. You may always think of evil things.

As first lord in ninth bhava: If Benefic

You will protect others. You are religious and would like to do righteous acts. You can expect to become a good orator.

As first lord in ninth bhava: If Malefic

You may not protect others. You may not be religious and would not like to do righteous acts. You can not expect to become a good orator.

As first lord in tenth bhava: If Benefic

You may be materialistic, well-built, fair looking. You will become famous by your good behaviour. You can expect to be honoured by eminent men. You may perform religious deeds.

As first lord in tenth bhava: If Malefic

You may not be materialistic, well-built, fair looking. You may not become famous by your good behaviour. You can not expect to be honoured by eminent men. You may not perform religious deeds.

As first lord in eleventh bhava: If Benefic

Your character will be good. You will be respectable with generous heart and good disposition. You will gladly discharge your duties towards your kith and kin. You will be fond of ambition. You will be blessed with forethought. You may have prominent eyes.

As first lord in eleventh bhava: If Malefic

Your temperament may not be good. You may not be respectable with generous heart and good disposition. You may not gladly discharge your duties towards your kith and kin. You will not be fond of ambition. You may not be blessed with forethought. You may not have prominent eyes.

As first lord in twelfth bhava: If Benefic

You will be learned and interested in occultism. You will take pride in helping others. You are religiously inclined and emotionally balanced. You dedicate your life for public weal and you will have a number of friends.

As first lord in twelfth bhava: If Malefic

You may roam about in exile.

(II) AS SECOND BHAVA LORD IN DIFFERENT BHAVAS
Wealth

As second lord in first bhava: If Benefic

You will earn wealth by your own effort, intelligence and learning or you will get inherited wealth.

As second lord in first bhava: If Malefic

You may earn wealth by your own exertions and generally by manual labour.

As second lord in second bhava: If Benefic

You will be able to earn considerable fortune through business or other occupations. Riches will be acquired without efforts. You will be pretty rich and will have much wealth with steady fortune. You will spend money on moral purposes.

As second lord in second bhava: If Malefic

Ancestral wealth will be spent rather wasted on extravagant purposes. You may earn wealth by self-exertion. You will sustain losses. You will be bad in saving money.

As second lord in third bhava: If Benefic

You may get wealth and be benefited by your co-borns and by learning fine arts viz. music and dancing and by travels and journeys.

As second lord in third bhava: If Malefic

You may lose wealth through relatives, co-borns and by being addicted to luxuries.

As second lord in fourth bhava: If Benefic

Unexpected wealth may come from mining, lottery, competitions or unexpected sources. You may get wealth by earning as an automobile dealer or agent or an agriculturist or landlord or commission agent. You may be benefited from your mother, maternal grand-father and inheritance. You will be highly frugal in dealing with money and will spend money for your own happiness. You may get wealth through house, landed property or vehicles.

As second lord in fourth bhava: If Malefic

You may lose through maternal uncles, dealership or agency. You may not have wealth through house, landed property or vehicles.

As second lord in fifth bhava: If Benefic

You may have unexpected wealth through lotteries, speculation, chance games or the favour of rulers or ancestral properties. You may get wealth through children.

As second lord in fifth bhava: If Malefic

You may not spend money even on children. You may not get wealth through children.

As second lord in sixth bhava: If Benefic

You can expect wealth from enemies and broker's business.

As second lord in sixth bhava: if Malefic:

You may amass wealth through blackmarketing, deceit, dissimulation and by creating misunderstandings and troubles between friends and relatives and through questionable and suspicious dealings and you may land in troubles be sentenced for such crimes. You may lose wealth from relatives.

As second lord in seventh bhava: If Benefic

You will gain wealth after marriage and also may be benefited by contact with women. You may undertake journeys to foreign countries, do business and become wealthy. There will be influx of money from foreign sources.

As second lord in seventh bhava: If Malefic

You are likely to waste much of your wealth on the gratification of senses and sickness of wife etc.

As second lord in eighth bhava: If Benefic

You will have influx of wealth from legacies. You can expect to gain wealth from enemies.

As second lord in eighth bhava: If Malefic

You are likely to have loss of inherited or accumulated wealth. There will hardly be any earnings.

As second lord in ninth bhava: If Benefic

You will have good inheritance and wealth from father. You may possess wealth by dealing in voyages and shipping. You can also expect benefits of wealth from different sources.

As second lord in ninth bhava: If Malefic

You may not have good inheritance and wealth from father. You may possess wealth by dealing in voyages and shipping. You can also expect benefits of wealth from different sources.

As second lord in tenth bhava: If Benefic

You will get wealth from profession, eminent people and government favours. You will do business or take to agriculture and also engage yourself in philosophical lectures and dissertations and will take to a number of useful avocations and thereby benefit financially.

As second lord in tenth bhava: If Malefic

You may get loss of wealth from profession, business etc. You may earn by your own exertions.

As second lord in eleventh bhava: If Benefic

You will get wealth by lending money or as a banker or by running a boarding house. You can also expect money from different means.

As second lord in eleventh bhava: If Malefic

You may earn wealth by unscrupulous means.

As second lord in twelfth bhava: If Benefic

You can expect to gain wealth by dealing with churches and servants.

As second lord in twelfth bhava: If Malefic

You may lose wealth by offending authorities and through governmental executions, fines and penalties. Your wealth may be lost by dealing with sources connected with churches. You are likely to gain money from unscrupulous means and illegal gratifications. You may be indebted sometimes.

(III) AS THIRD BHAVA LORD IN DIFFERENT BHAVAS
Courage

As third lord in first bhava: If Benefic

You will be brave and courageous. You will vanquish your enemies.

As third lord in first bhava: If Malefic

You may become vindictive.

As third lord in second bhava: If Benefic

You may not be unscrupulous or like mean deeds.

As third lord in second bhava: If Malefic

You may be unscrupulous and like mean deeds.

As third lord in third bhava: If Benefic

You will be brave.

As third lord in third bhava: If Malefic

You may not be brave.

As third lord in fourth bhava: If Benefic

You may be brave.

As third lord in fourth bhava: If Malefic

You may not be brave.

As third lord in fifth bhava: If Benefic
   You may be courageous.

As third lord in fifth bhava: If Malefic
   You may not be brave.

As third lord in sixth bhava: If Benefic
   You may not be tormented by enemies. You may not be deceitful.

As third lord in sixth bhava: If Malefic
   You may be tormented by enemies. You may be deceitful.

As third lord in seventh bhava: If Benefic
   You will be brave.

As third lord in seventh bhava: If Malefic
   You may not be brave.

As third lord in eighth bhava: If Benefic
   You may be brave.

As third lord in eighth bhava: If Malefic
   You may not be brave.

As third lord in ninth bhava: If Benefic
   You will be brave.

As third lord in ninth bhava: If Malefic
   You may not be brave.

As third lord in tenth bhava: If Benefic
   You will be brave.

As third lord in tenth bhava: If Malefic
   You may not be brave.

As third lord in eleventh bhava: If Benefic
You may not become vindictive.

As third lord in eleventh bhava: If Malefic
You may become vindictive.

As third lord in twelfth bhava: If Benefic
You may not be brave.

As third lord in twelfth bhava: If Malefic
You may be brave.

(IV) AS FOURTH BHAVA LORD IN DIFFERENT BHAVAS
Education

As fourth lord in first bhava: If Benefic
You will be highly learned.

As fourth lord in first bhava: If Malefic
You will be afraid to speak in public assemblies.

As fourth lord in second bhava: If Benefic
You will get education.

As fourth lord in second bhava: If Malefic
You may have problems in your educational pursuits.

As fourth lord in third bhava: If Benefic
You may progress in your education satisfactorily.

As fourth lord in third bhava: If Malefic
You may not progress in your education satisfactorily

As fourth lord in fourth bhava: If Benefic
You may be religiously inclined. You will have good education.

As fourth lord in fourth bhava: If Malefic
You may not be religiously inclined. You may not have good education.

As fourth lord in fifth bhava: If Benefic
Your education will be successful.

As fourth lord in fifth bhava: If Malefic
Your education may not be successful.

As fourth lord in sixth bhava: If Benefic
You may not have obstructions in your education.

As fourth lord in sixth bhava: If Malefic
You may have obstructions in your education.

As fourth lord in seventh bhava: If Benefic
You will have good education, may be abroad.

As fourth lord in seventh bhava: If Malefic
You may not have good education abroad.

As fourth lord in eighth bhava: If Benefic
Your educational pursuits may not be spoiled.

As fourth lord in eighth bhava: If Malefic
Your educational pursuits may be spoiled.

As fourth lord in ninth bhava: If Benefic
You may get education in far off places.

As fourth lord in ninth bhava: If Malefic
You may not get education in far off places.

As fourth lord in tenth bhava: If Benefic
Your education will help you in your profession.

As fourth lord in tenth bhava: If Malefic
Your education may not help you in your profession.

As fourth lord in eleventh bhava: If Benefic
You will get gains from good education.

As fourth lord in eleventh bhava: If Malefic
You may not get gains from good education.

As fourth lord in twelfth bhava: If Benefic
You may go to long distances – may be foreign – for education.

As fourth lord in twelfth bhava: If Malefic
You may have loss of education.

Houses, Landed Properties, Means of Conveyance

As fourth lord in first bhava: If Benefic
You may not be likely to lose inherited wealth.

As fourth lord in first bhava: If Malefic
You are likely to lose inherited wealth.

As fourth lord in second bhava: If Benefic
You may inherit property from maternal grand father.

As fourth lord in second bhava: If Malefic
You may not inherit property from maternal grand father.

As fourth lord in third bhava: If Benefic
You will acquire wealth by self-effort.

As fourth lord in third bhava: If Malefic
You may not acquire wealth by self-effort.

As fourth lord in fourth bhava: If Benefic
You will be rich.

As fourth lord in fourth bhava: If Malefic
You may not be rich.

As fourth lord in fifth bhava: If Benefic
You will become rich by self-effort and acquire vehicles.

As fourth lord in fifth bhava: If Malefic
You may not become rich by self-effort and acquire vehicles.

As fourth lord in sixth bhava: If Benefic
There may not be obstruction to acquire properties, houses and vehicles.

As fourth lord in sixth bhava: If Malefic
There may be obstruction to your acquiring properties, houses and vehicles.

As fourth lord in seventh bhava: If Benefic
You will command houses and lands.

As fourth lord in seventh bhava: If Malefic
You may not command houses and lands.

As fourth lord in eighth bhava: If Benefic
You are not likely to lose landed properties and you may not have to lose in litigations.

As fourth lord in eighth bhava: If Malefic
You are likely to lose landed properties and you may have to lose in litigations.

As fourth lord in ninth bhava: If Benefic

You will be generally fortunate, having happiness in regard to properties.

As fourth lord in ninth bhava: If Malefic

You may not be generally fortunate in having happiness in regard to properties.

As fourth lord in tenth bhava: If Benefic

You will have all comforts through houses, landed properties and vehicles.

As fourth lord in tenth bhava: If Malefic

You may not have all comforts through houses, landed properties and vehicles.

As fourth lord in eleventh bhava: If Benefic

You will be successful in selling and buying lands and cattle.

As fourth lord in eleventh bhava: If Malefic

You may not be successful in selling and buying lands and cattle.

As fourth lord in twelfth bhava: If Benefic

You may not be deprived of properties.

As fourth lord in twelfth bhava: If Malefic

You will be deprived of properties.

Happiness

As fourth lord in first bhava: If Benefic

You will be highly learned.

As fourth lord in first bhava: If Malefic

You are likely to lose inherited wealth.

As fourth lord in second bhava: If Benefic

You will inherit property from maternal grandfather. You will be highly fortunate and happy.

As fourth lord in second bhava: If Malefic

You may not inherit property from maternal grandfather. You may not be highly fortunate and happy.

As fourth lord in third bhava: If Benefic

You will acquire wealth through self-effort.

As fourth lord in third bhava: If Malefic

You may suffer from machinations from relatives. You may be sickly.

As fourth lord in fourth bhava: If Benefic

You will be religiously inclined. You will be rich, respected and happy.

As fourth lord in fourth bhava: If Malefic

You may not be religiously inclined. You may not be rich, respected and happy.

As fourth lord in fifth bhava: If Benefic

You will be loved and respected by others. You will become rich by self-effort. You will acquire vehicles.

As fourth lord in fifth bhava: If Malefic

You may not be loved and respected by others. You may not become rich by self-effort. You may not acquire vehicles.

As fourth lord in sixth bhava: If Benefic

You may not always be roaming about. You may not be short-tempered and may not have dissimulating habits.

As fourth lord in sixth bhava: If Malefic

You may be always roaming about. You may be short-tempered and may have dissimulating habits.

As fourth lord in seventh bhava: If Benefic

You will command houses and vehicles. You will be generally happy.

As fourth lord in seventh bhava: If Malefic

You may not command houses and vehicles. You may not be generally happy.

As fourth lord in eighth bhava: If Benefic

You may not be likely to lose landed property or to face litigation. You may have satisfaction in sex life. Your father may not suffer ill health. You may be comfortable.

As fourth lord in eighth bhava: If Malefic

You are likely to lose landed property or to face litigation. You may suffer in sex life. Your father may have ill health. You may not be comfortable.

As fourth lord in ninth bhava: If Benefic

You will be generally fortunate in finding happiness with regard to father and properties.

As fourth lord in ninth bhava: If Malefic

You may not be generally fortunate in finding happiness in regard to father and properties.

As fourth lord in tenth bhava: If Benefic

You will have political success. You will vanquish your enemies and make your personality felt by others. You may be an expert chemist.

As fourth lord in tenth bhava: If Malefic

You will have possible loss of reputation.

As fourth lord in eleventh bhava: If Benefic

You will be self-made. You will be successful in selling and buying cattle and lands.

As fourth lord in eleventh bhava: If Malefic

You may not be self-made. You may not be successful in selling and buying cattle and lands.

As fourth lord in twelfth bhava: If Benefic

You may not have ill health. You may not have bad finances and generally uncomfortable existence. You may not be deprived of property and happiness.

As fourth lord in twelfth bhava: If Malefic

You may have ill health sometimes. You may have bad finances and generally uncomfortable existence. You may be deprived of property and happiness.

(V) AS FIFTH BHAVA LORD IN DIFFERENT BHAVAS
Children

As fifth lord in first bhava: If Benefic

You may have a few children.

As fifth lord in first bhava: If Malefic

You may not have issues or may have limited children or develop misunderstandings with your children.

As fifth lord in second bhava: If Benefic

You will be blessed with well-behaved children.

As fifth lord in second bhava: If Malefic

You may have family troubles and misunder-standings with your children.

As fifth lord in third bhava: If Benefic

You may have birth of good children.

As fifth lord in third bhava: If Malefic

You may have ill health of children or misunderstanding with them.

A fifth lord in fourth bhava: If Benefic

You may have a few children and one of them may live by agriculture.

As fifth lord in fourth bhava: If Malefic

You may not have many children. There may be separation from children.

As fifth lord in fifth bhava: If Benefic

You may have children.

As fifth lord in fifth bhava: If Malefic

Your children may be limited or suffer ill health.

As fifth lord in sixth bhava: If Benefic

Issues may be born and you may not have to adopt one from maternal uncle's line. You may not have enmity with children.

As fifth lord in sixth bhava: If Malefic

Issues may not be born and you may have to adopt one from maternal uncle's line or you may have limited children or enmity with your children.

As fifth lord in seventh bhava: If Benefic

You may have children. Your children may live abroad and attain distinction, wealth and fame. You will be benefitted by your childrens' trip to and residence in foreign countries.

As fifth lord in seventh bhava: If Malefic

You may have ill health of children and one of them may suffer abroad even though they might attain name and fame. Misfortunes may befall on your children.

As fifth lord in eighth bhava: If Benefic

There may not be suffering in family or ill health of children or abortion to wife. You may not develop misunderstandings with children.

As fifth lord in eighth bhava: If Malefic

There may be suffering in family or ill health of children or abortions to wife. You may develop misunderstandings with children.

As fifth lord in ninth bhava: If Benefic

One of your children may attain distinction as orator or as author.

As fifth lord in ninth bhava: If Malefic

One of your children may not attain distinction as orator or as author.

As fifth lord in tenth bhava: If Benefic

One of your children may become gem of your family. You will receive joy from children.

As fifth lord in tenth bhava: If Malefic

One of your children may not become gem of your family. You may not be receipent of joy from children.

As fifth lord in eleventh bhava: If Benefic

You may have children and you will get gains and benefits through them.

As fifth lord in eleventh bhava: If Malefic

You may have misunderstandings with your children.

As fifth lord in twelfth bhava: If Benefic

You may be much attached to your children. You may not have misunderstandings with your children.

As fifth lord in twelfth bhava: If Malefic

You may not be much attached to your children. You may have misunderstandings with your children.

(VI) AS SIXTH BHAVA LORD IN DIFFERENT BHAVAS
Diseases

As sixth lord in first bhava: If Benefic

You may not suffer from diseases. You may not have sharp attacks of ill health. You may not suffer from boils and fevers.

As sixth lord in first bhava: If Malefic

You may suffer from diseases sometimes. You may have attacks of ill health. You may suffer from boils and fevers.

As sixth lord in second bhava: If Benefic

You may not have defective vision. You may not stammer. You may not suffer from dental and eye troubles.

As sixth lord in second bhava: If Malefic

You may have defective vision. You may stammer. You may suffer from dental and eye troubles.

As sixth lord in third bhava: If Benefic

You may not have ear complaints. You may not have injuries to neck and you may not suffer from throat complaints.

As sixth lord in third bhava: If Malefic

You may have ear complaints. You may have injuries to neck and you may suffer from throat complaints.

As sixth lord in fourth bhava: If Benefic

Your health may not be in jeopardy.

As sixth lord in fourth bhava: If Malefic
Your health may be in jeopardy sometimes.

As sixth lord in fifth bhava: If Benefic
Your children may not suffer ill health.

As sixth lord in fifth bhava: If Malefic
Your children may have ill health sometimes.

As sixth lord in sixth bhava: If Benefic
You will not generally have any major diseases.

As sixth lord in sixth bhava: If Malefic
You may suffer from ill health sometimes.

As sixth lord in seventh bhava: If Benefic
Your wife may not suffer ill health. You may not fall ill.

As sixth lord in seventh bhava: If Malefic
Your wife may suffer ill health. You may fall ill.

As sixth lord in eighth bhava: If Benefic
You may get redemption from ailments and suffering.

As sixth lord in eighth bhava: If Malefic
You may suffer from fevers or watery diseases.

As sixth lord in ninth bhava: If Benefic
You may not suffer from diseases.

As sixth lord in ninth bhava: If Malefic
You may suffer from diseases sometimes.

As sixth lord in tenth bhava: If Benefic
You may not suffer from diseases.

As sixth lord in tenth bhava: If Malefic
You may suffer from diseases sometimes.

As sixth lord in eleventh bhava: If Benefic
You may not suffer from diseases.

As sixth lord in eleventh bhava: If Malefic
You may suffer from diseases sometimes.

As sixth lord in twelfth bhava: If Benefic
You may not have colic diseases.

As sixth lord in twelfth bhava: If Malefic
You may have colic diseases.

Enemies

As sixth lord in first bhava: If Benefic
You may not have troubles from machinations of enemies and you may not be vexed by enemies.

As sixth lord in first bhava: If Malefic
You may have troubles from machinations of enemies and you may be vexed by enemies.

As sixth lord in second bhava: If Benefic
You may gain from enemies.

As sixth lord in second bhava: If Malefic
You may have loss of money from enemies. Your relatives and friends may turn into bitter enemies.

As sixth lord in third bhava: If Benefic
You may not have enmity or misunderstandings with your brothers. Your maternal uncle may not work against your interests.

As sixth lord in third bhava: If Malefic

You may have enmity or misunderstandings with your brothers. Your maternal uncle may work against your interests.

As sixth lord in fourth bhava: If Benefic

You may not quarrel with your mother. You may not have trouble with your servants. You may not be troubled by relatives. Your properties may not be auctioned or lost to enemies.

As sixth lord in fourth bhava: If Malefic

You may quarrel with your mother. You may have trouble with your servants. You may be troubled by relatives. Your properties may be auctioned or lost to enemies.

As sixth lord in fifth bhava: If Benefic

You may not have enmity with your children.

As sixth lord in fifth bhava: If Malefic

You may have enmity with your children.

As sixth lord in sixth bhava: If Benefic

You may not have enemies.

As sixth lord in sixth bhava: If Malefic

There may be increase of enmity with your kith and kin.

As sixth lord in seventh bhava: If Benefic

You will be free from troubles from enemies.

As sixth lord in seventh bhava: If Malefic

You may have misunderstandings or quarrels with partner. You may have trouble from enemies.

As sixth lord in eight bhava: If Benefic
You may not have enemies.

As sixth lord in eighth bhava: If Malefic
You may have enemies.

As sixth lord in ninth bhava: If Benefic
You may benefit from cousins.

As sixth lord in ninth bhava: If Malefic
You may have misunderstandings between you and your father. You may have danger from your cousins.

As sixth lord in tenth bhava: If Benefic
You may not have formidable enemies and may not be vexed by enemies.

As sixth lord in tenth bhava: If Malefic
You may have formidable enemies and may be vexed by enemies.

As sixth lord in eleventh bhava: If Benefic
You will conquer your enemies and overcome all opposition.

As sixth lord in eleventh bhava: If Malefic
You may get displeasure of your own elder brother.

As sixth lord in twelfth bhava: If Benefic
You will not have any untoward-things from enemies.

As sixth lord in twelfth bhava: If Malefic
You may have losses and destructions in your enemies' hands and you may suffer troubles.

Debts

As sixth lord in first bhava: If Benefic

You may not land in debts due to losses by theft, poverty, sharp attacks of misfortune and financial losses.

As sixth lord in first bhava: If Malefic

You may land in debts due to losses by theft, poverty, sharp attacks of misfortune and financial losses.

As sixth lord in second bhava: If Benefic

You may not incur debts due to loss of money from enemies.

As sixth lord in second bhava: If Malefic

You may incur debts due to loss of money from enemies.

As sixth lord in fourth bhava: If Benefic

Your ancestral property may not be involved in debts.

As sixth lord in fourth bhava: If Malefic

Your ancestral property may be involved in debts.

As sixth lord in fifth bhava: If Benefic

You may not be in debt due to children.

As sixth lord in fifth bhava: If Malefic

You may get into debts due to children.

As sixth lord in sixth bhava: If Benefic

You may not have debts.

As sixth lord in sixth bhava: If Malefic

You may be in debt.

As sixth lord in seventh bhava: If Benefic
You may not get into debt due to partner.

As sixth lord in seventh bhava: If Malefic
You may get into debt due to partner.

As sixth lord in eighth bhava: If Benefic
You may not have debts due to loss of money or diseases.

As sixth lord in eighth bhava: If Malefic
You may have debts due to loss of money or diseases sometimes.

As sixth lord in ninth bhava: If Benefic
You may get benefits from cousins.

As sixth lord in ninth bhava: If Malefic
You may be involved in debts due to losses, litigations, pecuniary troubles and due to father losing property sometimes.

As sixth lord in tenth bhava: If Benefic
You may not have debts due to low life.

As sixth lord in twelfth bhava: If Benefic
You may not have debts.

As sixth lord in twelfth bhava: If Malefic
You may incur losses and get indebted sometimes.

(VII) AS SEVENTH BHAVA LORD IN DIFFERENT BHAVAS
Marriage and Marital Relationship

As seventh lord in first bhava: If Benefic
You may marry someone you have known since

childhood or one who has been brought up in the same place. Your partner may be a stable and mature person.

As seventh lord in first bhava: If Malefic
You may be sensual. You may travel frequently.

As seventh lord in second bhava: If Benefic
You will get wealth from women or through marriage.

As seventh lord in second bhava: If Malefic
You may have a wavering mind and may be inclined sensually.

As seventh lord in third bhava: If Benefic
You may not indulge in adultery.

As seventh lord in third bhava: If Malefic
You may be sensual.

As seventh lord in fourth bhava: If Benefic
You will have a lucky and happy married partner with many children and comforts.

As seventh lord in fourth bhava: If Malefic
Your domestic harmony may be spoiled through an immature partner. Your partner's temperament may not be very good.

As seventh lord in fifth bhava: If Benefic
You may have an early marriage. Your partner may hail from an affluent and well-to-do family. Your partner will be mature and an advantage to you.

As seventh lord in fifth bhava: If Malefic
You may not have an early marriage. Your partner may not hail from an affluent and well-to-do family. Your partner may not be mature and an advantage to you.

As seventh lord in sixth bhava: If Benefic

You may marry a cousin such as an uncle's daughter.

As seventh lord in sixth bhava: If Malefic

You may have two marriages with both partners living. You may not have marital happiness. Your partner may be sickly and jealous by nature, denying you happiness from marriage. You may desert or lose married partner through some indiscreet act.

As seventh lord in seventh bhava: If Benefic

You will have a charming and magnetic personality and you will be sought after for alliance. Your partner will be just and honourable person, coming from a family of reputation and social standing. Your marriage may take place early in life. You will have a very favourable partner who will be beautiful with good social background.

As seventh lord in seventh bhava: If Malefic

You may have lonely life devoid of marriage or the marriage negotiations may fail or there may be loss through marriage.

As seventh lord in eighth bhava: If Benefic

Your marriage may take place with relative or your partner may be a rich person.

As seventh lord in eighth bhava: If Malefic

You are likely to have a sickly and ill-tempered life partner leading to estrangement and separation.

As seventh lord in ninth bhava: If Benefic

You will get an accomplished partner who will enable you to lead a righteous life.

As seventh lord in ninth bhava: If Malefic

Your married partner may drag you from the righteous course of life and you waste away your wealth and suffer penury.

As seventh lord in tenth bhava: If Benefic

You will get a devoted and faithful life partner. Your partner may also be employed and contribute to your income or may help you in advancement of your career.

As seventh lord in tenth bhava: If Malefic

Your partner may be avaricious and overambitious but without sufficient capacity and consequently your career may suffer and deteriorate.

As seventh lord in eleventh bhava: If Benefic

Your partner may hail from a rich background or bring in much wealth.

As seventh lord in eleventh bhava: If Malefic

You may have more than one marriage or you may associate with others of opposite sex.

As seventh lord in twelfth bhava: If Benefic

You may not have more than one marriage. There may not be death or separation of your partner. Your partner may not hail from a low family. You may not dream of opposite sex and may marry. You may not be lacking in marital happiness.

As seventh lord in twelfth bhava: If Malefic

You may have more than one marriage. There may be separation from your partner. Your partner may hail from a low family. You may dream of opposite sex but may never marry. You may be lacking in marital happiness.

(VIII) AS EIGHTH BHAVA LORD IN DIFFERENT BHAVAS
Longevity

As eighth lord in first bhava: If Benefic

You may not suffer bodily complaints such as disease and disfiguration. Your constitution may not be weak. You may have bodily comforts.

As eighth lord in first bhava: If Malefic

You may suffer bodily complaints. Your constitution may be weak. You may have no bodily comforts.

As eighth lord in second bhava: If Benefic

You may not suffer severe illness. You may not have eye and tooth trouble.

As eighth lord in second bhava: If Malefic

You may suffer illness. You may have eye and tooth troubles.

As eighth lord in third bhava: If Benefic

Your ears may not cause problems. You may not suffer from mental anguish and hallucinations.

As eighth lord in third bhava: If Malefic

Your ears may cause problems. You may suffer from mental anguish and hallucinations sometimes.

As eighth lord in fourth bhava: If Benefic

Your mental peace may not shatter.

As eighth lord in fourth bhava: If Malefic

Your mental peace may shatter sometimes.

As eighth lord in fifth bhava: If Benefic

You may not suffer much bodily ill health. You may

not have nervous debility or breakdown or mental aberrations.

As eighth lord in fifth bhava: If Malefic

You may suffer bodily ill health. You may have nervous debility or breakdown or mental aberrations sometimes.

As eighth lord in sixth bhava: If Benefic

You may not suffer ill health.

As eighth lord in sixth bhava: If Malefic

You may suffer ill health sometimes.

As eighth lord in seventh bhava: If Benefic

You may not suffer from diseases.

As eighth lord in seventh bhava: If Malefic

You may suffer from diseases sometimes.

As eighth lord influencing eighth bhava: If Benefic

You may have good life span.

As eighth lord influencing eighth bhava: If Malefic

You may not have very good long life span.

(IX) AS NINTH BHAVA LORD IN DIFFERENT BHAVAS
Prosperity

As ninth lord in first bhava: If Benefic

You will become self-made and earn much money through own efforts. You will acquire means of conveyance, wealth, riches and every kind of comfort. You will inherit paternal property and will build it up with own efforts as well. You will work in top levels of government service and occupy a post equivalent to king or minister and you will get position of authority and power. Many of your relatives will depend on your hospitality for their living and shelter. You will become famous both for your generous instincts and achievements in career. You will be fortunate with riches and happiness. You will lead a happy life.

As ninth lord in first bhava: If Malefic

You may get results contrary to your expectations. You may suffer penury and instead of maintaining others you may be forced to depend on others.

As ninth lord in second bhava: if Benefic

Your father will be rich and influential and you will acquire wealth from him. You will get unlimited wealth through family business or property. You will eat very good food and enjoy a luxurious life. You will have many relatives who will hold you in regard and affection. Your face gets a radiant glow and you will have eloquent speech.

As ninth lord in second bhava: If Malefic

You may ruin and destroy your paternal property. Your resources and inheritance may dwindle on account of family squabbles. You may suffer disgrace and humiliation.

As ninth lord in third bhava: if Benefic

You will make your fortune through writing, speeches and oratorial abilities. Your father may be a man of moderate means. You will advance your fortune through your co-borns. Your brothers will prosper. You will have an inclination for writing on religion and spirituality. You may earn through music and musical instruments. You will make many trips abroad as well as to holy spots and pilgrim centres. You will go to foreign lands where you will serve the government or the ruler.

As *ninth lord in third bhava: If Malefic*

You may land in trouble through your writings which may be irrational and even obscene. You may be forced to sell your paternal property because of troubles occuring through your writings. Your fortune may be mediocre.

As *ninth lord in fourth bhava: If Benefic*

You will have vast landed properties and beautiful bungalows. You will earn through estate and land dealings. Your mother will be a rich and fortunate woman. You will inherit father's immovable properties. You will become a president or ruler of a country or head of a centre of learning or research.

As *ninth lord in fourth bhava: If Malefic*

You may have any domestic unhappiness. Your early life may be crossed by miseries due to hard-hearted father or disharmony between parents. Your mother may be living separately from your father. Good results in all respects will be experienced to a lesser scale.

As *ninth lord in fifth bhava: If Benefic*

You will have a prosperous and famous father. Your children may also be fortunate in life and enjoy success and distinction. You will experience great clarity of thought and consequent tranquillity. Your father will help you with money and in other ways also to advance your career and interests. Your children will distinguish themselves in academics and bring much happiness to you. Your children may become very famous and earn governmental patronage. Your children will also prosper very well and enjoy all kinds of luxuries.

As *ninth lord in fifth bhava: If Malefic*

You may not have a prosperous and famous father. Your children may not also be fortunate in life and enjoy success and distinction. You may not experience great clarity of thought and consequent tranquillity. Your father may not help you with money and in other ways also to advance your career and interests. Your children may not distinguish themselves in academics nor bring much happiness to you. Your children may not become very famous and earn governmental patronage. Your children may not also prosper very well and enjoy all kinds of luxuries.

As ninth lord in sixth bhava: If Benefic

You may gain wealth through successful termination of father's legal problems and by way of compensation, costs, etc. You will get generally good results in all respects. You will earn well and advance in career. Your father's health will improve. You may get a post of judicial or similar officer. You will have many servants and men at your beck and call. You will inherit landed property. You may profit through royalty on books and through legal bequests.

As ninth lord in sixth bhava: If Malefic

You may have sickly father or your father may suffer. You may contract debts and be drawn into litigation.

As ninth lord in seventh bhava: If Benefic

You may go abroad and prosper there. Your father may also prosper in foreign lands. You will get a noble and lucky married partner. You may seek spiritual guidance and fulfilment abroad. You will earn wealth in foreign lands. You will be sent abroad on diplomatic and similar assignments. You will be born in a prosperous family. You will get all sorts of luxurious comforts. You will get every kind of enjoyment. You will earn landed property and earn through women abroad. Fortune booms after marriage; your partner will be a rich and noble person, hailing from a respectable family.

As ninth lord in seventh bhava: If Malefic

Your father may meet with his suffering abroad. Your partner may be sickly, although gracious and gentle. You may have to defray expenses on account of liabilities and litigations, even though earning well.

As ninth lord in eighth bhava: If Benefic

You may inherit substantial paternal property. Your father may leave you a large inheritance.

As ninth lord in eighth bhava: If Malefic

You may not only suffer bereavements but also lose your wealth and lands. You may wander aimlessly from place to place and suffer hunger and thirst. Your father may suffer ill health. You may suffer poverty and heavy responsibility due to father's separation. You may abandon traditions or damage religious institutions and trusts set up by the family.

As ninth lord in ninth bhava: If Benefic

You will have a long-lived and prosperous father. You will be religiously inclined and charitable. You will travel abroad and earn money and distinction thereby. You will be lucky. You may marry a very eligible and good-natured partner. You will invest wisely in father's business and expand it beyond expectations. You will earn wealth. You may win in elections and become a great political personage. Your father may become famous in foreign lands. You will be pious and dutiful towards your parents.

As ninth lord in ninth bhava: If Malefic

You may indulge in vile acts. You may suffer from stomach complaints. You may lose your parents or be separated from them.

As ninth lord in tenth bhava: If Benefic

You will become very famous and powerful. You will

be generous and occupy posts of authority. You will
earn much wealth and acquire every kind of comfort
and luxury. Your means of livelihood will be righteous
and you will be a law-abiding citizen. You will become
renowned for your learning. You will get settled in your
career and will lead a very successful life. You will do
charitable deeds such as building rest-houses and
hospitals. You will earn wealth through your service to
government. You will be honoured many times.

As ninth lord in tenth bhava: If Malefic

You may lose your job. If in profession, you may earn
the wrath of people and be forced to close down your
practice. You may lead an unrighteous life and seek to
earn through illegal and shady means. You may lose
your property and may suffer punishment by the ruler
or the government.

As ninth lord in eleventh bhava: If Benefic

You will be exceedingly rich. You will have powerful
and influential friends. Your father will be a well-
known and well-placed man. You will prosper in the
family business.

As ninth lord in eleventh bhava: If Malefic

Your unfaithful friends may destroy your wealth
through selfish scheming and fraud.

As ninth lord in twelfth bhava: If Benefic

You will lead a pure and honest life. You will be
spiritually inclined and spend your wealth in charity.
You will be religious and noble but always in want.

As ninth lord in twelfth bhava: If Malefic

You may have a poor background. You may suffer
much and may have to work very hard in life and even
then success may not come to you. Your father may
leave you penniless or your father may live far away
from you. You may lose money by foolishly investing it.

You may be robbed of your money. You may lose your cattle, pets and also your servants and workers.

(X) AS TENTH BHAVA LORD IN DIFFERENT BHAVAS
Profession

As tenth lord in first bhava: If Benefic

You will live by sheer dint of perseverance. You will be self-employed or pursue a profession of independence. You will become very famous and a pioneer in your field of work. You will found a public institution and be engaged in social projects and will be renowned. You will occupy top position in government and exercise much power and authority. You will be noble and engage yourself in charitable deeds. You will be a just and peace-loving person.

As tenth lord in first bhava: If Malefic

You may suffer disgrace and humiliation.

As tenth lord in second bhava: If Benefic

You will be fortunate. You will rise well in life and make lots of money. You may engage in family trade and develop it. You may prosper in catering and restaurant business. You will earn riches. Your fame for your riches will spread widely. You may work for the government in an influencial job with many servants at your beck and call. Your power and authority will have no limit.

As tenth lord in second bhava: If Malefic

You may suffer from losses and be responsible for winding up the family business. You may be beset with various kinds of troubles and lose your money.

As tenth lord in third bhava: If Benefic

You may have to travel constantly on short journeys. You may be a speaker or writer of celebrity. Your

brothers may be instrumental in advancing your career.
Your prosperity will boom. You will become famous as
a bold writer. You will rise swiftly in your career with
frequent promotions. You will acquire musical talent
and become famous in this field. You may work for
newspapers or publishing houses.

As tenth lord in third bhava: If Malefic

Your rise in life may be slow and you may be beset
with obstacles. Rivalry between your brothers may lead
to reversals, obstacles etc. in your career. You may
have a mediocre period. You may wander aimlessly.

As tenth lord in fourth bhava: If Benefic

You may engage in agricultural pursuits or in
dealings with immovable properties. You may wield
great political authority as a president or head of a
government. Your income may be from lands and
buildings. You may head an educational institution or a
research organisation.

As tenth lord in fourth bhava: If Malefic

You may be forced to take to a life of servitude. You
may take wrong decisions which may affect your
reputation adversely.

As tenth lord in fifth bhava: If Benefic

You may shine well as a broker and engage in
speculation and similar business. You may lead a
simple and pious life of prayers and pious activities.
You may become the head of an orphanage or remand
house. You may rise to the rank of a minister. You may
even become ruler of a country and may be elected to
office. You may innovate many reforms helpful to
society.

As tenth lord in fifth bhava: If Malefic

You may not attain a high position of the rank of a
minister but may be a mere member of the assembly.

Good results regarding your profession may be greatly reduced.

As tenth lord in sixth bhava: If Benefic

You may have an occupation bearing on judiciary, prisons or hospitals. You will hold a post of authority. You may be a court official. You may become a high court or supreme court judge. You may become a skilled surgeon or physician also.

As tenth lord in sixth bhava: If Malefic

You may suffer disgrace in your career. You may be exposed to criminal action and face imprisonment.

As tenth lord in seventh bhava: If Benefic

You will get a mature married partner who will assist you in your work. You will travel abroad on diplomatic missions. You will be known for your skill in undertaking and achieving your objectives. You will make profits through partnerships and cooperative ventures. You will work abroad where you will get distinction and recognition. Your work may be connected with means of conveyance. You may work as pilot. You may work for railways or in automobile companies.

As tenth lord in seventh bhava: If Malefic

You may follow a profession that may not fetch much money and as a consequence you may suffer penury.

As tenth lord in eighth bhava: If Benefic

You may occupy a high office in your field but only for a short period. You may become a mystic or spiritual teacher. You may be suspended and then reinstated.

As tenth lord in eighth bhava: If Malefic

You may have criminal propensities and commit offences. You may lose your job in humiliating circumstances. You may hold low jobs or take a career connected with crimes. You may spoil your agricultural income.

As tenth lord in ninth bhava: If Benefic

You will be a spiritual stalwart and will be a beacon light to spiritual seekers. You will be generally fortunate and well-to-do. You may follow a hereditary profession or that of a preacher, teacher or healer. You will do many charitable deeds. You will lead a life of righteousness. You will earn through fair means. You may embark on a spiritual sadhana (exercise to attain perfection). You may work as government officer or take up medical profession. You may work as an auditor and banker in government or in some big undertaking. You may go abroad and do research. You may be head of industrial or other concern, employing labour.

As tenth lord in ninth bhava: If Malefic

You may be forced to work in a low position.

As tenth lord in tenth bhava: If Benefic

You will achieve distinction in your profession but only after a hard struggle. You will acquire power, status and eminence. There will be many people working under you, who will respect your word as law. You will do charitable deeds. You will found institutions relating to your field.

As tenth lord in tenth bhava: If Malefic

You may suffer poverty. You may lose your job and drift about in misery.

As tenth lord in eleventh bhava: If Benefic

You will earn immense riches. You will engage in meritorious deeds. You will give employment to many people. You will have many business enterprises and all your ventures will turn out successful. You will have many men at your command. You will be a popular figure in social circles. You may earn through trade in sea products, milk or restaurants. Your income may come from woollen factories, match industries, gold market or chemicals. You may earn as a great intellectual and thinker. You may head many institutions of learning as a chairman or trustee or you may be a newspaper magnate or prosperous publisher.

As tenth lord in eleventh bhava: If Malefic

Your friends may turn out enemies and cause you every sort of hardship and worry. You may have professional losses. You may have moderate success and wealth.

As tenth lord in twelfth bhava: If Benefic

You may become a spiritual seeker. You may head a medical institution or a prison or a remand house. You may pursue your spiritual inclinations with zeal.

As tenth lord in twelfth bhava: If Malefic

You may have to work in a far-off place. You may indulge in nefarious activities. You may suffer humiliation. You may lose your job and if in business, losses may accrue to you. You may have unconventional profession and people may revile at you. You may wander aimlessly.

(XI) AS ELEVENTH BHAVA LORD IN DIFFERENT BHAVAS
Gains and Income

As eleventh lord in first bhava: If Benefic

You will be born in a rich family. You will earn much wealth.

As eleventh lord in first bhava: If Malefic

You may lose elder brother or develop misunderstanding with him.

As eleventh lord in second bhava: If Benefic

You will earn through commercial concerns and banking business. Your business with friends will bring good profits.

As eleventh lord in second bhava: If Malefic

You may suffer losses on account of friends in business.

As eleventh lord in third bhava: If Benefic

You may be a concert singer or musician and may earn thereby. You will gain through brothers, many friends and helpful neighbours.

As eleventh lord in third bhava: If Malefic

You may get contrary results regarding your gains.

As eleventh lord in fourth bhava: If Benefic

You will profit through landed estates, rentals and products of earth. You will get comfort and enjoy all joys in life. You will be renowned for your learning and scholarship of various subjects. You will have a devoted and charming partner.

As eleventh lord in fourth bhava: If Malefic

You may not profit through landed estates, rentals and products of earth. You may not get comfort and enjoy all joys in life. You may not be renowned for your learning and scholarship of various subjects. You may not have a devoted and charming partner.

As eleventh lord in fifth bhava: If Benefic

You may have children who will come up in life. You will be pious and observe many resolves and vows which will enhance your prosperity. You will indulge in speculation and gain money.

As eleventh lord in fifth bhava: If Malefic

You may be a gambler and you may indulge in foolish ventures.

As eleventh lord in sixth bhava: If Benefic

You may gain money through maternal relatives, litigation or running nursing homes.

As eleventh lord in sixth bhava: If Malefic

You may lose through maternal relatives, litigation etc.

As eleventh lord in seventh bhava: If Benefic

You may marry only once, but a rich and influential person. You may prosper in foreign countries.

As eleventh lord in seventh bhava: If Malefic

You may engage in immoral activities.

As eleventh lord in eighth bhava: If Benefic

You may be rich at birth and you may not suffer many calamities and lose money. You may not suffer from thieves, cheats and swindlers.

As eleventh lord in eighth bhava: If Malefic

Though rich at birth you may suffer calamities and lose money. You may suffer from thieves, cheats and swindlers.

As eleventh lord in ninth bhava: If Benefic

You will inherit large paternal fortune and will be lucky in life. You will possess many houses, means of conveyance and every kind of luxury. You will set up charitable institutions.

As eleventh lord in ninth bhava: If Malefic

You may not inherit large paternal fortune and may not be lucky in life. You may not possess many houses, means of conveyance and every kind of luxury. You may not set up charitable institutions.

As eleventh lord in tenth bhava: If Benefic

You will prosper well in business and make good profits. Your elder brother may also help you in your business. You will earn some prize money for original contribution to the subject of your study or profession.

As eleventh lord in tenth bhava: If Malefic

You may not prosper well in business and make good profits. Your elder brother may not help you in your business. You may not earn some prize money for original contribution to the subject of your study or profession.

As eleventh lord in eleventh bhava: If Benefic

You will have many friends and elder brothers who will help you throughout your life. You will have a happy life with partner, house, children and comforts.

As eleventh lord in eleventh bhava: If Malefic

You may not have many friends and elder brothers to help you throughout your life. You may not have a happy life with partner, house, children and comforts.

As eleventh lord in twelfth bhava: If Benefic

You may not suffer losses in business. You may not incur much expenditure on account of illness of elder brother. You may not have to pay fines and penalties frequently and may not be burdened with many domestic responsibilities.

As eleventh lord in twelfth bhava: If Malefic

You may suffer losses in business. You may incur much expenditure on account of illness of elder brother. You may have to pay fines and penalties frequently and may be burdened with many domestic responsibilities.

(XII) AS TWELFTH BHAVA LORD IN DIFFERENT BHAVAS
Losses and Expenditure

As twelfth lord in first bhava: If Benefic

You will be generally travelling about. Evil effects will be reduced. Even if you lose money you will try to work hard and regain it.

As twelfth lord in first bhava: If Malefic

You may be imprisoned. You may be living abroad. You may be miserly. You may be hated by all. You may be devoid of intelligence and grow dull. You may have a weak constitution with a feeble mind. You may lose affection of others. You may lose your wealth through short-sighted schemes. You may be associated with evil persons and addicted to bad habits.

As twelfth lord in second bhava: If Benefic

You may not suffer financial loss. You may not get involved in nefarious activities. You may eat timely meals and good food. Your eyesight may not be poor. Your family life may not be marked by lack of harmony. You may not be gossiping and quarrelling. There may not be constant bickerings in the family. You may not be ill-tempered and commit many indiscretions. You may not have some ailment of tongue or throat. You may not live at others' expense. You may not be lacking domestic peace.

As twelfth lord in second bhava: If Malefic

You may suffer financial loss. You may get involved in nefarious activities. You may not eat timely meals and good food. Your eyesight may be poor. Your family life may be marked by lack of harmony. You may be gossiping and quarrelling. There may be constant bickerings in the family. You may be ill-tempered and commit many indiscretions. You may have some ailment of tongue or throat. You may live at others' expense. You may be lacking domestic peace.

As twelfth lord in third bhava: If Benefic

You may not be timid and quiet. You may not have loss of brother or your brother may not take to evil course and face hardships. You may not be shabbily dressed. You may not have ear ailments. You may not have to spend much money on younger brothers. You may not be unsuccessful as writer. You may not work in some commonplace job and earn very little.

As twelfth lord in third bhava: If Malefic

You may be timid and quiet. You may have a loss of brother or your brother may take to evil course and face hardships. You may be shabbily dressed. You may have ear ailments. You may have to spend much money on younger brothers. You may be unsuccessful as writer. You may work in some commonplace job and earn very little.

As twelfth lord in fourth bhava: If Benefic

You may own your own conveyance but it may give trouble. You may have to undertake lot of journeys within the country. You may face troubles but overcome them. Adverse indications will be mitigated.

As twelfth lord in fourth bhava: If Malefic

Your mother may suffer crisis in life and may have unhappy days. You may have unnecessary worry and mental restlessness. You may develop enmities with your relatives. You may be living abroad. You may be suffering from constant harassment from your landlord. Your residence may be in an ordinary house. You may have troubles on account of your properties which may get lost or be destroyed.

As twelfth lord in fifth bhava: If Benefic

You will be religiously inclined. You may undertake pilgrimages.

As twelfth lord in fifth bhava: If Malefic

You may have either difficulty to beget progeny or unhappiness and pain from children. You may have loss of children or your children may face troubles. You may be weak-minded and may suffer mental aberrations sometimes. You may feel that you are miserable. You may not succeed in agriculture as your crops may suffer from pests and diseases. Your friends may desert you. You may lose association of an influential person. Your father may pass through difficulties while you yourself may rouse the wrath of a powerful person. You may face troubles in your work or occupation. Your life may be disrupted due to political disturbances.

As twelfth lord in sixth bhava: If Benefic

You will be happy and prosperous. You will enjoy many comforts. You will possess a healthy and handsome physique. You will vanquish your enemies. You may involve in litigation which may come to an end to your advantage. You will be happy with joyous festivites. You will become fortunate in all walks of life. You will get much wealth. You will marry a noble and good person. Your children will be a source of happiness to you.

As twelfth lord in sixth bhava: If Malefic

You may be suffering unhappiness on account of your children. You may hate your mother. You may be ill-tempered. Your immoral tendencies may land you in distress.

As twelfth lord in seventh bhava: If Benefic

You will have acquisition of money. Your partner may be surviving.

As twelfth lord in seventh bhava: If Malefic

Your married partner may come from a poor family. Your married life may be unhappy and may end in

separation. Later on you may take to asceticism. You
may be weak in health and suffer from phlegmatic
troubles. You may be without learning or property.
Your partner may have to face some danger or the
other. You may face some ill health. Your partner may
live abroad. You may wander aimlessly, get tired and
may lack physical comforts. You may be beset with
sorrows and ailments. Your married life may be marred
with slanderous talk.

As twelfth lord in eighth bhava: If Benefic

You will be rich and celebrated. You will enjoy
luxurious life with many servants waiting on you. You
will get a legacy. You will be interested in occult
subjects and devoted to Lord Vishnu. You will be
righteous, famous and a good speaker, being endowed
with good qualities of head and heart. You will have
luck but sometimes you may land in some troubles. You
will generally have happiness. You will succeed in your
ventures though results may be coming slowly.
Marriage and happy celebrations will take place in
your house. Much money and authority will be secured.

As twelfth lord in eighth bhava: If Malefic

You may not be rich and celebrated. You may not
enjoy luxurious life with many servants waiting on you.
You may not get legacy. You may not be interested in
occult subjects and devoted to Lord Vishnu. You may
not be righteous, famous and a good speaker though
endowed with good qualities of head and heart. You
may have luck but sometimes you may land in some
troubles. You may not generally have happiness. You
may succeed in your ventures though results may come
slowly. Marriage and happy celebrations may not take
place in your house. Much money and authority may not
be secured.

As twelfth lord in ninth bhava: If Benefic

You may reside abroad and prosper well. You may

acquire much property in foreign lands. You will be honest, generous and large-hearted. You will be interested in physical culture. You will have a steady career. You will develop interest in piety and lead a virtuous life.

As twelfth lord in ninth bhava: If Malefic

You may not have any spiritual leaning. You may not like your partner sometimes. You may have misunderstanding with father. You may have loss of job and luck. Your maternal property may be on a low keel.

As twelfth lord in tenth bhava: If Benefic

You will spend money on charitable purposes. You will be detached and develop spirituality.

As twelfth lord in tenth bhava: If Malefic

You will have to work hard and undertake tedious journeys for your occupation. You may be a jailor or doctor or you may work in cemetry and such places. You may spend money on agricultural pursuits in which you may not make profits. You may have no happiness or physical comforts from your children. Your paternal property may slip out of your hands or get spoiled through fire or other accidents. You may be dreaded for your evil powers.

As twelfth lord in eleventh bhava: If Benefic

You may earn well by trading in pearls, rubies and other precious stones. You may spend much money on religious and charitable deeds even at the cost of your own well-being.

As twelfth lord in eleventh bhava: If Malefic

You may engage yourself in business but do not make much profit. Your trade may bring in much losses to you. You may land in loss in business due to misunderstandings with elder brother or partners who are in the business. You may have few friends and

many enemies. You may be troubled by extravagant
brothers and your funds may dwindle on this account.
You may get loss of money through theft, fire or
accident. You may have financial setbacks.

As twelfth lord in twelfth bhava: If Benefic

You will spend much on religious and righteous
purposes. You will have good eyesight. You will enjoy
pleasures of touch. You may be engaged in agriculture
and generally get favourable results. You may reside
abroad. You will have delightful journeys. You will
have general good fortune. You may have a good father
to take care of your wants and to spend any amount of
money. You will have much wealth. You will do
honourable expenditure. You will be religiously
inclined. You will feed many holy men and seek their
company. You will always be engaged in spiritual
thoughts and will lead a comfortable life.

As twelfth lord in twelfth bhava: If Malefic

You may be restless and always roaming about. You
may leave the country for fear of the law or life. You
may lead vagrant life as an incognito. You may eke out
your livelihood through serving in low position. You
may spend money in illegal or questionable ways. You
may expend your wealth on illegal gratifications, races,
gambling or other vices. Your earning may get
dissipated in many ways. You will get loss of prestige.
You may have untoward expenditure. Though born in
an illustrious family you may become obscure and may
take to evil ways and lead an uncomfortable existence.

PREDICTIONS OF INFLUENCE OF DIFFERENT OTHER BHAVA LORDS ON DIFFERENT BHAVAS

(I) AS DIFFERENT BHAVA LORDS INFLUENCING FIRST BHAVA
Temperament and Personality

Note: **For the Influence of a Bhava Lord on the Same Bhava, see the Previous Section.**

As second lord influencing first bhava: If Benefic

You will be conscious of time sense and will try to complete your works on time. You would like to earn by own effort and exertions through your intelligence and learning.

As second lord influencing first bhava: If Malefic

You may develop misunderstandings with your own people. You may not be able to control your passions.

As third lord influencing first bhava: If Benefic

Due to your bold nature you want to stand on your own feet and earn livelihood by self-exertion. You are likely to become an expert in fine arts.

As third lord influencing first bhava: If Malefic

You may become vindictive sometimes. You may be sickly. You may be serving others.

As fourth lord influencing first bhava: If Benefic

You will be learned.

As fourth lord influencing first bhava: If Malefic

You will be scared to face public and address meetings.

As fifth lord influencing first bhava: If Benefic

You may take to some religious or ascetic order. You may command a number of servants. Temperamentally you would like to behave in such a manner as to make others feel happy.

As fifth lord influencing first bhava: If Malefic

You may develop a tendency to talk evil about one person to another person and thereby land with many enemies.

As sixth lord influencing first bhava: If Benefic

You will have a commanding personality.

As sixth lord influencing first bhava: If Malefic

You may suffer from diseases. You may not have a good temperament.

As seventh lord influencing first bhava: If Benefic

You will be capable of weighing pros and cons through your intelligence while undertaking any job.

As seventh lord influencing first bhava: If Malefic

You will be fond of travelling. You are likely to be sensual.

As eighth lord influencing first bhava: If Benefic

Your constitution may not be weak and you may not suffer from bodily complaints. Your behavioural pattern may not lead to the displeasure of your superiors and higher ups.

As eighth lord influencing first bhava: If Malefic

Your constitution may be weak and you may suffer from bodily complaints. Your behavioural pattern may lead to the displeasure of your superiors and higher ups.

As ninth lord influencing first bhava: If Benefic

You will be a self-made person earning money through your own efforts. Due to your generous instincts you will become famous.

As ninth lord influencing first bhava: If Malefic

You may not be a self-made person earning money through your own efforts. In spite of your generous instincts you may not become famous.

As tenth lord influencing first bhava: If Benefic

Your perseverance will lead you to rise in life through your self-employment or independent profession. You may become an established figure in your field of work. Due to your noble nature you may be engaged in social projects and charitable deeds and become renowned.

As tenth lord influencing first bhava: If Malefic

Your perseverance may not lead you to rise in life through your self-employment or independent profession. You may not become an established figure in your field of work. In spite of your noble nature you may not be engaged in social projects and charitable deeds nor become renowned.

As eleventh lord influencing first bhava: If Benefic

You will have good relations with brothers. You will lead a happy and prosperous life.

As eleventh lord influencing first bhava: If Malefic

You may not have good relations with brothers. You may not lead a very happy and prosperous life.

As twelfth lord influencing first bhava: If Benefic

You will talk nicely and sweetly and you are likely to have a handsome and charming personality.

As twelfth lord influencing first bhava: If Malefic

You may lack intelligence and become dull due to your weak constitution and feeble mind. You will be generally roaming about, may be to far-off places. You are likely to be miserly and short-sighted thereby developing hatred of others.

(II) AS DIFFERENT BHAVA LORDS INFLUENCING SECOND BHAVA

Wealth

As first lord influencing second bhava: If Benefic

You are likely to be wealthy because of more gains, your forethought and your ambitious nature. You will be well-disposed with money. There will be gains from business. You will not experience financial stress.

As first lord influencing second bhava: If Malefic

You are likely to lose wealth because of being teased or worried by enemies, being generous hearted and gladly discharging your duties towards your kith and kin.

As third lord influencing second bhava: If Benefic

You will get wealth with effort. You may make advances on the wealth of others. There will be a likelihood of getting wealth from the sources pertaining to your brothers and sisters.

As third lord influencing second bhava: If Malefic

You may lose your wealth by your mean and unscrupulous deeds.

As fourth lord influencing second bhava: If Benefic

You may inherit property from maternal grand-father's side. You may earn wealth by your courageous nature and also by your success in selling and buying lands. You will be highly fortunate.

As fourth lord influencing second bhava: If Malefic

You may not inherit property from maternal grandfather's side. You may not earn wealth by your courageous nature and also by your success in selling and buying lands. You may not be highly fortunate.

As fifth lord influencing second bhava: If Benefic

You will have aquisition of riches and gains from business. You may get money from a new job. You may gain in your wealth from government or king, children, speculation. Being learned, a good astrologer and author you may get your riches.

As fifth lord influencing second bhava: If Malefic

You are likely to lose your wealth through business, reverses in official life, misunderstandings, government displeasure, family troubles, speculation and cousins. Your generous nature will also give you some losses in your wealth.

As sixth lord influencing second bhava: If Benefic

You may become wealthy through your enemies and sometimes while suffering from diseases. You may get money by doing service and by getting loans.

As sixth lord influencing second bhava: If Malefic

You may lose wealth through enemies or by spending on your diseases. You are likely to spend your wealth to clear your debts.

As seventh lord influencing second bhava: If Benefic

You may get wealth from women or through marriage or by marrying a working person. Your partner may be from a rich family and may bring in much wealth to you. You are likely to succeed in good business partnership and gain in wealth. There is also a likelihood of gaining in wealth through agency in distant lands. The relations of your partner may also help you in your wealth.

As seventh lord influencing second bhava: If Malefic

Your wealth may be reduced through women or through your marriage. You may earn your wealth through unfair means. You will be inclined to be sensual and spend your money. Your partnership business may also give you some losses in your wealth.

As eighth lord influencing second bhava: If Benefic

You are likely to get legacies.

As eighth lord influencing second bhava: If Malefic

You may lose wealth through troubles and problems of all sorts including ill health. Your business may suffer losses and run into debts and you may lose your wealth.

As ninth lord influencing second bhava: If Benefic

You may acquire wealth from your rich and influential father. You are likely to get wealth through your family business or property.

As ninth lord influencing second bhava: If Malefic

You may ruin or destroy paternal property and lose wealth. Your resources and inheritance may dwindle on account of family squabbles and litigation.

As tenth lord influencing second bhava: If Benefic

You may work in an influential job and earn money. You may have many businesses and all your ventures may turn out successful and consequently you may be wealthy. You may rise well in life and make a lot of wealth.

As tenth lord influencing second bhava: If Malefic

You may lose wealth from family misunderstandings and various kinds of troubles. You may suffer losses and may be responsible for winding up the business.

As eleventh lord influencing second bhava: If Benefic

You may earn and get wealth through commercial concerns and banking business. Your business with friends may bring good profits. You may expect to get wealth from elder brothers and sisters. You may acquire much property and earn large sums of money.

As eleventh lord influencing second bhava: If Malefic

You may suffer loss of wealth through domestic bickerings and on account of friends. Your elder brothers and sisters also may cause some loss to your wealth.

As twelfth lord influencing second bhava: If Benefic

You will have financial stability. You may earn well by trading in pearls, rubies and other precious stones or you may acquire such precious stones. You will spend your money for good causes. The evil indications of financial losses will be greatly reduced.

As twelfth lord influencing second bhava: If Malefic

Your funds may dwindle on account of troubles from your extravagant brothers. You may engage in business but will not make much profit. You may take loans and get involved in nefarious activity and lose money. You may suffer financial losses.

(III) AS DIFFERENT BHAVA LORDS INFLUENCING THIRD BHAVA
Courage

As first lord influencing third bhava: If Benefic
You will be highly courageous.

As first lord influencing third bhava: If Malefic
You may not be courageous.

As second lord influencing third bhava: If Benefic
You will be brave.

As second lord influencing third bhava: If Malefic
   You may not be brave.

As fourth lord influencing third bhava: If Benefic
   You may be brave.

As fourth lord influencing third bhava: If Malefic
   You may not be brave.

As fifth lord influencing third bhava: If Benefic
   You will have courage due to strong mental personality.

As fifth lord influencing third bhava: If Malefic
   You may not have courage due to weak mental personality.

As sixth lord influencing third bhava: If Benefic
   You may not lose self-confidence.

As sixth lord influencing third bhava: If Malefic
   You may lose self-confidence.

As seventh lord influencing third bhava: If Benefic
   You may not lose courage.

As seventh lord influencing third bhava: If Malefic
   You may lose courage.

As eighth lord influencing third bhava: If Benefic
   You may not be beset by all sorts of fears and mental anguish.

As eighth lord influencing third bhava: If Malefic
   You may be beset by all sorts of fears and mental anguish.

As *ninth lord influencing third bhava: If Benefic*
You will be brave.

As *ninth lord influencing third bhava: If Malefic*
You may not be brave.

As *tenth lord influencing third bhava: If Benefic*
You may not become timid.

As *tenth lord influencing third bhava: If Malefic*
You may become timid due to your suffering from mental aberrations.

As *eleventh lord influencing third bhava: If Benefic*
You will be brave.

As *eleventh lord influencing third bhava: If Malefic*
You may be timid.

As *twelfth lord influencing third bhava: If Benefic*
You may not be timid and quiet.

As *twelfth lord influencing third bhava: If Malefic*
You will be timid and quiet.

(IV) AS DIFFERENT BHAVA LORDS INFLUENCING FOURTH BHAVA
Education

As *first lord influencing fourth bhava: If Benefic*
You will have acquaintance with learned men and discussions with them. You will get good education.

As *first lord influencing fourth bhava: If Malefic*
You may not have acquaintance with learned men and discussions with them. You may not get good education.

As second lord influencing fourth bhava: If Benefic

You may learn or be interested in fine arts, music or dancing.

As second lord influencing fourth bhava: If Malefic

You may not learn or be interested in fine arts, music or dancing.

As third lord influencing fourth bhava: If Benefic

You may be learned or interested in science or politics.

As third lord influencing fourth bhava: If Malefic

You may not be learned or interested in science or politics.

As fifth lord influencing fourth bhava: If Benefic

You will have successful education.

As fifth lord influencing fourth bhava: If Malefic

You may not have successful education.

As sixth lord influencing fourth bhava: If Benefic

You may not have breaks in education and you may not fail in examinations.

As sixth lord influencing fourth bhava: If Malefic

You may have breaks in education and you may fail in examinations.

As seventh lord influencing fourth bhava: If Benefic

You will have the benefit of high academic qualification. Your education may begin paying in foreign lands.

As seventh lord influencing fourth bhava: If Malefic

You may not have the benefit of high academic

qualification. Your education may not begin paying in foreign lands.

As eighth lord influencing fourth bhava: If Benefic
  Your education may go smooth.

As eighth lord influencing fourth bhava: If Malefic
  Your education may not go smooth.

As ninth lord influencing fourth bhava: If Benefic
  You will be learned. You may get foreign education.

As ninth lord influencing fourth bhava: If Malefic
  You may not be learned and may not get foreign education.

As tenth lord influencing fourth bhava: If Benefic
  You will be highly learned in various subjects. You will be famous for your learning.

As tenth lord influencing fourth bhava: If Malefic
  You may not be highly learned in various subjects. You may not be famous for your learning.

As eleventh lord influencing fourth bhava: If Benefic
  You will be renowned for your learning and scholarship of varied subjects. You will acquire excellent education. You will get awards and distinctions.

As eleventh lord influencing fourth bhava: If Malefic
  You may not be renowned for your learning and scholarship of varied subjects. You may not acquire excellent education. You may not get awards and distinctions.

As twelfth lord influencing fourth bhava: If Benefic
  You may have a chance of foreign education.

As twelfth lord influencing fourth bhava: If Malefic

You may not have a chance of foreign education.

Houses, Landed Property and Means of Conveyance

As first lord influencing fourth bhava: If Benefic

You will acquire considerable landed properties especially through maternal sources. You will possess houses and lands and vehicles. You will construct a new house.

As first lord influencing fourth bhava: If Malefic

You may not acquire considerable landed properties especially through maternal sources. You may not possess houses and lands and vehicles. You may not construct a new house.

As second lord influencing fourth bhava: If Benefic

You will have vehicles, houses. You may inherit property from mother or maternal grand-father.

As second lord influencing fourth bhava: If Malefic

You may lose your vehicles and lands.

As third lord influencing fourth bhava: If Benefic

You will acquire vehicles.

As third lord influencing fourth bhava: If Malefic

You may lose your lands and may have to live in houses of others.

As fifth lord influencing fourth bhava: If Benefic

You will acquire new conveyance and immovable property.

As fifth lord influencing fourth bhava: If Malefic

You may not acquire new conveyance and immovable property.

As sixth lord influencing fourth bhava: If Benefic

Your ancestral property may not be involved in debts. Your immovable properties may not be auctioned or lost to enemies.

As sixth lord influencing fourth bhava: If Malefic

Your ancestral property may be involved in debts. Your immovable properties may be auctioned or lost to enemies.

As seventh lord influencing fourth bhava: If Benefic

You will own many vehicles and obtain cars.

As seventh lord influencing fourth bhava: If Malefic

You may run into problems on account of vehicles.

As eighth lord influencing fourth bhava: If Benefic

You may not be beset with problems regarding your house, land and conveyance. Your lands and immovable property may not slip from your hands due to circumstances beyond your control. Your conveyance may not get lost or be destroyed.

As eighth lord influencing fourth bhava: If Malefic

You may be beset with problems regarding your house, land and conveyance. Your lands and immovable property may slip from your hands due to circumstances beyond your control. Your conveyance may get lost or be destroyed.

As ninth lord influencing fourth bhava: If Benefic

You will have landed properties and beautiful bungalows. You will inherit father's immovable properties. You will acquire many vehicles and lands.

As ninth lord influencing fourth bhava: If Malefic

You may not have vast landed properties and beautiful bungalows. You may not inherit father's immovable properties. You may not acquire many vehicles and lands.

As tenth lord influencing fourth bhava: If Benefic

You will have immovable properties, lands and buildings.

As tenth lord influencing fourth bhava: If Malefic

You may lose your lands.

As eleventh lord influencing fourth bhava: If Benefic

You will get profits through landed estates, rentals, and products of earth. You will gain through lands, vehicles and houses.

As eleventh lord influencing fourth bhava: If Malefic

You may not get profits through landed estates, rentals, and products of earth. You may not gain through lands, vehicles and houses.

As twelfth lord influencing fourth bhava: If Benefic

You will have substantial immovable property and you may own your own conveyance.

As twelfth lord influencing fourth bhava: If Malefic

Your conveyance may give trouble. You may get trouble on account of properties which may get lost or be destroyed.

Happiness

As first lord influencing fourth bhava: If Benefic

You will get respect from friends and relatives. You will have acquaintance with learned men and discussion with them. You will form new friendships. You will be rich. You will get happiness from parents. You will be happy.

As first lord influencing fourth bhava: If Malefic

You may not construct new houses. You may not get respect from friends and relatives. You may not have acquaintance with learned men and discussion with them. You may not form new friendships. You may not be very rich. You may not get much happiness from parents. You may not be happy.

As second lord influencing fourth bhava: If Benefic

You will get unexpected wealth through mining, lotteries, competitions and unexpected sources. You will be benefited by your sisters and by learning fine arts, music or dancing. You may earn well as an automobile dealer or agent or agriculturist or landlord or commission agent. You will be benefited by maternal uncles. You will get money through mother or maternal grandfather. You will have inheritance, acquisition of lands, cars, houses and financial advantages through literary and intellectual activities.

As second lord influencing fourth bhava: If Malefic

You may get losses through dealings in lands, vehicles, lotteries etc.

As third lord influencing fourth bhava: If Benefic

You will be learned and rich. Your brothers will shine well. You will become head of political or scientific organisation. You will have vehicles. Life will be happy on the whole.

As third lord influencing fourth bhava: If Malefic

You may lose lands and property and your crops may be destroyed. Your partner may not be even-tempered. Your brothers may cause unpleasantness and losses. Your family may break up and brothers may separate. You may sustain an accident by falling from a vehicle.

As fifth lord influencing fourth bhava: If Benefic

You may become an adviser to ruler or his preceptor.

You will get happiness from ruling class. Your mother
may live long. You may have a few sons. You will
acquire political power.

As fifth lord influencing fourth bhava: If Malefic

You may face wrath of ruler and suffer displeasure.
You may not have any sons and may be conferred with
only daughters. There is likelihood of loss of issues or
separation from children.

As sixth lord influencing fourth bhava: If Benefic

You may not have breaks in education and you may
not fail in examinations. You may live in a good
building. You may not quarrel with your mother or may
separate from her. Your ancestral property may not be
involved in debts. You may work in good position and
lead a very comfortable life. You may not have a
troublesome home and your domestic affairs may be
smooth. You may not get troubles through servants.
Your immovable property may not be auctioned or lost
to enemies. You may not meet with accidents by falling
from vehicles. Your mother may not suffer.

As sixth lord influencing fourth bhava: If Malefic

You may have breaks in education and you may fail
in examinations. You may not live in a good building.
You may quarrel with your mother or may separate
from her. Your ancestral property may get involved in
debts. You may not work in good position. You may not
lead a very comfortable life. You may have a
troublesome home and your domestic affairs may not
be smooth. You may get troubles through servants. Your
immovable property may be auctioned or lost to
enemies. You may meet with accidents by falling from
vehicles. Your mother may suffer.

As seventh lord influencing fourth bhava: If Benefic

You will have a lucky and happy married life with
good partner, children and comforts. You will have

domestic harmony. You will celebrate auspicious events like marriages, engagement etc. You may have benefit of high academic qualification. Your education may begin paying mostly in foreign lands. You may obtain vehicles.

As seventh lord influencing fourth bhava: If Malefic

Your domestic harmony may be spoiled on account of immature partner. Your partner's temperament may not be good. Your mother may pass through a crisis. You may run into problems on account of vehicles.

As eighth lord influencing fourth bhava: If Benefic

You may not have domestic bickerings. Your financial and other problems may not increase. Your mother's health may not suffer and cause great concern. You may not be beset with problems connected with house, land and conveyance. Your pets may not get diseases or die. You may not be forced to seek fortune abroad where you may not meet with all sorts of troubles and losses. You may not have displeasure of superiors and reverses in profession.

As eighth lord influencing fourth bhava: If Malefic

You may have domestic bickerings. Your financial and other problems may increase. Your mother's health may suffer and cause great concern. You may be beset with problems connected with house, land and conveyance. Your pets may get diseases or die. You may be forced to seek fortune abroad where you may meet with troubles and losses. You may have displeasure of superiors and reverses in profession.

As ninth lord influencing fourth bhava: If Benefic

You may have landed properties and beautiful bungalows. You may earn through estate and land dealings. Your mother may be rich and fortunate. You may inherit father's immovable properties. You may acquire means of conveyance and lands. You may become a president or ruler of a country. You will be learned and may become head of centre of learning or research. You will be very happy.

As ninth lord influencing fourth bhava: If Malefic

You may have domestic unhappiness. Your life may be crossed by miseries due to hard-hearted father or disharmony between parents. Your mother may be living separately from your father.

As tenth lord influencing fourth bhava: If Benefic

You may be lucky and highly learned in various subjects. You will be famous both for your learning and generosity. You will be respected wherever you go and receive royal honours and favour. You will wield great political authority as president or head of government. You will get income from lands and buildings. You may head an educational or research organisation. You will gain fame through immovable properties. You will enjoy mental happiness.

As tenth lord influencing fourth bhava: If Malefic

You may lose your lands and be forced to take to life of servitude. You may take wrong decisions which may affect your reputation adversely. You may have mental vacillation.

As eleventh lord influencing fourth bhava: If Benefic

You will profit through landed estates, rentals and products of earth. You will be renowned for your learning and scholarship of various subjects. You will live in comfort and enjoy all joys in life. You will have devoted and charming partner. You will acquire excellent education. You will become famous and will get many awards and distinctions. You will gain through lands, vehicles, and houses. You will have domestic harmony and bliss. You will be very happy.

As eleventh lord influencing fourth bhava: if Malefic

You may not profit through landed estates, rentals and products of earth. You may not be renowned for your learning and scholarship of various subjects. You may not live in comfort and enjoy all joys in life. You may not have devoted and charming partner. You may not acquire excellent education. You may not become famous and may not get many awards and distinctions. You may not gain through lands, vehicles, and houses. You may not have domestic harmony and bliss. You may not be very happy.

As twelfth lord influencing fourth bhava: If Benefic

You may own immovable property and conveyance. You may be happy.

As twelfth lord influencing fourth bhava: If Malefic

Your mother may suffer some crisis in life. You may have mental restlessness and unnecessary worry. You may have enmity with your relatives. You may be suffering constant harassment from landlord. You may own your own conveyance but it may give trouble. You may get trouble on account of property which may get lost or destroyed.

(V) AS DIFFERENT BHAVA LORDS INFLUENCING FIFTH BHAVA
Children

As first lord influencing fifth bhava: If Benefic

There will be birth of a child.

As first lord influencing fifth bhava: If Malefic

You may not have much happiness from children.

As second lord influencing fifth bhava: If Benefic

Your children will prosper and you will get their help and financial assistance.

As second lord influencing fifth bhava: If Malefic

You may be hating family. You may not be spending money even on children.

As third lord influencing fifth bhava: If Benefic

Much pleasure may be derived from children. Friction will not prevail in domestic life.

As third lord influencing fifth bhava: If Malefic

Much pleasure may not be derived from children. Friction may prevail in domestic life.

As fourth lord influencing fifth bhava: If Benefic

You will be loved and respected by children.

As fourth lord influencing fifth bhava: If Malefic

You may not be loved and respected by children.

As sixth lord influencing fifth bhava: If Benefic

Your children may not frequently suffer ill health. You may not develop enmity with your children.

As sixth lord influencing fifth bhava: If Malefic

Your children may suffer ill health. You may develop enmity with your children.

As seventh lord influencing fifth bhava: If Benefic

Your children will be happy and wealthy.

As seventh lord influencing fifth bhava: If Malefic

There may be no children or mishaps may befall on your children. You may have female progeny. You may get into crisis through the conduct of your partner.

As eighth lord influencing fifth bhava: If Benefic

Your children may not get into trouble and they may not commit some crime and invite situations that could affect your reputation. Your child may not fall sick and suffer thereby.

As eighth lord influencing fifth bhava: If Malefic

Your children may get into trouble and they may commit some crime and invite situations that could affect your reputation. Your child may fall sick and suffer thereby causing grief to you.

As ninth lord influencing fifth bhava: If Benefic

Your children may be very fortunate in life and enjoy success and distinction. Your children will distinguish themselves in academics and bring much happiness to you. Your children may become very famous and earn governmental patronage. Your children will also prosper very well and enjoy all kinds of luxuries.

As ninth lord influencing fifth bhava: If Malefic

Your children may not be very fortunate in life and enjoy success and distinction. Your children may not distinguish themselves in academics and bring much happiness to you. Your children may not become very famous and earn governmental patronage. Your children may not also prosper very well and enjoy all kinds of luxuries.

As tenth lord influencing fifth bhava: If Benefic

You will have good children.

As tenth lord influencing fifth bhava: If Malefic

You may not have good children.

As eleventh lord influencing fifth bhava: If Benefic

You will have children who will come up well in life.

As eleventh lord influencing fifth bhava: If Malefic

You may have mental anguish, anxiety and monetary loss on account of your children.

As twelfth lord influencing fifth bhava: If Benefic

You may not expect either difficulty to beget progeny or unhappiness from children. Your children may not face trouble and you may not suffer much pain on their account.

As twelfth lord influencing fifth bhava: If Malefic

You can expect either difficulty to beget progeny or unhappiness from children. Your children may face trouble and you will suffer pain on their account.

(VI) AS DIFFERENT BHAVA LORDS INFLUENCING SIXTH BHAVA
Diseases

As first lord influencing sixth bhava: If Benefic

You may not suffer from physical ailments. You may not get wounds and may not have physical distress.

As first lord influencing sixth bhava: If Malefic

You may suffer from physical ailments such as wounds and may have physical distress sometimes.

As second lord influencing sixth bhava: If Benefic

You may not suffer from diseases or defects in arms and thighs.

As second lord influencing sixth bhava: If Malefic

You may suffer from defects in arms and thighs sometimes.

As third lord influencing sixth bhava: If Benefic

You may not fall ill and suffer from diseases. You may not get ear trouble.

As third lord influencing sixth bhava: If Malefic

You may fall ill and suffer from ear trouble sometimes.

As fourth lord influencing sixth bhava: If Benefic
You may not suffer from diseases.

As fourth lord influencing sixth bhava: If Malefic
You may suffer from physical ailments sometimes.

As fifth lord influencing sixth bhava: If Benefic
You may not have any diseases.

As fifth lord influencing sixth bhava: If Malefic
You may suffer from ailments sometimes.

As seventh lord influencing sixth bhava: If Benefic
You may not suffer from impotency and other diseases. Your partner may not be sickly.

As seventh lord influencing sixth bhava: If Malefic
You may suffer from impotency sometimes. Your partner may be sickly.

As eighth lord influencing sixth bhava: If Benefic
You may not suffer from ill health.

As eighth lord influencing sixth bhava: If Malefic
You may suffer from ill health sometimes.

As ninth lord influencing sixth bhava: If Benefic
You may not have a sickly father.

As ninth lord influencing sixth bhava: If Malefic
You may have a sickly father.

As tenth lord influencing sixth bhava: If Benefic
You will be generally healthy.

As tenth lord influencing sixth bhava: If Malefic
You may not be generally healthy.

As eleventh lord influencing sixth bhava: If Benefic
You will be generally healthy.

As eleventh lord influencing sixth bhava: If Malefic
You may not be generally healthy.

As twelfth lord influencing sixth bhava: If Benefic
You will be healthy and you will have handsome physique.

As twelfth lord influencing sixth bhava: If Malefic
You may not be healthy and you may not have handsome physique.

Enemies

As first lord influencing sixth bhava: If Benefic
You will vanquish your enemies. You will succeed in litigation.

As first lord influencing sixth bhava: If Malefic
You may have enmity with rulers and mis-understandings with cousins.

As second lord influencing sixth bhava: If Benefic
You may get income from enemies and earn through litigation.

As second lord influencing sixth bhava: If Malefic
You may incur enmity of moneyed people. You may have misunderstandings and troubles with friends and relatives. You may have expenditure from enemies.

As third lord influencing sixth bhava: If Benefic
You will be benefited by maternal uncles.

As third lord influencing sixth bhava: If Malefic
Your brother may become enemy. You may hate your

brothers and relatives and may get difficulties from them.

As fourth lord influencing sixth bhava: If Benefic

You will get happiness from mother.

As fourth lord influencing sixth bhava: If Malefic

You may have enmities of rulers and mother. You may have troubles from authorities. Your short temper, evil thoughts and intentions may increase your enemies.

As fifth lord influencing sixth bhava: If Benefic

You may get benefits from maternal uncles.

As fifth lord influencing sixth bhava: If Malefic

You may have enmity with your children. You may be a victim of ruler's wrath.

As seventh lord influencing sixth bhava: If Benefic

You may not have troubles from law suits. Your wife may not be jealous by nature, denying happiness from marriage.

As seventh lord influencing sixth bhava: If Malefic

You may have troubles from law suits. Your partner may be jealous by nature, denying happiness from marriage.

As eighth lord influencing sixth bhava: If Benefic

You will be able to overcome all troubles and enemies. Attempts made by ill-wishes of enemies may not harm you.

As eighth lord influencing sixth bhava: If Malefic

You may get into trouble from courts and police.

As ninth lord influencing sixth bhava: If Benefic

Your attempts to make your fortune may not be frustrated through litigation involving your father. You may not be drawn into endless litigation.

As ninth lord influencing sixth bhava: If Malefic

Your attempts to make your fortune may be frustrated through litigation involving your father. You may be drawn into endless litigation.

As tenth lord influencing sixth bhava: If Benefic

You may not be exposed to criminal actions and face imprisonment.

As tenth lord influencing sixth bhava: If Malefic

You may be exposed to criminal actions and face imprisonment.

As eleventh lord influencing sixth bhava: If Benefic

You may gain money through litigations. No amount of skill or treachery on part of ill-wishes of your enemies can do you any harm.

As eleventh lord influencing sixth bhava: If Malefic

You may not gain money through litigations. Some amount of skill or treachery on part of ill-wishes of your enemies may cause you harm.

As twelfth lord influencing sixth bhava: If Benefic

You will vanquish your enemies. You may become involved in litigation which may come to an end to your advantage.

As twelfth lord influencing sixth bhava: If Malefic

You may have troubles by adverse criticism and enemies.

Debts

As first lord influencing sixth bhava: If Benefic
Your debts will be liquidated.

As first lord influencing sixth bhava: If Malefic
You may take loans for your personal purpose sometimes.

As second lord influencing sixth bhava: If Benefic
You may not be indebted due to expenditure from enemies.

As second lord influencing sixth bhava: If Malefic
You may be indebted due to expenditure from enemies.

As third lord influencing sixth bhava: If Benefic
You may not get into debts due to your younger brothers or sisters.

As third lord influencing sixth bhava: If Malefic
You may have debts due to your younger brothers or sisters.

As fourth lord influencing sixth bhava: If Benefic
You may not get into debts due to your house, property or vehicles.

As fourth lord influencing sixth bhava: If Malefic
You may be indebted due to your house, property or vehicles.

As fifth lord influencing sixth bhava: If Benefic
You may not be indebted due to your children.

As fifth lord influencing sixth bhava: If Malefic
You may have debts due to your children.

As seventh lord influencing sixth bhava: If Benefic

Your debts may not crop up due to trouble from law suits. You may not have losses through theft and deceit.

As seventh lord influencing sixth bhava: If Malefic

Your debts may crop up due to trouble from law suits. You may have losses through theft and deceit.

As eighth lord influencing sixth bhava: If Benefic

You may not suffer loss of money through theft and trouble through court and police and you may not land in debts.

As eighth lord influencing sixth bhava: If Malefic

You may suffer loss of money through theft and trouble through court and police and you may land in debts.

As ninth lord influencing sixth bhava: If Benefic

Your attempts to make fortune may not be frustrated through litigation involving your father or debts contracted by him. You may not contract debts and be drawn into endless litigation.

As ninth lord influencing sixth bhava: If Malefic

Your attempts to make fortune may be frustrated through litigation involving your father or debts contracted by him. You may contract debts and be drawn into endless litigation.

As tenth lord influencing sixth bhava: If Benefic

You may not have debts for your professional purpose.

As tenth lord influencing sixth bhava: If Malefic

You may have debts for your professional purpose.

As eleventh lord influencing sixth bhava: If Benefic

You may not be indebted due to expenditure on medical bills and law suits. You may not have debts due to your elder brothers or sisters.

As eleventh lord influencing sixth bhava: If Malefic

You may be indebted due to expenditure on medical bills and law suits. You may get into debts due to your elder brothers or sisters.

As twelfth lord influencing sixth bhava: If Benefic

You may not be indebted due to expenditure.

As twelfth lord influencing sixth bhava: If Malefic

You may be indebted due to expenditure.

(VII) AS DIFFERENT BHAVA LORDS INFLUENCING SEVENTH BHAVA
Marriage And Marital Relationship

As first lord influencing seventh bhava: If Benefic

You may have marriage, if unmarried.

As first lord influencing seventh bhava: If Malefic

Your partner may suffer. You may a puppet in the hands of parent-in-law.

As second lord influencing seventh bhava: If Benefic

You will benefit by contact with others. You will gain after marriage. You will get good wealth from father-in-law.

As second lord influencing seventh bhava: If Malefic

Laxity of good temperament may mark your partner. There may be loss from sickness of partner.

As third lord influencing seventh bhava: If Benefic

Your marriage union may not be unfortunate. You

may not land in second marriage.

As third lord influencing seventh bhava: If Malefic
Your marriage union may be unfortunate.

As fourth lord influencing seventh bhava: If Benefic
You will be generally happy.

As fourth lord influencing seventh bhava: If Malefic
You may not be generally happy.

As fifth lord influencing seventh bhava: If Benefic
You may have a charming personality and marriage may take place if not already married and a new family may be set up.

As fifth lord influencing seventh bhava: If Malefic
You may not have a charming personality and marriage may not take place, if not already married.

As sixth lord influencing seventh bhava: If Benefic
You may marry a person from relations' family.

As sixth lord influencing seventh bhava: If Malefic
Your partner's temperament may not be good. You may have a sickly partner. There may be troubles from disrespectful persons.

As eighth lord influencing seventh bhava: If Benefic
Your partner may not suffer ill health.

As eighth lord influencing seventh bhava: If Malefic
Your partner may suffer ill health.

As ninth lord influencing seventh bhava: If Benefic
You may get a noble and lucky life partner. You may get every kind of sensual pleasures. Fortune booms

after marriage. Your partner may hail from a rich and respectable family.

As *ninth lord influencing seventh bhava: If Malefic*

You may not get a noble and lucky life partner. You may not get every kind of sensual pleasures. Fortune may not boom after marriage. Your partner may not hail from a rich and respectable family.

As *tenth lord influencing seventh bhava: If Benefic*

You may get a mature married partner who may assist you in your work.

As *tenth lord influencing seventh bhava: If Malefic*

You may not get a mature married partner who may assist you in your work.

As *eleventh lord influencing seventh bhava: If Benefic*

You may marry a rich and influential person.

As *eleventh lord influencing seventh bhava: If Malefic*

You may marry more than once. You may carry liaison with persons of ill-repute. You are likely to indulge in immoral activities. You and your partner may seek to earn money by questionable means. Your partner may desert you.

As *twelfth lord influencing seventh bhava: If Benefic*

Your partner may survive a crisis.

As *twelfth lord influencing seventh bhava: If Malefic*

Your partner may not come from a rich family. Your married life may not be very happy or may end in separation and later on you may take to asceticism. Your partner may have to face some danger or the other. Your partner may live abroad. Your married life may be marred by slanderous talk.

(VIII) AS DIFFERENT BHAVA LORDS INFLUENCING EIGHTH BHAVA
Longevity

As first lord influencing eighth bhava: If Benefic
You may have a peaceful and sudden end.

As first lord influencing eighth bhava: If Malefic
You may not have a peaceful and sudden end.

As third lord influencing eighth bhava: If Benefic
You may not have trouble on account of disease.

As third lord influencing eighth bhava: If Malefic
You may have trouble on account of disease sometimes.

As fourth lord influencing eighth bhava: If Benefic
There may not be a likelihood of suffering.

As fourth lord influencing eighth bhava: If Malefic
There is a likelihood of suffering.

As fifth lord influencing eighth bhava: If Benefic
You may not have lung troubles and you may not be peevish.

As fifth lord influencing eighth bhava: If Malefic
You may have lung troubles and you may be peevish.

As sixth lord influencing eighth bhava: If Benefic
You will have redemption from ailments and you will have good span of life.

As sixth lord influencing eighth bhava: If Malefic
You will have disease and distress of mind.

As seventh lord influencing eighth bhava: If Benefic
You may not meet with an accident. You may not suffer at a distant place.

As seventh lord influencing eighth bhava: If Malefic
You may meet with an accident. You may suffer at a distant place.

As ninth lord influencing eighth bhava: If Benefic
You may have good life span.

As ninth lord influencing eighth bhava: If Malefic
You may not have very good long life span.

As tenth lord influencing eighth bhava: If Benefic
You may have good life span.

As tenth lord influencing eighth bhava: If Malefic
You may not have good long life span.

As eleventh lord influencing eighth bhava: If Benefic
You may have good life span.

As eleventh lord influencing eighth bhava: If Malefic
You may not nave very good long life span.

As twelfth lord influencing eighth bhava: If Benefic
You may have good life span.

As twelfth lord influencing eighth bhava: If Malefic
You may not have very good long life span.

(IX) AS DIFFERENT BHAVA LORDS INFLUENCING
NINTH BHAVA
Prosperity

As first lord influencing ninth bhava: If Benefic

You will be generally fortunate. You will be protector of others. You will be a good orator. You will get happiness on account of wife and children. You will inherit good ancestral and paternal property. You will be rich. Your father will be famous, philanthrophic and god fearing. Your father will be happy. You will do religious acts and will be devoted to your parents and elders. You will have influx of wealth and expenditure on desirable and deserving causes.

As first lord influencing ninth bhava: If Malefic

You may develop atheistic tendencies. There may be litigation with regard to ancestral property.

As second lord influencing ninth bhava: If Benefic

You will have wealth and become happy. You will have good inheritance. There will also be benefits through different sources. You will have financial gains from father, voyages and shipping. Your father will have very good fortune. You will be skilful. You will earn righteously. You will cultivate the friendship of learned men and will have the opportunity of holding intellectual discussions with them.

As second lord influencing ninth bhava: If Malefic

You may have ill health sometimes but you may recover.

As third lord influencing ninth bhava: If Benefic

Your fortune will improve after marriage. Your brother will inherit ancestral property and you yourself will get benefited by your brother. Your brother will become fortunate and prosperous. Your father's property will increase. You will become religious.

As third lord influencing ninth bhava: If Malefic

You may have misunderstandings with your father.

As fourth lord influencing ninth bhava: If Benefic

You will be generally fortunate, favouring happiness in regard to father and prosperity. You may get sudden fortune and wealth.

As fourth lord influencing ninth bhava: If Malefic

You may get contrary and unfavourable results pertaining to your prosperity against your expectations.

As fifth lord influencing ninth bhava: If Benefic

You may become a teacher or preceptor. You may renovate ancient temples, wells, choultries and gardens. One of your sons may attain distinction as orator or an author. You will have happiness from father during childhood. There will be inheritance of paternal or ancestral property. You may get a good administrative or honorary post. Your father will be in the good books of the ruling classes. There will be unexpected dawn of property and fortune. You may become author of books. There will be acquisition of wealth through a new administrative job, your own occupation or through female sources.

As fifth lord influencing ninth bhava: If Malefic

You may earn the divine wrath and consequent destruction of fortune.

As sixth lord influencing ninth bhava: If Benefic

Your father may become a judge. Your maternal uncle will become highly fortunate. There will be benefits from cousins.

As sixth lord influencing ninth bhava: If Malefic

There may be misunderstandings between you and your father. You may be ungrateful towards preceptors and engage in irreligious deeds. You may have misfortunes through relatives. You may do sinful acts. You may not be very rich.

As seventh lord influencing ninth bhava: If Benefic

Your father may live abroad while you make fortune in foreign lands. You will get an accomplished partner who will enable you to lead a righteous life. Your fortune comes through marriage. You will undertake pilgrimages and give away much money in charities. There will be inclination to be pious and virtuous. You will amass a fortune through just and honest means. You will acquire property and enjoy every kind of comfort. Your married partner will be a noble person and lead you on a righteous path. Your work will prosper abroad. Fame and distinction will follow you.

As seventh lord influencing ninth bhava: If Malefic

Your father may suffer. You married partner may drag you from right course of life and you may waste away your wealth. Your partner may lead you astray and away from your duties. You may harbour ill-will and hatred for others and indulge in wicked deeds. Evil results may be intensified.

As eighth lord influencing ninth bhava: If Benefic

You will acquire father's property. Your relations with your father will be harmonious.

As eighth lord influencing ninth bhava: If Malefic

You may lose your father's property. Mis-understandings with father may arise. Your father may suffer. You may suffer all kinds of hardships, misery and unhappiness. Your friends and kinsmen may desert you while your superiors may find fault with you.

As tenth lord influencing ninth bhava: If Benefic

You will become a spiritual stalwart and you will be a beacon of light to spiritual seekers. You will be generally fortunate and well-to-do. You will follow a hereditary profession as that of a teacher, preceptor or healer. Your father will have great influence on you. You will be dutiful and do many charitable deeds. You will lead a righteous life. You will earn by fair means and will become well-known for your sense of fair play and justice. You may embark on a life of spiritual sadhana (exercise to attain perfection). You will work for government or take up medical profession. You may work as an auditor, banker in government or in some big undertaking. You may acquire immovable property from your father. You may go abroad for education and do research. You will prosper along with your father. You may get gold, precious stones, conveyance and all kinds of comforts. You may head an industrial or other concern employing labour.

As tenth lord influencing ninth bhava: If Malefic

You may be forced to work in a low position.

As eleventh lord influencing ninth bhava: If Benefic

You will inherit a large paternal fortune. You will be very lucky in life. You will possess many houses, means of conveyance and every other kind of luxury. You will be religious-minded and disseminate religious literature. You will be charitable and set up charitable institutions. You will have an exalted and aristocratic father and background. You will hail from a rich family and will continue the family business extending it beyond expectations. You will have a colourful social life and move on equal terms with rulers and other dignitaries. Your regard for religion will increase and you will be victorious and of good conduct. Foreign collaborations will bring you both distinction and money.

As eleventh lord influencing ninth bhava: If Malefic

You may not inherit a large paternal fortune. You may not be very lucky in life. You may not possess many houses, means of conveyance and every other kind of luxury. You may not be religiously minded and disseminate religious literature. You may not be charitable and set up charitable institutions. You may not have an exalted and aristocratic father and background. You may not hail from a rich family and may not continue the family business extending it beyond expectations. You may not have a colourful social life and move on equal terms with rulers and other dignitaries. Your regard for religion may not increase nor will you be victorious and of good conduct. Foreign collaborations may not bring you both distinction and money.

As twelfth lord influencing ninth bhava: If Benefic

You may reside abroad and get prosperous. You may acquire much property in foreign lands. You will be honest, generous and large-hearted. You will be interested in physical culture. You will have a steady career. You will have interest in piety and lead a virtuous life.

As twelfth lord influencing ninth bhava: If Malefic

You may not have any spiritual leanings. You may not be liking your partner, friends and preceptors. You are likely to separate from your father. You may have a loss of job and luck. Your material prosperity may be on a low keel.

(X) AS DIFFERENT BHAVA LORDS INFLUENCING TENTH BHAVA
Profession

As first lord influencing tenth bhava: If Benefic

You will have professional success. You may be a research scholar or specialist in a branch of knowledge. '

As first lord influencing tenth bhava: If Malefic

You may not have professional success. You may not be a research scholar or a specialist in a branch of knowledge.

As second lord influencing tenth bhava: If Benefic

You will earn by your own exertions. You will take to number of avocations. You will do business or take to agriculture and also engage yourself in philosophical lectures and dissertations and thereby benefit financially. You will get government favours. You will secure high political or administrative position and emoluments consistent with office. You will earn huge profits as a business person. You may become a diplomat. You will be well-versed in intrigue and hypocrisy.

As second lord influencing tenth bhava: If Malefic

You may have loss from every source. You may abuse your position and cause pain to others. You may exhort money by way of bribes. You may have reversals and losses.

As third lord influencing tenth bhava: If Benefic

You will gain from journeys connected with profession. Your brother may attain distinction in political fields. You may become rich.

As third lord influencing tenth bhava: If Malefic

You may meet with frustrations and disappointments. Your daily mode of life may be upset. You may become immoral and commit sins. Your brothers may take to questionable means of earning money.

As fourth lord influencing tenth bhava: If Benefic

You will have political success. You may be an expert chemist. You will vanquish your enemies and make your personality felt by the world. You may become a minister or high-placed government servant. There will be access to wealth through trade and business.

As fourth lord influencing tenth bhava: If Malefic

There is a possibility of loss of your reputation.

As fifth lord influencing tenth bhava: If Benefic

You will earn goodwill of rulers or government. You will construct temples and perform religious sacrifices. You may join the crime investigation department. You will acquire kingdom or become head of state or a minister if a politician or may reach the highest position if in government. You will have palmy days as a businessman. If agriculturist, you will earn enormous profits in your own avocations.

As fifth lord influencing tenth bhava: If Malefic

You may face wrath of rulers or government. You may get contrary results regarding your prosperity beyond your expectations. You may not be generally very prosperous.

As sixth lord influencing tenth bhava: If Benefic

Evil results regarding your prosperity will be lessened. You may be moderately prosperous.

As sixth lord influencing tenth bhava: If Malefic

Your day to day professional activities may be dislocated. You may have low life. You may take to occupations considered low and degrading by current social values. You will incur displeasure of government or your superiors. You may become a victim of calumny (defamation and scandal).

As seventh lord influencing tenth bhava: If Benefic

You may flourish in a profession abroad or your career may involve constant travelling. Your married partner will also be employed and contribute to your income and may help in the advancement of your career. You will gain much fame and reputation abroad. Your profession will flourish well and you will obtain distinction in your field of your activity.

As seventh lord influencing tenth bhava: If Malefic

Your married partner may be avaricious and overambitious but without sufficient capacity and consequently your career may suffer and deteriorate. You may expect contrary results in respect of profession.

As eighth lord influencing tenth bhava: If Benefic

You may have unexpected gains due to the death of the superiors or elders. Evil influences on your prosperity will be greatly reduced.

As eighth lord influencing tenth bhava: If Malefic

You may have slow advancement in your career. You may face obstacles and impediments in your activities. You may be superceded by your subordinates and your merit may go unnoticed. You may resort to deceit and unrighteous means to gain your ends. Your thinking may be clouded and your actions may invite the wrath of the government or the law. Your reputation may suffer.

As ninth lord influencing tenth bhava: If Benefic

You will become famous and powerful. You will be generous and occupy posts of authority. You will earn wealth and acquire every kind of comfort and luxury. Your means of livelihood would be righteous. You will be a law-abiding citizen. You will be settled in your career and lead a successful life. You will do charitable deeds. You may earn much wealth through your service to government. You will be honoured many times.

As ninth lord influencing tenth bhava: If Malefic

You may lose your job. If in profession, you may earn the wrath of people and may be forced to close down your practice. You may lead an unrighteous life and seek to earn through illegal and shady means. You may suffer punishment by the ruler or government. You may not have very good prosperity.

As eleventh lord influencing tenth bhava: If Benefic

You will prosper well in your business and will earn good profits. Your elder brother may also help you in your business. You will earn some prize money for your original contribution to the subject of your study or profession. You will earn through fair means. You will have a highly successful and distinguished career. You will have more than one occupation.

As eleventh lord influencing tenth bhava: If Malefic

You may earn through foul means. You may become powerful and rich but you may be unscrupulous, indulging in every kind of despicable act to achieve your ends. You may suffer repercussions. You may lose your wealth and power.

As twelfth lord influencing tenth bhava: If Benefic

You may reside abroad and prosper. You may be interested in physical culture.

As twelfth lord influencing tenth bhava: If Malefic

You may be detached and you may develop spirituality.

(XI) AS DIFFERENT BHAVA LORDS INFLUENCING ELEVENTH BHAVA
Gains and Income

As first lord influencing eleventh bhava: If Benefic

If a businessman you will gain in business. You will not experience financial straits. You owe your prosperity to your elder brother. You will earn enormous business profits. You will get much gain from trade.

As first lord influencing eleventh bhava: If Malefic

If a businessman, you may not gain in business. You may experience financial straits. You may not owe your prosperity to your elder brother. You may not earn enormous business profits. You may not get much gain from trade.

As second lord influencing eleventh bhava: If Benefic

You will earn considerable wealth. You may earn by lending money or as a banker or by running a boarding house. You will gain from different means.

As Second lord influencing eleventh bhava: If Malefic

You may not earn considerable wealth. You may not earn by lending money or as a banker or by running a boarding house. You may not gain from different means.

As third lord influencing eleventh bhava: If Benefic

You will have earnings without efforts. Generally favourable results will be provided.

As third lord influencing eleventh bhava: If Malefic

You may not have earnings without efforts. Generally favourable results may not be provided.

As fourth lord influencing eleventh bhava: If Benefic

You will be selfmade. You will have success in selling and buying cattle and lands. You will earn in trade and commerce.

As fourth lord influencing eleventh bhava: If Malefic

You may not be selfmade. You may not have success in selling and buying cattle and lands. You may not earn in trade and commerce.

As fifth lord influencing eleventh bhava: If Benefic

You may get benefits from children and success in all your undertakings. You will become rich and learned. You may have children. You may become an author. You may acquire riches and gain from business. You will gain through sea products or ship-building. You will gain through your children or government sources or elder brother. You may acquire a new job. You will have immense wealth and fortune will flow in.

As fifth lord influencing eleventh bhava: If Malefic

You may get losses in business. You may have reversals in official life. You may get disappointments, financial troubles, misunderstandings and upheavals.

As sixth lord influencing eleventh bhava: If Benefic

You will gain from maternal uncle.

As sixth lord influencing eleventh bhava: If Malefic

You may not be very rich and may not have comfortable life. You may be suffering on account of convictions. Your gains in business, agriculture or your occupation in general may be below normal.

As seventh lord influencing eleventh bhava: If Benefic

Your married partner will hail from a rich background or bring in much wealth. You will fare well in trade and partnership business. Your business may expand well and even spread abroad.

As seventh lord influencing eleventh bhava: If Malefic

Your married partner may not hail from a rich background or bring in much wealth. You may not fare well in trade and partnership business. Your business may not expand well and spread abroad.

As eighth lord influencing eleventh bhava: If Benefic

You will get help from friends and elder brother to overcome troubles.

As eighth lord influencing eleventh bhava: If Malefic

Your business may suffer losses and run into debts.

As ninth lord influencing eleventh bhava: If Benefic

You will be rich. You will have powerful and influential friends. Your father will be a well-known and well-placed man. You will prosper in family business.

As ninth lord influencing eleventh bhava: If Malefic

Your unfaithful friends may destroy your wealth through selfish scheming and fraud. You may be forced to beg for survival.

As tenth lord influencing eleventh bhava: If Benefic

You will earn riches. You will be fortunate in every respect. You will do meritorious deeds. You will give employment to many persons and will be endowed with a high sense of humour. You will have many powerful friends in government and upper classes. You will become rich and prosperous. You will have many kinds of business and all your ventures will turn out successful. You will be a popular figure in social circles. You will have men at your command. You will possess many mansions.

As tenth lord influencing eleventh bhava: If Malefic

Your friends may turn out enemies and cause you every sort of hardship and worry.

As twelfth lord influencing eleventh bhava: If Benefic

You may earn through trading in pearls, rubies and other precious stones.

As twelfth lord influencing eleventh bhava: If Malefic

You may engage in business but may not make much profit. You may have few friends and many enemies. Your funds may dwindle on account of invalid and extravagant brothers. You may have financial setbacks. Your trade may bring losses. You may have loss of money through theft, fire or accident. If you are in business, you will have loss due to misunderstanding with elder brother or partners who are in business. Your wealth may be dissipated by children.

(XII) AS DIFFERENT BHAVA LORDS INFLUENCING TWELFTH BHAVA
Losses and Expenditure

As first lord influencing twelfth bhava: If Benefic

You will be learned and interested in occultism. You will take pride in helping others. You will have a number of friends. You will be religiously inclined and will have a peaceful and sudden end. You will visit holy places. You will spend inherited riches on charities and other deserving causes. You will be emotionally balanced and will dedicate yourself to public weal.

As first lord influencing twelfth bhava: If Malefic

You may have gambling tendencies and many losses. You may not have success in business enterprises.

As second lord influencing twelfth bhava: If Benefic

You will become a respectable person. You may be a government servant. Your income may be through dealings connected with churches.

As second lord influencing twelfth bhava: If Malefic

You may be deprived of the happiness of elder brother. You may lose money through churches. Your domestic affairs may take an unfortunate turn apart from financial losses.

As third lord influencing twelfth bhava: If Benefic

You will get fortune through marriage.

As third lord influencing twelfth bhava: If Malefic

You may get sorrow through relatives. You would like to have seclusion. You may face great ups and downs. You may not have a prosperous father. Your youngest brother may not be of good temperament and you will suffer because of him or your younger brother may suffer. You may meet a series of misfortunes. You may have fear from enemies. You may have ear diseases. You may have to sell or mortgage all your jewels. There may be mental affliction also.

As fourth influencing twelfth bhava: If Benefic

You may not be deprived of properties and happiness. Your mother may not suffer. You may not have bad finances and generally you may not have a miserable existence. You may not have mental worry. You may not get losses of cattle. You may not bring misfortunes to mother and involvement in troubles.

As fourth influencing twelfth bhava: If Malefic

You may be deprived of properties and happiness. Your mother may suffer. You may have bad finances and generally you may not have a comfortable life. You may have mental worry. You may get loss of cattle. You may bring misfortunes to mother and involvement in troubles.

As fifth lord influencing twelfth bhava: If Benefic

Your quest for knowing the ultimate reality will be pronounced. You will lead a life of non-attachment. You will become spiritual. You will move from place to place and ultimately attain Moksha (enlightenment). You will become wiser and spend money on deserving causes.

As fifth lord influencing twelfth bhava: If Malefic

Your children may suffer. There may be mental afflictions, almost bordering on lunacy. Misunderstandings may arise with father and children. You may incur the displeasure of the rulers or the government.

As sixth lord influencing twelfth bhava: If Benefic

You will be all-right and no untoward things may happen.

As sixth lord influencing twelfth bhava: If Malefic

You may get difficulties and sorrows through your destructive nature. You may cause harm to others. You may not have a very comfortable existence. You may suffer from troubles, losses and destruction in your enemy's hands. You may become immoral.

As seventh lord influencing twelfth bhava: If Benefic

There may not be more than one marriage in your life. You not may marry a second time clandestinely while the first partner is still alive or may not marry a second time after losing the first partner by death or separation. You may not suffer while travelling. Your marriage partner may not hail from a low family. You may not be generally poor. You may not be lacking marital happiness. You may not go abroad and may not be unhappy there with constant troubles and worries.

As *seventh lord influencing twelfth bhava: If Malefic*

There may be more than one marriage in your life. You may marry a second time clandestinely while the first partner is still alive or may marry a second time after losing the first partner by death or separation. You may suffer while travelling. Your marriage partner may hail from a low family. You may be generally not very rich. You may be lacking marital happiness. You may go abroad but may be unhappy there with constant troubles and worries.

As *eighth lord influencing twelfth bhava: If Benefic*

You will get Rajayoga (all-round improvement). You will gain in religion and piety. Some post or seat of authority may be thrust on you with all its attendant paraphernalia.

As *eighth lord influencing twelfth bhava: If Malefic*

Treachery of friends may result in many problems and grief. Unexpected expenditure may arise and there may be pecuniary losses. You may resort to various clandestine acts.

As *ninth lord influencing twelfth bhava: If Benefic*

You will lead a pure and honest life. You will be religious and noble. You will be spiritually inclined. You will spend your wealth in charity.

As *ninth lord influencing twelfth bhava: If Malefic*

You may have a poor background. You may suffer much and may have to work very hard in life and even then success may not come to you. You may always be in want. Your father may leave you penniless or you may be living far away from father. You may lose money through foolishly investing it. You may be robbed of your valuables in a dacoity. You may lose your ancestral lands and money.

As tenth lord influencing twelfth bhava: If Benefic

You will pursue your spiritual inclinations with zeal. You will become a spiritual seeker. You may head a medical institution or prison or a remand house.

As tenth lord influencing twelfth bhava: If Malefic

You may have to work in a far-off place. You may wander about without success. You may indulge in nefarious activities. You may lack comforts and face many difficulties in life. You may be separated from your family. There may be sorrow for the family and relatives. You may have humiliation. You may lose your job and if in business losses may accrue to you. You may have unconventional professions and people may revile at you. You may wander aimlessly with no domestic peace.

As eleventh lord influencing twelfth bhava: If Benefic

You may not suffer losses in business. You may not incur much expenditure on account of illness of your elder brother. You may not have to pay fines and penalties and you may not be burdened with many domestic responsibilities. You may not land in losses through varied expenditure. Your wealth may not be squandered. Your elder brother may not pass through a troubled phase, suffering from much monetary loss. You may not run into debts.

As eleventh lord influencing twelfth bhava: If Malefic

You may suffer losses in business. You may incur much expenditure on account of illness of your elder brother. You may have to pay fines and penalties and you may be burdened with many domestic responsibilities. You may land in losses through varied expenditure. Your wealth may be squandered. Your elder brother may pass through a troubled phase suffering from much monetary loss. You may run into debts.

CHAPTER VI

Model Horoscope

The model horoscope given is taken out of a computer print-out specially programmed for this benefic and malefic analysis of planets and bhavas along with predictions. The complete Vimsottari Dasas tables of main, sub- and inter-period planets are not given in the model horoscope to restrict the number of pages in this book, though the computer print-out gives all detailed tables of all Dasas upto the full cycle of 120 years of the Vimsottari Dasa System. The reader can calculate these tables from any standard book on astrology.

The model horoscope gives the Planetary degrees, Rasi chart, Navamsa chart, Bhava chart, Planetary Relationships, Benefic and Malefic Analysis of Planets and Bhavas, Broad Life Predictions, Yearly Predictions of Current, Main Period Planet, Sub-period Planet in the Main Period Planet and Inter-period Planets in the Sub-period Planet. The results of the subsequent periods are not given due to space restrictions.

The intention of the model horoscope is to give an idea of the application of this new theory of Benefic and Malefic Analysis of Planets and Bhavas and subsequent reading of the predictions accordingly.

INTRODUCTION

We, at Bharathi Jyothishi Centre (C/o P. Bharati Rayudu, 67 Vinayanagar, Saidabad, Hyderabad-500659, India. Phone: 527354), have studied the various computer software packages available on Hindu astrology in India and formulated our own software package based on south Indian style of Hindu astrology with our past non-professional, service oriented research experience of about twenty-five years. The software utilises the Raman's 110-years ephemeris along with the Lahiri's Ayanamsa for calculation part. It works out the Rasi chart, Navamsa chart, Bhava chart, Vimsottari dasa tables of main, sub- and inter-periods of the planets, general life readings and yearly predictions.

Compared to the other softwares available, the uniqueness of our software is that it distinguishes mathematically each planet as benefic or malefic towards the horoscope in study with analysis checking the various aspects of astrological principles as normally done by any serious astrologer and then proceeds to apply these benefic or malefic tendencies while giving the predictions.

In the general reading of the horoscope the significations of all the twelve bhavas covering all the important aspects of life are given. In the yearly predictions all the different results of the main period, sub-period and inter-period of planets are given.

The aspects covered in the predictions are body, health, temperament, personality, wealth, courage, education, houses, landed, property, conveyance, happiness, children, diseases, enemies, debts, marriage, marital relationship, longevity, prosperity, profession, gains, income, losses and expenditure.

The results attributable to your social, economical, circumstantial and environmental factors are only to be taken.

It may be appreciated that the results based on the basic horoscope of Rasi chart and Navamsa chart and the detailed horoscope covering many other varga charts may differ since more conditions will be considered in the detailed horoscope.

It may also be appreciated that the horoscope available with you may differ from our casting due 'to the differences in Ayanamsa and Ephemeris. Also the periods of the planets, that is, the timing of the events may vary upto six months to one year sometimes. It may also to be noted that the transit results of the planets are not given which may influence the predictions to some extent. The accuracy of the calculations and predictions depends upon the accuracy of the birth time, which is not always available with high degree of accuracy. Also astrological predictions cannot be simply based upon strict hypothetical principles or vague guesses but a certain amount of intuitive capacity must be brought to bear upon such attempts.

The various rules given for future predictions are merely intended for your guidance. As such, this centre does not guarantee the certainty of the results nor own any responsibility for your decisions based upon the indications and any claim or cause of action for any damages or otherwise against this centre shall not be entertained.

BASIC BIRTH DATA

Name	P.V.R. Rayudu
Sex	Male
Place of birth	Vizianagram
State	Andhra Pradesh
Country	India
Date of Birth	07 Sep., 1938
Day of Birth	Wednesday
Time of Birth (I.S.T.)	09:03:44
Longitude	083:26:00 East

Latitude   018:07:00 North
Lunar Thithi   13
Lunar Paksha   Shukla
I.S.T. To L.M.T. Correction   00:03:43
Time Birth (L.M.T.)   09:07:27
Siderial Time at Birth   08:09:41
Ayanamsa   022:59:40
Tenth House   Cancer 07:14:44
Ascendant (Lagna)   Libra
Birth Rasi (Moon Rasi)   Capricorn
Birth Star (Moon Star)   Shravana Pada - 4
Balance of Dasa at Birth   Moon 2 years 3 months
                                  15 days

PLANETARY INFORMATION

Planet	Rasi	Degrees	Retro	Exalt	Star	Pada	Rlord	St. lord
Sun	Leo	20:57:0	No	–	Poorva-phalguna	3	Sun	Venus
Mars	Leo	06:33:2	No	–	Magha	2	Sun	Ketu
Mercury	Leo	06:07:5	Yes	–	Magha	2	Sun	Ketu
Jupiter	Aquarius	02:08:1	No	–	Dhanistha	3	Saturn	Mars
Venus	Libra	06:59:5	No	–	Svati	1	Venus	Rahu
Saturn	Pisces	23:51:3	Yes	–	Revati	3	Jupiter	Mercury
Rahu	Libra	27:57:4	Yes	–	Vishakha	3	Venus	Jupiter
Ketu	Aries	27:57:4	Yes	–	Krittika	1	Mars	Sun
Moon	Capricorn	20:16:4	No	–	Sravana	4	Saturn	Moon
Ascendant	Libra	07:39:5	No	–	Svati	1	Venus	Rahu

Rasi Chart

Saturn (R)	Ketu		
Jupiter (R)		Rasi	
Moon			Mercury (R) Sun Mars
		Ascendant Venus Rahu	

Navamsa Chart

		Mars Mercury	Rahu
Saturn		Navamsa	Moon
Ascendant Venus Ketu		Sun Jupiter	

CUSP AND BHAVA DEGREES

Bhava	Bhava	Start	Bhava	Cusp	Star	Star-lord
1	Virgo	22:35:46	Libra	07:39:59	Svati	Rahu
2	Libra	22:35:46	Scorpion	07:31:34	Anuradha	Saturn
3	Scorpio	22:27:21	Sagittarius	07:23:09	Moola	Ketu
4	Sagittarius	22:18:56	Capricorn	07:14:44	Uttara	Sun
5	Capricorn	22:18:56	Aquarius	07:23:09	Satabhisha	Rahu
6	Aquarius	22:27:21	Pisces	07:31:34	Uttara	Saturn
7	Pisces	22:35:46	Aries	07:39:59	Asvini	Ketu
8	Aries	22:35:46	Taurus	07:31:34	Krittika	Sun
9	Taurus	22:27:21	Gemini	07:23:09	Ardra	Rahu
10	Gemini	22:18:56	Cancer	07:14:44	Pushya	Saturn
11	Cancer	22:18:56	Leo	07:23:09	Magha	Ketu
12	Leo	22:27:21	Virgo	07:31:34	Uttara	Sun

Bhava Chart

	Saturn (R)	Ketu	
Jupiter (R)		Bhava	
Moon			Mercury(R) Mars
		Ascendant Venus Rahu in 2nd bhava	Sun

PLANETARY RELATIONSHIP

Permanent Relationship

Planet	Friends	Neutrals	Enemies
Sun	Moon Mars Jupiter	Mercury	Saturn Venus Ketu Rahu
Mars	Sun Moon Jupiter	Venus Saturn Ketu Rahu	Mercury
Mercury	Sun Venus Ketu Rahu	Mars Jupiter Saturn	Moon
Jupiter	Sun Moon Mars	Saturn Ketu Rahu	Mercury Venus
Venus	Mercury Saturn Ketu Rahu	Mars Jupiter	Moon Sun
Saturn	Venus Mercury Ketu Rahu	Jupiter	Sun Moon Mars
Rahu	Venus Saturn Merury Ketu	Mars Jupiter	Sun Moon
Ketu	Venus Saturn Mercury Rahu	Mars Jupiter	Sun Moon
Moon	Sun Mercury	Mars Jupiter Venus Saturn	Rahu Ketu

Functional Relationship

Planet	Friends	Enemies
Sun		Merury Saturn Ketu
Mars	Venus Rahu	Saturn Ketu Mercury
Mercury	Venus Rahu	Mars Jupiter Saturn Ketu
Jupiter	Moon Saturn Ketu	Rahu Mercury Venus
Venus	Mercury Mars	Jupiter
Saturn	Ketu Jupiter	Sun Mars
Rahu	Merury Mars	Jupiter
Ketu	Saturn Jupiter	Mars Sun
Moon	Jupiter Venus Saturn	Mars

VIMSOTTARI DASA TABLE

Balance of MOON Dasa at birth: 02 Yrs 03 mons 15 days
Current date is: 07 Sep 1990

Current main period:	Saturn	from	22/12/1981	to	22/12/2000
Current sub period:	Venus	from	13/10/1988	to	13/12/1991
Current inter period:	Jupiter	from	22/05/1990	to	24/10/1990

Note : Periods of planets given below are for the full cycle of 120 years of Vimsottari dasa. However, it does not determine the longevity of the horoscope. The dates show the beginning of dasa. All the dates are in the format of date/month/year.

PLANETS MAIN PERIODS

Moon	07/09/1938	Mars	22/12/1940	Rahu	22/12/1947	Jupiter	22/12/1965
Saturn	22/12/1981	Mercury	22/12/2000	Ketu	22/12/2017	Venus	22/12/2024
Sun	22/12/2044						

Planets Sub-periods

Moon-Ketu	07/09/1938	Moon-Venus	22/10/1938	Moon-Sun	22/06/1940
Mars-Mars	22/12/1940	Mars-Rahu	19/05/1941	Mars-Jupiter	07/06/1942
Mars-Saturn	13/05/1943	Mars-Mercury	22/06/1944	Mars-Ketu	19/06/1945
Mars-Venus	16/11/1945	Mars-Sun	16/01/1947	Mars-Moon	22/05/1947
Rahu-Rahu	22/12/1947	Rahu-Jupiter	04/09/1950	Rahu-Saturn	28/01/1953
Rahu-Mercury	04/12/1955	Rahu-Ketu	22/06/1958	Rahu-Venus	10/07/1959
Rahu-Sun	10/07/1962	Rahu-Moon	04/06/1963	Rahu-Mars	04/12/1964
Jupiter-Jupiter	22/12/1965	Jupiter-Saturn	10/02/1968	Jupiter-Mercury	22/08/1970
Jupiter-Ketu	28/11/1972	Jupiter-Venus	04/11/1973	Jupiter-Sun	04/07/1976
Jupiter-Moon	22/04/1977	Jupiter-Mars	22/08/1978	Jupiter-Rahu	28/07/1979
Saturn-Saturn	22/12/1981	Saturn-Mercury	25/12/1984	Saturn-Ketu	04/09/1987
Saturn-Venus	13/10/1988	Saturn-Sun	13/12/1991	Saturn-Moon	25/11/1992
Saturn-Mars	25/06/1994	Saturn-Rahu	04/08/1995	Saturn-Jupiter	10/06/1998
Mercury-Mercury	22/12/2000	Mercury-Ketu	19/05/2003	Mercury-Venus	16/05/2004
Mercury-Sun	16/03/2007	Mercury-Moon	22/01/2008	Mercury-Mars	22/06/2009
Mercury-Rahu	19/06/2010	Mercury-Jupiter	07/01/2013	Mercury-Saturn	13/04/2015
Ketu-Ketu	22/12/2017	Ketu-Venus	19/05/2018	Ketu-Sun	19/07/2019
Ketu-Moon	25/11/2019	Ketu-Mars	25/06/2020	Ketu-Rahu	22/11/2020
Ketu-Jupiter	10/12/2021	Ketu-Saturn	16/11/2022	Ketu-Mercury	25/12/2023
Venus-Venus	22/12/2024	Venus-Sun	22/04/2028	Venus-Moon	22/04/2029
Venus-Mars	22/12/2030	Venus-Rahu	22/02/2032	Venus-Jupiter	22/02/2035
Venus-Saturn	22/10/2037	Venus-Mercury	22/12/2040	Venus-Ketu	22/10/2043
Sun-Sun	22/12/2044	Sun-Moon	10/04/2045	Sun-Mars	10/10/2045
Sun-Rahu	16/02/2046	Sun-Jupiter	10/01/2047	Sun-Saturn	28/10/2047
Sun-Mercury	10/10/2048	Sun-Ketu	16/08/2049	Sun-Venus	22/12/2049

Planets Inter Periods

Saturn-Ketu-Saturn	13/06/1988	Saturn-Ketu-Mercury	16/08/1988	Saturn-Venus-Venus	13/10/1988
Saturn-Venus-Sun	23/04/1989	Saturn-Venus-Moon	20/06/1989	Saturn-Venus-Mars	25/09/1989
Saturn-Venus-Rahu	01/12/1989	Saturn-Venus-Jupiter	22/05/1990	Saturn-Venus-Saturn	24/10/1990
Saturn-Venus-Mercury	24/04/1991	Saturn-Venus-Ketu	05/10/1991	Saturn-Sun-Sun	13/12/1991

Note: The other inter-periods are intentionally deleted to save space
though the computer print-out gives all the inter-periods from
the beginning of the birth upto 120 years.

NATURAL AND LORDSHIPS BENEFICS AND MALEFICS

Natural Benefics for Your Chart
Jupiter Venus Moon

Natural Malefics for Your Chart
Saturn Sun Mars Rahu Ketu Mercury

Lordship Benefics for Your Chart
Mars Saturn Mercury Venus

Lordship Malefics for Your Chart
Sun Moon Jupiter Rahu Ketu.

BENEFIC AND MALEFIC ANALYSIS OF PLANETS

Note: The following analysis takes into account various influences that the planets are subjected to in your horoscope and assigns suitable weightages while giving the benefic and malefic percentages.

Analysis of Sun

Benefic due to
is in own sign
is in lordship benefic's star
is in natural benefic's star
associated with lordship benefic
aspected by natural benefic
as lordship malefic in 6th, 8th or 12th bhavas.

Malefic due to
is a natural malefic
is a lordship malefic

    is in association with functional enemy

    is associated with natural malefic

    is aspected by lordship malefic

    as a natural malefic in 3, 6, 10 or 11 bhavas
    in debilitation in navamsa

Net benefic percentage: 54.55%

Net malefic percentage: 45.45%

Analysis of Mars

Benefic due to

    lordship benefic

    is a funcational friend of ascendant lord

    associated with lordship benefic

    aspected by natural benefic

    as a natural malefic in 3, 6, 10 or 11 bhavas

    as lordship benefic not in 6, 8 or 12 bhavas

    is in functional friends sign in navamsa.

Malefic due to

    is a natural malefic

    is in lordship malefics sign

    is in natural malefics sign

    is in functional enemies star

    is in lordship malefics star

    is in natural malefics star

    is in association with functional enemy

      is associated with lordship malefic

      is associated with natural malefic

      is aspected by lordship malefic.

Net benefic percentage: 40.00%.

Net malefic percentage: 60.00%.

Analysis of Mercury

Benefic due to

      lordship benefic

      is a functional friend of ascendant lord

      associated with lordship benefic

      aspected by natural benefic

      as a natural malefic in 3, 6, 10 or 11 bhavas

      as lordship benefic not in 6, 8 or 12 bhavas

      is in functional friend's sign in navamsa.

Malefic due to

      is a natural malefic

      is in lordship malefic's sign

      is in natural malefic's sign

      is in lordship malefic's star

      is in natural malefic's star

      is in association with functional enemy

      is associated with lordship malefic

      is associated with natural malefic

      is aspected by functional enemy

      is aspected by lordship malefic.

Net benefic percentage: 40.00%.

Net malefic percentage: 60.00%.

Analysis of Jupiter

Benefic due to

    natural benefic

    is in functional friend's sign

    is in lordship benefic's sign

    is in lordship benefic's star

    aspected by lordship benefic

    as a natural benefic not in 12 bhava.

Malefic due to

    is a lordship malefic

    is in natural malefic sign

    is in natural malefic star

    is a functional enemy of ascendant lord

    is aspected by functional enemy

    is aspected by lordship malefic

    is aspected by natural malefic

    as a lordship malefic not in 6, 8 or 12 bhavas

    is in functional enemies sign in navamsa.

Net benefic percentage: 44.00%.

Net malefic percentage: 56.00%.

Analysis of Venus

Benefic due to

    natural benefic

    lordship benefic

    is in own sign

aspected by natural benefic

as a natural benefic not in 12 bhavas

as lordship benefic not in 6, 8 or 12 bhavas.

Malefic due to

is in lordship malefic's star

is in natural malefic's star

is associated with lordship malefic

is associated with natural malefic

is aspected by functional enemy

is aspected by lordship malefic

is in functional enemies sign in navamsa.

Net benefic percentage: 44.44%.

Net malefic percentage: 55.56%.

Analysis of Saturn

Benefic due to

lordship benefic

is in functional friend's sign

natural benefic's sign

is in lordship benefic's star

aspected by lordship benefic

as lordship benefic not in 6, 8 or 12 bhavas

in own sign in navamsa.

Malefic due to

is a natural malefic

is in lordship malefic's sign

is in natural malefic's star

is aspected by functional enemy

is aspected by natural malefic

as a natural malefic not in 3, 6, 10 or 11 bhavas.

Net benefic percentage: 61.11%.

Net malefic percentage: 38.89%.

Analysis of Rahu

Benefic due to

is in lordship benefic's sign

is in natural benefic's sign

is in natural benefic's star

associated with lordship benefic

associated with natural benefic

aspected by natural benefic

is in functional friend's sign in navamsa.

Malefic due to

is a natural malefic

is a lordship malefic

is in functional enemies' star

is in lordship malefic's star

is aspected by functional enemy

is aspected by lordship malefic

as a natural malefic not in 3, 6, 10 or 11 bhavas

as a lordship malefic not in 6, 8 or 12 bhavas.

Net benefic percentage: 45.00%.

Net malefic percentage: 55.00%.

Analysis of Ketu

Benefic due to
  is in lordship benefic's sign
  aspected by lordship benefic
  aspected by natural benefic
  as lordship benefic in 6, 8 or 12 bhavas
  is in functional friend's sign in navamsa.

Malefic due to
  is a natural malefic
  is a lordship malefic
  is in functional enemy's sign
  is in natural malefic's sign
  is in functional enemy's star
  is in lordship malefic's star
  is in natural malefic's star
  as a natural malefic not in 3, 6, 10 or 11 bhavas.

Net benefic percentage: 47.06%.
Net malefic percentage: 52.94%.

Analysis of Moon

Benefic due to
  natural benefic
  is in functional friend's sign
  is in lordship benefic's sign
  is in own star
  as a natural benefic not in 12 bhavas
  in own sign in navamsa.

Malefic due to

   is a lordship malefic

   is in natural malefic's sign

   as a lordship malefic not in 6, 8 or 12 bhavas.

Net benefic percentage: 69.23%.

Net malefic percentage: 30.77%.

BROAD LIFE PREDICTIONS

Important Information

The general characteristics of the Ascendant (Lagna) you are born in are given. The various planets influencing your various bhavas are analysed with respect to their benefic and malefic tendencies and the net effect of the bhavas are given with due weightages.

When the bhava percentage is between 50% to 55% malefic, moderate results of the bhava are given. When the percentage of the bhava is 50% or more benefic, benefic results of the bhava are given. When the percentage of the bhava is 55% or more malefic, malefic results of the bhava are given.

In general the twelve bhavas represent the various aspects of your life covering body, health, temperament, personality, wealth, education, landed property, conveyance, happiness, children, diseases, enemies, debts, marriage, marital relationship, longevity, prosperity, profession, gains, income, losses and expenditure.

Broad general reading of the above aspects are only given which will indicate the overall effects in your life in general. The various planets influencing your various aspects will, however, give the special effects pertaining to their characteristics during their operating periods.

GENERAL CHARACTERISTICS OF LIBRA ASCENDANT (LAGNA)

Body

You may have middle-sized stature or sometimes tall and lean body. You may have a handsome appearance with broad face and fine eyes. Your features may be regular with broad chest and prominent nose. You may have a youthful appearance.

Health

You will have a sensual disposition. You will suffer in some limb. You may get setbacks in health due to slight causes but you will easily recover.

Temperament and Personality

You will be idealistic, quickwitted, vindictive, forceful and positive. You will be a keen observer of human nature. You will have sensual disposition. You will have keen foresight and reason out things from the standpoint of your own views. You will love justice, peace, order and you will be an agreeable person. You will be intelligent, clean, very active and devoted to gods and brahmins. You will be ambitious. You will be firm in convictions and unmoved by mean motives. You will be somewhat susceptible to feelings of others' minds. You will be more idealist than realist or practical person and often contemplate upon schemes like building castles in the air. You will be clever in purchase and sale of goods. You will be skilful and act impartially as arbitrator. You will not be sensitive to what others say of you. You will exert tremendous influence over the masses as political leaders and religious reformers. Sometimes your zeal and enthusiasm may go to such a high pitch that you will force your views upon others of opposite thought not realising the baneful after-effects of such a practice. You will not hesitate to sacrifice even your living at the altars of freedom and fair play. You will love excitement. You will not be easily amenable to reason sometimes. You will be a great lover of music. You will have special liking for trust and honesty.

ANALYSIS OF BHAVAS

First Bhava Represents:

Complexion, Body, Health, Temperament and Personality.

Planets Influencing Your First Bhava:

> Planets in First bhava: Venus
>
> Lord of First bhava: Venus
>
> Planets aspecting First bhava: Jupiter Saturn
>
> Lord of the First bhava cusp star: Rahu
>
> Planets associated with First bhava lord: Rahu
>
> Planets aspecting First bhava lord: Jupiter
>
> Karakas of First bhava: Sun

Thus planets influencing your First Bhava are: Venus, Jupiter, Saturn, Rahu, Sun.

The net benefic malefic analysis of your First bhava:

> Benefic percentage: 46.2%
>
> Malefic percentage: 53.8%

The net analysis of the planets influencing your First bhava is benefic 46.2% and malefic 53.8%, i.e. it can be taken as Moderate.

General Effects of First Bhava Significations

You are likely to have medium body structure. You may not expect very good health. Your temperament and personality may be of moderate nature.

Similarly other Bhavas are analysed.

Second Bhava Represents:

Wealth, Speech, Family, Food.

The net analysis of the planets influencing your Second bhava is benefic 44.3% and malefic 55.7%, i.e. it can be taken as Malefic.

General Effects of Second Bhava Significations

You may not be wealthy. Your speech may not be good. You may have a troubled family. Your face and eyes may not be attractive. You may not be able to enjoy good food.

Third Bhava Represents:

Courage, Younger brothers and sisters, Relatives, Friends, Communications.

The net analysis of the planets influencing your Third bhava is benefic 43.3% and malefic 56.7%, i.e. can be taken as Malefic.

General Effects of Third Bhava Significations

You may not be courageous. You may not have younger brothers and sisters or your relations with them may not be good. There may be problems in your throat, arms and shoulders. You may not be good at communicating with others. You may not have many friends and relatives.

Fourth Bhava Represents:

Education, Mother, Houses, Landed Property and Conveyance, Happiness.

The net analysis of the planets influencing your Fourth bhava is benefic 51.9% and malefic 48.1%, i.e. it can be taken as Benefic.

General Effects of Fourth Bhava Significations

You will get good education. You will possess houses, landed property and conveyance. You will have a good mother. Your chest and heart will not give problems. You will enjoy good general happiness.

Fifth Bhava Represents:

Children, Wisdom, Intelligence.

The net analysis of the planets influeneing your Fifth bhava is benefic 46.2% and malefic 53.8%, i.e. it can be taken as Moderate.

General Effects of Fifth Bhava Significations

You may have limited children. Your wisdom and intelligence may be satisfactory. Your stomach may function in a moderate fashion.

Sixth Bhava Represents:

Diseases, Enemies, Debts.

The net analysis of the planets influencing your Sixth bhava is benefic 46.0% and malefic 54.0%, i.e. it can be taken as Moderate.

General Effects of Sixth Bhava Significations

Your diseases may not give you much trouble. You may have limited enemies or you may be able to deal with your enemies. Your debts may be moderate and under control.

Seventh Bhava Represents:

Marriage, Wife/husband, Marital Relationship.

The net analysis of the planets influencing your Seventh bhava is benefic 46.9% and malefic 53.1%, i.e. it can be taken as Moderate.

General Effects of Seventh Bhava Significations

Your partner may be just normal and your marital relationship may be satisfactory. You may have moderate success in your business partnership.

Eighth Bhava Represents:

Longevity, Legacies.

The net analysis of the planets influencing your Eighth bhava is benefic 47.8% and malefic 52.2%, i.e. it can be taken as Moderate.

General Effects of Eighth Bhava Significations

You may have normal life span. You may inherit legacies of moderate nature. You may have to guard against diseases of your secret organs.

Ninth Bhava Represents:

Prosperity, Father, Devotion to God, Long travels.

The net analysis of the planets influencing your Ninth bhava is benefic 44.8% and malefic 55.2%, i.e. it can be taken as Malefic.

General Effects of Ninth Bhava Significations

You may not expect overall good prosperity. You may not have highly prosperous father. You may not be interested in gods or religious preceptors. You may not have long journeys often. You may suffer in your hips and thighs.

Tenth Bhava Represents:

Profession, Respect, Travels, Status, Position, Life, Activity.

The net analysis of the planets influencing your Tenth bhava is benefic 55.1% and malefic 44.9%, i.e. it can be taken as Benefic.

General Effects of Tenth Bhava Significations

You will have a good profession. Your status and position will increase. You will be respected. You can expect good travels. Your life and activity will be jubiliant. You will have strong knees and back.

Eleventh Bhava Represents:

Gains and Income, Elder brothers and sisters.

The net analysis of the planets influencing your Eleventh bhava is benefic 43.9% and malefic 56.1%, i.e. it can be taken as Malefic.

General Effects of Eleventh Bhava Significations

You may not expect much gains and income. You may not have elder brothers and sisters or you may not maintain good relations with them. The calves of your legs may be weak.

Twelfth Bhava Represents:

Losses and Expenditure, Moksha, Foreign Travels, Sexual Enjoyment, Confinement/Imprisonment.

The net analysis of the planets influencing your Twelfth bhava is benefic 45.8% and malefic 54.2%, i.e. it can be taken as Moderate.

General Effects of Twelfth Bhava Significations

You may have tolerable expenditure and losses. You may expect to get Moksha (enlightenment). You may have a chance of foreign travels. Your sexual enjoyment may be normal. There may be a chance of being confined or imprisoned. You may have decay of teeth.

MAJOR SIGNIFICATOR PLANETS
FOR VARIOUS BHAVAS

Significator	Bhavas
Sun	0 1 2 3 4 5 6 7 8 9 10 11
Mars	1 2 3 4 5 6 8 10 11
Mercury	1 2 3 4 5 6 8 9 10 11
Jupiter	0 1 2 3 4 5 6 7 8 9 10 11
Venus	0 3 6 7
Saturn	0 1 3 4 5 6 7 8 9 11
Rahu	0 1 4 7 8
Ketu	2 6 7 10
Moon	3 9

Note: "0" represents the First bhava, "1" represents the Second bhava, "2" represents the Third bhava and so on.

YEARLY PREDICTIONS

Important

The planets during their main periods, sub-periods and inter-periods give benefic or malefic results pertaining to the affairs they rule depending on the extent of their benefic or malefic nature towards your horoscope. If the planets are towards the benefic nature, the maximum good results come to pass and the evil results are not felt or are at their minimum. Conversely, if the overall malefic influence of the planets is more, the good effects are felt at their minimum and unfavourable ones are at their maximum. Thus both the benefic and malefic results are felt but only the extent of the effect will vary depending on the percentages of the benefic and malefic tendencies of the planets.

It is also to be noted that in the main period of a benefic planet, sub-period of a benefic planet, inter-period of a benefic planet you will get excellent results. Similarly in the main period of a malefic planet, subperiod of a malefic planet, interperiod of a malefic planet you will experience intense malefic results. The results vary as per the extent of the nature of benefic and malefic tendencies of the planets of the main period, sub-period and inter-period.

When the period is more than 55% malefic only, the malefic results have been given. However, you are cautioned to note that when malefic results are given, some benefic results may also occur. Similarly, when malefic results are given, some benefic results may also occur.

Almost all the possible results that a planet may give under the circumstances have been given and some of them may not suit you. You are therefore advised to pick and choose the results depending on your social, economical, circumstantial and environmental factors.

Current date is: 07 September 1990

Current main period: Saturn   From 22/12/1981 to 22/12/2000
Current sub period: Venus   From 13/10/1988 to 13/12/1991
Current inter period: Jupiter   From 22/05/1990 to 24/10/1990

MAIN PERIOD OF SATURN
From 22/12/1981 to 22/12/2000
Net benefic 61.11%, Net malefic 38.89%

Body

You may be good looking.

Health

You will be strong-minded and will maintain good health.

Temperament and Personality

Your moral stability is an asset. Your disposition will be calm. You will be strong-minded exploring, methodical, industrious and self-confident. You will have much consideration for the welfare of the others. You may be thrifty.

Being in Pisces:

You will be endowed with many good qualities such as clever, pushful, gifted, good diplomat and good manners. You will command respect and trust in government.

As fourth lord influencing first bhava:

You will be learned.

As fifth lord influencing first bhava:

You may take to some religious or ascetic order. You may command a number of servants. Temperamentally you would like to behave in such a manner to make others feel happy.

Wealth

You will gain wealth by success in estate, mines, investment, coal, lead or refrigeration. You may get wealth by dealing in gambling, oils, seeds, pots, woollen fabrics, iron, cereals, atmosphere, air, mountains, hills, forest regions, sapphire, elderly people, black grain, barley, astringent, jails, bricklaying, negroes, architecture or vehicles. You can expect gains in wealth from western direction.

Being in Pisces:

You will have wealth.

As fourth lord influencing second bhava:

You may inherit property from maternal grandfather's side. You may earn wealth by your courageous nature and also by your success in selling and buying lands. You will be highly fortunate.

As fifth lord influencing second bhava:

You will have aquisition of riches and gains from business. You may get money from a new job. You may gain in your wealth from government or king, children, speculation. You may get your riches by being learned, a good astrologer and author.

Education

You may get education connected with mines, oils, woollen fabrics, architectural skill, iron, lead, atmosphere, air, mountains, hills, forests, mass leadership or labour.

Being in Pisces:

Your education may lead you to become a diplomat.

As fourth lord in seventh bhava:

You will have good education, may be abroad.

As fourth lord influencing fourth bhava:

You may be religiously inclined and may have good education.

As fifth lord influencing fifth bhava:

You will have successful education.

Houses, Landed property, Conveyance

You will have conveyance.

As fourth lord in seventh bhava:

You will command houses and lands.

As fourth lord influencing fourth bhava:

You will become rich.

As fifth lord influencing fourth bhava:

You will acquire new conveyance and immovable property.

Happiness

You will have good patrimony. You will succeed in foreign countries. You will have conveyance. You will gain through oilseeds or black grains. You may get treasure.

Being in Pisces:

You will have a good-married partner. You will go on pilgrimage to sacred shrines and holy places. You will become chief and get respect from your friends and relatives. You will have good children. You may become the head of an institution, village or town. You will command respect and trust in government. You will be happy.

As fourth lord in seventh bhava:

You will command houses and vehicles. You will be generally happy.

As fourth lord influencing fourth bhava:

You will be religiously inclined and will be respected. You will be rich and happy.

As fifth lord influencing fourth bhava:

You may become an adviser to ruler or his preceptor. You will acquire new conveyance and immovable property. You will get happiness from ruling class. Your mother may live long. You may have a few sons. You will acquire political power.

Children

You may have children. You may not get still born child or there might not be premature death of a child. There may not be abortions or ill health of children or their death. You may not adopt a child. You may not suffer for want of sons. You may not have troubles connected with children.

As fifth lord in seventh bhava:

You may have children. Your children may live abroad and attain distinction, wealth and fame. You will be benefited by your childrens' trip to and residence in foreign countries.

As fourth lord influencing fifth bhava:

You will be loved and respected by children.

As fifth lord influencing fifth bhava:

There may be birth of children.

Diseases

You will maintain good digestive power.

As fourth lord influencing sixth bhava:

You may not suffer from diseases.

As fifth lord influencing sixth bhava:

You may not have any diseases.

Enemies

You will triumph over enemies and you will get victory over them.

As fourth lord influencing sixth bhava:

You will get happiness from mother.

As fifth lord influencing sixth bhava:

You may get benefits from maternal uncles.

Debts

You may not be indebted due to loss through animals and poultry. You may not incur debts due to servants.

As fourth lord influencing sixth bhava:

You may not get into debts due to your house, property or vehicles.

As fifth lord influencing sixth bhava:

You may not be in debt due to your children.

Marriage and Marital Relationship

You will be steady in your affections. You will have stable marriage.

As fourth lord influencing seventh bhava:

You will be generally happy.

As fifth lord influencing seventh bhava:

You may have a charming personality and marriage may take place if not already married and a new family may be set up.

Longevity

You will have good digestive parts and you will have long life.

Being in Pisces:

You will have a good end to life and peaceful death.

As fourth lord influencing eighth bhava:
There may not be a likelihood of suffering.

As fifth lord influencing eighth bhava:
You may not have lung troubles and you may not be peevish.

Prosperity

You will be founder of charitable institutions. You will be thrifty in domestic life. You will renovate temples. You will be fond of occult studies. You will get legal success. You will be successful in geology, minerology, occult subjects or metaphysics. You will be rich and happy. You will also get happiness from children. You will have a philosophical turn of mind. You may possess emerald. You may get prosperity from western direction.

Being in Pisces:
You will be happy. You will have a good-married partner. You may be a good jeweller or diplomat. You will be a chief among friends and relatives. You will have good children. You may become head of an institution, village or town. You will command respect and trust in government. You will be wealthy.

As fourth lord influencing ninth bhava:
You will be generally fortunate favouring happiness in regard to father and prosperity. You may get sudden fortune and wealth.

As fifth lord in influencing ninth bhava:
You may become a teacher or preceptor. You may renovate ancient temples, wells, choultries and gardens. One of your sons may attain distinction as orator or an author. You will have happiness from father during chilhood. There will be inheritance of paternal or ancestral property. You may get a good administrative or honorary post. Your father will be in

the good books of the ruling classes. There will be
unexpected dawn of prosperity and fortune. You may
become author of books. There will be acquisition of
wealth through a new administrative job, your own
occupation or through female sources.

Profession

You will be a great worker. You will be good farmer.
You will have professional success and you will get
promotions. You will be successful in your
undertakings. You will get position of authority. You
will have works connected with agriculture or products
derived from the bowels of earth such as minerals, oils
etc. You will occupy a high position in life. You will be
head of an institution or at the helm of affairs in your
sphere of activity. You will get speedy promotion to
high level. You will be head of religious institution.
You will become a ruler or minister. You will work for
down-trodden masses. You will be judicious and work
in the capacity of a judge. You will become ascetic in
later life. Your work may be connected with oils,
woollen fabrics, architecture, iron, lead, atmosphere,
air, mountains, hills, forests regions, coal and fuel of
every kind, petrol, real estate business, leather goods
farm or factory labour. You may be miner, craftsman, architect, building contractor, philosopher,
agriculturist, artisan, mechanic, compositor, mill
worker, brick layer or mass leader.

Being in Pisces:

You will be a good diplomat.

As fourth lord influencing tenth bhava:

You will have political success. You may be an
expert chemist. You will vanquish your enemies and
make your personality felt by the world. You may
become a minister or high placed government servant.
There will be access to wealth through trade and
business.

As fifth lord influencing tenth bhava:

You will earn goodwill of rulers or government. You will construct temples and perform religious sacrifices. You may join the crime investigation department. You will acquire kingdom or become head of state or a minister, if a politician or may reach the highest position, if in government. You will have palmy days as a businessman. If an agriculturist, you will earn enormous profits in your own avocations.

Losses and Expenditure

You will be learned in occult science. You will be dexterous. You will be attracted toward Yoga in later life. You will have less expenditure and enemies. You will have good longevity.

As fourth lord influencing twelfth bhava:

You may not be deprived of properties and happiness. Your mother may not suffer. You may not have bad finances and generally you may not have a miserable existence. You may not have mental worry. You may not get losses of cattle. You may not suffer misfortunes of mother and involvement in troubles.

As fifth lord influencing twelfth bhava:

Your quest for knowing the ultimate reality will be pronounced. You will lead a life of non-attachment. You will become spiritual. You will move from place to place and ultimately attain Moksha (enlightenment). You will become wiser and spend money on deserving causes.

To mitigate any evil influencing or to strengthen the benefic aspects of this period of Saturn, you are advised to pray to God Venkateshwara, wear sapphire, use dark colour and/or operate on number 8.

SUB-PERIOD OF VENUS IN THE MAIN-PERIOD OF SATURN
From 13/10/1988 to 13/12/1991
Net benefic 52.78%, Net malefic 47.22%

Note: The following results of the sub-period planet are in addition to those given under the main period planet.

Body

You will have magnetic power and handsome appearance. You may improve complexion.

Being in Libra:

You may be handsome.

Health

Your health will improve and your body will get energised.

Temperament and Presonality

You will be ambitious, bold, practical, affectionate, intelligent, poetical and persevering. You will have a pleasing and charming personality. Power of attracting others will be an important asset. Being of cheerful temperament and responsive to emotional side of nature you will generally be liked . You will have liking for scents and flowers. You are fond of dress of various colours. You will be of Rajasika temperament, that is, you are fond of pleasures of the senses, money and gay life. You will be easy going and of accommodating type.

Being in Libra:

You will be liked and respected by society and state due to your statesmanly, generous, philosophical, intuitive faculties. You will be clever in defending and protecting your interest and active in work even in difficult times through your strong and fearless nature. You may be devotional to Gods and Brahmins. You will get good reputation and become famous. You will have a handsome personality.

As first lord in first bhava:

You may live by your own exertions and independent spirit.

As first lord influencing first bhava:

Your spirit of independence will lead you to live by your own exertions.

As eighth lord influencing first bhava:

Your constitution may not be weak and you may not suffer from bodily complaints. Your behavioural pattern may not lead to the displeasure of your superiors and higher ups.

Education

You will be learned and successful in your educational pursuits. You will acquire new knowledge. You are likely to be interested in music. You may be fond of scientific education. You may be successful in education connected with poetical faculty, singers, musicians, dress, fine arts, actors, artists, botanists, authorship, rains, dancings, lakes, sugarcane, trade, medicine, wool, silk or cotton, computers.

Being in Libra:

Your interest may be in poetry.

As first lord influencing fourth bhava:

You will have acquaintance with learned men and discussions with them. You will get good education.

As eighth lord influencing fourth bhava:

Your education may go smooth.

Houses, Landed Property, Conveyance

You will easily get inheritance. You will possess estates and own cars. You will have acquisition of house and vehicles.

Being in Libra:

You will possess vehicles.

As first lord influencing fourth bhava:

You will acquire considerable landed properties especially through maternal sources. You will command a number of conveyance. You will possess houses and lands and vehicles. You will construct a new house.

As eighth lord influencing fourth bhava:

You may not be beset with problems regarding your house, land and conveyance. Your lands and immovable property may not slip from your hands due to circumstances beyond your control. Your conveyance may not get lost or be destroyed.

Happiness

You will be learned and successful in educational pursuits. You will have an affectionate mother. You will be endeared by relatives and friends. You will acquire houses, vehicles, property and cattle. You will have perfect domestic harmony. You will get friendship with good people and gain through them. You will have good ornaments and clothes. You will be successful in achievement of your desires. You will get good position and become famous and popular. You will lead a comfortable life. You will easily get inheritance. You will get plenty of milk and milky products. You will be respected.

Being in Libra:

You will gain wealth from royal patronage or government. You will get all comforts and enjoyments in life. You will have a successful marriage and there will be matrimonial felicity. You will be respected. You will get a good name due to devotion to gods and brahmins. You will be liked well in society and the state. You will possess vehicles. You will get great reputation. You will be wealthy.

As first lord influencing fourth bhava:

You will acquire landed properties specially through maternal sources. You will construct new houses. You will get respect from friends and relatives. You will have acquaintance with learned men and discussion with them. You will form new friendships. You will command a number of conveyance. You will be rich. You will get happiness from parents, You will be happy.

As eighth lord influencing fourth bhava:

You may not have domestic bickerings. Your financial and other problems may not increase. Your mother's health may not be bad and cause great concern. You may not be beset with problems connected with house, land and conveyance. Your pets may not get diseases or die. You may be forced to seek fortune abroad where you may not meet with all sorts of troubles and losses. You may not have displeasure of superiors and reverses in profession.

Marriage and Marital Relationship

You will have happy marriage and domestic harmony with loving and devoted partner. You will get a good beautiful partner. You will have stability in marriage. Both you and your partner will be successful and distinguished in your occupations. You will have good marital relations.

Being in Libra:

You will have a successful marriage and matrimonial felicity.

As first lord influencing seventh bhava:

You may have marriage, if unmarried.

As eighth lord influencing seventh bhava:

Your partner may not suffer ill health.

Longevity

You may not have diseases of urinary tract and you may not have trouble in mind. You may not suffer from muscular rheumatism. You may have long life.

As eighth lord in first bhava:

. You may not suffer bodily complaints such as disease and disfiguration. Your constitution may not be weak. You may have bodily comforts.

As first lord influencing eighth bhava:

You may have a peaceful and sudden end.

As eighth lord influencing eighth bhava:

You may have good life span.

To mitigate any evil influences or to strengthen the benefic aspects of this period of Venus, you are advised to pray to Goddess Lakshmi, wear diamond, use variegated colour and/or operate on number 6.

INTER-PERIOD OF JUPITER IN THE SUB-PERIOD OF VENUS AND MAIN-PERIOD OF SATURN

From 22/05/1990 to 24/10/1990

Net benefic 49.85%, Net malefic 50.15%

Note: The following results of the inter-period planet are in addition to those given under the main- and sub-period planets.

Body

You will have magnetic appearance, good body, abundant life force, attractive and adorable face. You will practise exercises that build-up your constitution and health. You may improve your complexion.

Health

You will have good health. You may practise exercises that build-up your constitution and health. You will have abundant life force.

Temperament and Personality

You will have a magnetic personality. You will be of Satwika temperament, that is, you will have pure thoughts and will be inclined to acts of religious merit. You will have optimistic spirit, jovial disposition, pleasant manners and pleasing personality. You would like to execute any work after matured deliberation, that is, after considering pros and cons. You will be wise, mild, knowledgeable, charitable, diplomatic. You will like to command respect.

Being in Aquarius:

You will become popular being compassionate, sympathetic, amenable, prudent, active and humanitarian. You may develop meditative and philosophical temperament. Whatever you do you may be acting intentionally.

As third lord influencing first bhava:

Due to your bold nature you want to stand on your own feet and earn livelihood by self-exertion. You are likely to become an expert in fine arts.

As sixth lord influencing first bhava:

You will have a commanding personality.

Wealth

You may get wealth through essence of your knowledge, wisdom, intellect and education. You may acquire silver and topaz. You may get wealth from children, sons, grandsons, learned men, grandfather or through your position as minister or adviser. You may become wealthy by dealing with banks, insurance companies, scriptures, benzion, quick silver, tin or cardamoms. Your wealth will increase by possessing lands, estates, buildings and vehicles. You will engage in trade, commerce, good business and successful career and become wealthy through your perseverance and vitality. In general, your financial position will improve. You can expect wealth from north-eastern direction.

As third lord influencing second bhava:

You will get wealth with effort. You may make advances on the wealth of others. There will be a likelihood of getting wealth from the sources pertaining to your brothers and sisters.

As sixth lord influencing second bhava:

You may become wealthy through your enemies and sometimes while suffering from diseases. You may get money by doing service and by getting loans.

Courage

You will get gains through your courage having mental calibre and leadership.

As third lord in fifth bhava:

You may be courageous.

As first lord influencing third bhava:

You will be highly courageous.

As sixth lord influencing third bhava:

You may not lose self-confidence.

Education

You will be well- read and educated. You will have acquisition of new knowledge. You will have great philosophical and spiritual advancement. You will have success in education connected with Vedas, Vedangas, legal affairs, diplomacy, proficiency in arts and sciences, law, philosophy, asceticism, bankers, philanthrophists, restaurants, hotels, insurance, travel or research and academic institutions.

Being in Aquarius:

You will be learned.

As third lord influencing fourth bhava:

You may be learned or interested in science or politics.

As sixth lord influencing fourth bhava:

You may not have breaks in education and you may not fail in examinations.

Houses, Landed Property, Conveyance

You will have successful estates. You will be in possession of buildings, vehicles etc. You will gain from lands. You will have good conveyance.

As third lord influencing fourth bhava:

You will acquire vehicles.

As sixth lord influencing fourth bhava:

Your ancestral property may not be involved in debts. Your immovable properties may not be auctioned or lost to enemies.

Happiness

You will have good inheritance, conveyance, buildings, successful estates and gains from lands. You will be wealthy. You will have success in education and you will be well-read. You will be a founder of charitable institution. You will have a good mother and friends. You will get fame and prosperity. You will lead a comfortable life. You will possess favour of ruling class. You will be a terror to your enemies. You will be religiously inclined. You will be fortunate and respected. You will have a peaceful domestic environment and great spiritual advancement. You will get gains from parents. You will get happiness in respect of mother, friends, servants, partner and agricultural products. You will have a happy end.

Being in Aquarius:

You will become head of your group. You will be much respected.

As third lord influencing fourth bhava:

You will be learned and rich. Your brothers will

shine well. You will become head of political or scientific organisation. You will have vehicles. Life will be happy on the whole.

As sixth lord influencing fourth bhava:

You may not have breaks in education and you may not fail in examinations. You may live in a good building. You may not quarrel with your mother or may separate from her. Your ancestral property may not be involved in debts. You may work in good position and lead a comfortable life. You may not have a troublesome home and your domestic affairs may be smooth. You may not get troubles through servants. Your immovable property may not be auctioned or lost to enemies. You may not meet with accidents by falling from vehicles. Your mother may not suffer.

Children

There will be a number of children and they will be good. You will be happy with your children.

As third lord influencing fifth bhava:

Much pleasure may be derived from children. Friction will not prevail in domestic life.

As sixth lord influencing fifth bhava:

Your children may not frequently suffer ill health. You may not develop enmity with your children.

Diseases

You will maintain good health and may not fall sick. You may gain during unhealthy periods. If disposed you will be well-attended.

As sixth lord influencing fifth bhava:

Your children may not suffer ill health.

As third lord influencing sixth bhava:

You may not fall ill and suffer from diseases. You may not get ear trouble.

As sixth lord influencing sixth bhava:

You will generally not get any diseases.

Enemies

You will have success over enemies and overpower them. You will be· free from enemies. You will have victory in elections.

As sixth lord in fifth bhava:

You may not have enmity with your children.

As third lord influencing sixth bhava:

You will be benefited by maternal uncles.

As sixth lord influencing sixth bhava:

You may not have enemies.

Debts

You may not get into debts due to children, sons, grandsons and grandfather. You may not expect to get money from learned men as debts.

As sixth lord influencing fifth bhava:

You may not be indebted due to children.

As third lord influencing sixth bhava:

You may not get into debts due to your younger brothers or sisters.

As sixth lord influencing sixth bhava:

You will not have any debts.

Marriage and Marital Relationship

You will have good, virtuous, good looking and chaste partner. Your partner will be well-behaved and truthful. You will gain through your partner. You will have a happy partner.

As third lord influencing seventh bhava:

Your marriage union may not be unfortunate. You may not land in second marriage.

As sixth lord influencing seventh bhava:

You may marry a person from a relative's family.

Longevity

You will live long.

As third lord influencing eighth bhava:

You may not have trouble on account of disease.

As sixth lord influencing eighth bhava:

You will have redemption from ailments and you will have good span of life.

Prosperity

You will have good children. You will have long-lived and fortunate father. You will be successful in your undertakings. You will occupy position in life as adviser or minister or consultant. You will have association with learned men and worship gods and brahmins. You may have association with foreigners also. You will be performing religious austerities. You will acquire wealth. You will get reputation and will be famous. You will have correct intuition and clear thought. You will have good travels. You may become a strong leader. You will possess good knowledge and wisdom. You may acquire topaz and silver. You may get prosperity from sons, grandsons, children or grandfather. You may get prosperity from north-eastern direction.

Being in Aquarius:

You will be learned. You will become head of your group. You will get much respect.

As third lord influencing ninth bhava:

Your fortune will improve after marriage. Your brother will inherit ancestoral property and you yourself will get benefited by your brother. Your brother will become fortunate and prosperous. Your father's property will increase. You will become religious.

As sixth lord influencing ninth bhava:

Your father may become a judge. Your maternal uncle will become highly fortunate. There will be benefits from cousins.

Profession

You will have good relations with higher officials. You will do meritorious deeds. You may become head of a village. You will command many servants. You will get timely promotion. You will be a good agriculturist. You will get success in business. You will be a high official in government. You will head research, academic and educational institution. You will have political life. You will be a sportsperson. Your work will be connected with Vedas, Vedangas, legal affairs, diplomacy, arts and science, philosophy, asceticism, restaurants, hotels, travel, research, law and academies. You may be a preceptor, minister, lawyer, banker, philonthrophist, counsellor, lecturer, publisher, writer, astrologer, travel agent, priest and temple trustee, official, cashier, philosopher, literateur, grocer, tobacconist, historian, mathematician, scientist, doctor, astronomer, psychologist, psychoanalyst or judge.

Being in Aquarius:

You may be a philosopher. You may become head of your group.

As third lord influencing tenth bhava:

You will gain from journeys connected with profession. Your brother may attain distinction in political field. You may become rich.

As sixth lord influencing tenth bhava:

Evil results regarding your prosperity will be
reduced. You may be moderately prosperous.

Gains and Income·

You will be a lover of music. You will be wealthy.
You will have accumulated funds. You will do good
deeds. You will have many friends. You will have gain
and accumulation of wealth. You will get birth of good
children. You will acquire good house, conveyance etc.
You will be respected by people from high position and
authority. You will have a large income. You will have
servants. You will have good friends. You will gain
through social success. You will realise your ambitions.
You will learn music and master it. You will enjoy all
comforts. You will be well-placed in life. You will be
able, statesmanly, god fearing, charitable, influential,
philanthrophic, famous, bold and fearless. You will be
long lived. You will gain from your wisdom, knowledge,
intellect and education. You will get topaz and silver.
You will gain from children. You may gain as minister
and adviser and from insurance companies. You may
gain from north-eastern direction.

As third lord influencing eleventh bhava:

You will have earnings without efforts. Generally
favourable results will be provided.

As sixth lord influencing eleventh bhava:

You will gain from maternal uncle.

Losses and Expenditure

You will be honest and pay taxes and tolls properly.
You will gain through law, medicines, occult subjects or
service in public institutions. You will visit hospitals
and asylums. You will have connections with
foreigners. You will be pious and in the end of life you
will attain Moksha (enlightenment). You will be devoid

of attachment. You will be inclined to ascetism in the later life. You will have artistic taste. You will travel a lot. You will be eloquent in speech. You will get happiness on account of children. You will be religiously inclined to chastity and benevolence. You will accumulate money. You will have good wealth, children and profession.

As third lord influencing twelfth bhava:

You will get fortune through marriage.

As sixth lord influencing twelfth bhava:

You will be alright and no untoward things may happen.

To mitigate any evil influences or to strengthen the benefic aspects of this period of Jupiter, you are advised to pray to God Brahma, wear topaz, use yellow colour and/or operate on number 3.

INTER-PERIOD OF SATURN IN THE SUB-PERIOD OF VENUS AND MAIN-PERIOD OF SATURN

From 24/10/1990 to 24/04/1991

Net benefic 55.56%, Net malefic 44.44%

Note: The following results of the inter-period planet are in addition to those given under the main- and sub-period planets.

The results of this inter-period of Saturn will be similar to those already given earlier under the main-period of Saturn except for the change in the benefic and malefic percentage.

INTER-PERIOD OF MERCURY IN THE SUB-PERIOD OF VENUS AND MAIN-PERIOD OF SATURN

From 24/04/1991 to 05/10/1991

Net benefic 48.52%, Net malefic 51.48%

Note: The following results of the inter-period planet are in addition to those given under the main- and sub-period planets.

Wealth

You may get wealthy by dint your of intelligence and gains through teaching, writing or by commissions, advertising, stationery or books. You may become wealthy by dealing with mercantile activity, trade, imports and exports, industries, architecture, weaving, vegetation, base metals, betel leaves, edible oils, nuts, limestone, green grams, emerald, lead, oil seeds or alloys. You may get money by being an accountant, mathematician, orator, bookseller, publisher, broker, poet or through your shrewdness and intellect. You can expect wealth from your maternal uncles, maternal grandfather or paternal relatives. You may gain wealth from commerce, aerial and landed journeys, churches, schools, parks, gambling dens or by being a doctor or tradesman. Your wealth may come from northern direction.

Being in Leo:

You can expect acquisition of wealth from various countries.

As ninth lord influencing second bhava:

You may acquire wealth through your family business or property.

As twelfth lord influencing second bhava:

You will have financial stability. You may earn well by trading in pearls, rubies and other precious stones or you may acquire such precious stones. You will spend your money for good causes. The evil indications of financial losses will be greatly reduced.

Courage

When once a work is undertaken, you will do it to finish and will never be discouraged. You will be brave and powerful with your power of speech and eloquence.

As ninth lord influencing third bhava:
You will be brave.

As twelfth lord influencing third bhava:
You may not be timid and quiet.

Education

You will be successful in your educational pursuits. You are inclined to pursue literary activities. You may have taste for music and for other fine arts. You may have proficiency in astrology. Your education may lead you to shine well as educationist or diplomat. You may be educated in fields connected with science, research, inspection of accounts, atomic energy, mathematics, electrical/electronic engineering, currency, alloys, water reserviors, poetry, business management, mercantile activity, journalism, commerce, weaving, aerial and land journeys or vegetation.

Being in Leo:
You will have good progress in knowledge.

As ninth lord influencing fourth bhava:
You will be learned. You may get foreign education.

As twelfth lord influencing fourth bhava:
You may have a chance of foreign education.

Houses, Landed Property, Conveyance

You will gain from landed property and estate.

As ninth lord influencing fourth bhava:
You will have landed properties and beautiful bungalows. You will inherit father's immovable properties. You will acquire many means of conveyance and lands.

As twelfth lord influencing fourth bhava:

You will have substantial immovable property and you may own your own conveyance.

Happiness

You will have robust health. You will have success in your educational pursuits. You will be learned and held in great esteem. You will have good mother and bring happiness to her. You will gain new friends. You will command good conveyance, material comforts and you will gain from landed properties. You will get promotion in profession or gains in profession. You will have prosperity and happiness in domestic life. You will get happiness from relatives. You will have princely appearance. You will acquire emarald. You will have good education with your intellect, wisdom and shrewdness. You will have power of speech and eloquence. You will have good enjoyments. You will possess or live in palatial buildings. You will have good relations with your maternal uncles, maternal grandfather and paternal relatives and you may gain from them. You will be good at poetry and may become a good poet. You will be happy.

Being in Leo:

You will have a remunerative profession. There will be elevation in your position. You will acquire wealth from various countries. You will get progress in knowledge and great reputation. You will be married.

As ninth lord influencing fourth bhava:

You may have landed properties and beautiful bungalows. You may earn through estate and land dealings. Your mother may be rich and fortunate. You may inherit father's immovable properties. You may acquire conveyances and lands. You may become a president or ruler of a country. You will be learned and may become head of centre of learning or research. You will be very happy.

As twelfth lord influencing fourth bhava:

You may own immovable property and conveyance. You may be happy.

Children

You will have good and intelligent children. There will be number of children.

As ninth lord influencing fifth bhava:

Your children may be very fortunate in life and enjoy success and distinction. Your children will distinguish themselves in academics and bring much happiness to you. Your children may become very famous and earn governmental patronage. Your children will also prosper very well and enjoy all kinds of luxuries.

As twelfth lord influencing fifth lord:

You may not expect either difficulty to beget progeny or unhappiness from children. Your children may not face trouble and you may not suffer much pain on their account.

Diseases

You will study hygiene and may take preventive measures not to get diseases.

As ninth lord influencing sixth bhava:

You may not have a sickly father.

As twelfth lord influencing sixth bhava:

You will be healthy and you will have handsome physique.

Enemies

You may be a terror to enemies and there may not be any enemies.

As ninth lord influencing sixth bhava:

Your attempts to make your fortune may not be frustrated through litigation involving your father. You may not be drawn into endless litigation.

As twelfth lord influencing sixth bhava:

You will vanquish your enemies. You may become involved in litigation which may come to an end to your advantage.

Debts

You may get debts from maternal uncles, maternal grandfather and paternal relatives but you may not be in debt due to them.

As ninth lord influencing sixth bhava:

Your attempts to make fortune may not be frustrated through litigation involving your father or debts contracted by him. You may not contract debts and be drawn into endless litigation.

Marriage and Marital Relationship

You may have an early marriage. Your partner may be good looking. You may gain through your partner. Your marriage may be with a wealthy person. Your partner may be more intelligent and shrewd, younger and may be employed. Your marriage may take place due to advertisement.

Being in Leo:

You are likely to have early marriage.

As ninth lord influencing seventh bhava:

You may get a noble and lucky life partner. You may get every kind of sensual pleasures. Fortune booms after marriage. Your partner may hail from a rich and respectable family.

As twelfth lord influencing seventh bhava:

Your partner may survive a crisis.

Prosperity

You will be studious, scientific-minded and highly educated. You will be lover of music and literateur. You will do virtuous acts. You may be author of books or work in diplomatic service. You will have high position in life. You will be popular, well-known and respected by public. You will be endowed with children and wealth. You will have a fortunate father. You may engage in trade and commerce. You will have success in long journeys and life in foreign places. You will be successful in all kinds of work. You will have happiness and prosperity. You may acquire emerald. You may get property from maternal uncles, maternal grandfather and paternal relations. You will have currency. You may get prosperity from northern direction.

Being in Leo:

You will have remunerative profession. You will get elevation in your career. You will acquire wealth from various sources. You will get married, if not married. You will get great reputation and fame.

As ninth lord in eleventh bhava:

You will be exceedingly rich. You will have powerful and influential friends. Your father will be a well-known and well-placed man. You will prosper in the family business.

As ninth lord influencing ninth bhava:

You may have a long-lived and prosperous father. You will be religiously inclined and charitable. You will travel abroad and earn money and distinction thereby. You will be lucky. You will marry a very eligible and good-natured partner. You will invest wisely in father's business and expand it beyond expectations. You will earn great wealth. You may win in elections and become a great political acumen. Your father may become famous in foreign lands. You will become pious and dutiful towards your parents.

As twelfth lord influencing ninth bhavas:

You may reside abroad and get prosperous. You may acquire much property in foreign lands. You will be honest, generous and large-hearted. You will be interested in physical culture. You will have a steady career. You will have interest in piety and lead a virtuous life.

Profession

You will succeed in long journeys. You will take additional charge of duties. You may be engaged in public life. You may work as reporter, electrician or in railways. You will succeed in profession and business. You will get promotion. You will get involved in religious activity and spiritual evolution. You will have success in education. You will be interested in research or antiquities. You may be a copyist or proof reader. Your profession may be connected with currency, alloys, water reservoirs, poetry, authorship, mercantile activity, trade and trading association, commerce, aerial and land journeys, weaving, vegetation, inferior or base metals, accounts, schools, parks, science, research, inspection of accounts, business management, atomic energy, mathematics, electrical/electronic engineering, documentation and recording and all jobs connected with such work like teaching, writing, radio or communication media. You may be a journalist, accountant, mathematician, orator, public speaker, ambassador, bookseller, merchant, publisher, stationer, grocer, printer, manufacturing representative, architect, correspondent, interpreter, reporter, historian, scientist, philosopher, doctor, astronomer, psychologist, psychoanalyst, judge or lawyer.

Being in Leo:

You will have a remunerative profession. You may have work connected with various countries. You may be a mountaineer.

As ninth lord influencing tenth bhava:

You will become famous and powerful. You will be

generous and occupy posts of authority. You will earn wealth and acquire every kind of comfort and luxury. Your means of livelihood would be righteous. You will be a law-abiding citizen. You will be settled in your career and lead a successful life. You will do charitable deeds. You may earn much wealth through your service to government. You will be honoured many times.

As twelfth lord influencing tenth bhava:

You may reside abroad and prosper. You may be interested in physical culture.

Gains and Income

You will be wealthy and happy. You will have mathematical faculty. You may be a good astrologer. You will have many friends among famous men. You will possess many lands. You will be logical and scientific. You will succeed in trade. There will be influx of wealth in large scale. You will lead a prosperous and contended life. You will do virtuous deeds and will be respected. You will be famous. You will be truthful and you will have a number of obedient servants. You will be endowed with various worldly comforts. You will get happiness in respect of children. You will triumph over enemies. You will own much property. You will have increased wealth. You will have many acquaintances but only a few permanent friends. You will associate with yougsters. You will be generous and charitable. You will be prosperous and respected. You will be good in mathematics or astrology. You will gain from dealings connected with commerce, chemistry, green grams, emerald, lead, oil-seeds, edible oils, intellect, education, authorship, power of speech and eloquence, currency or palatial buildings. You may gain as doctor or tradesperson. You may gain also from maternal uncles, maternal grandfather and paternal relations. You may gain from northern direction.

Being in Leo:

You will be wealthy.

As ninth lord influencing eleventh bhava:

You will be rich. You will have powerful and influential friends. Your father will be a well-known and well-placed man. You will prosper in family business.

As twlefth lord influencing eleventh bhava:

You may earn through trading in pearls, rubies and other precious stones.

Losses and Expenditure

You will become philosophical, intelligent, obliging, gifted, and religiously inclined. You will have a pleasing personality. You will speak sweetly. You will spend on good deeds. You will acquire new skills.

Being in Leo:

You will acquire wealth from various countries.

As twelfth lord in eleventh bhava:

You may earn well by trading in pearls, rubies and other precious stones. You may spend much money on religious and charitable deeds even at the cost of your own well-being.

As ninth lord influencing twelfth bhava:

You will lead a pure and honest life. You will be religious and noble. You will be spiritually inclined. You will spend your wealth in charity.

As twelfth lord influencing twelfth bhava:

You will be always engaged in spiritual thoughts and talks. You will lead a comfortable life. You will spend much on religious and righteous purposes. You will have good eyesight. You will enjoy pleasures of couch. You may be engaged in agriculture and get much wealth. You will not have untoward things. You will incur honourable expenditure. You will be religiously inclined. You will feed many holy men and seek their company.

To mitigate any evil influences or to strengthen the benefic aspects of this period of Mercury, you are advised to pray to the God Vishnu, wear emerald, use green colour and/or operate on number 5.

INTER-PERIOD OF KETU IN THE SUB-PERIOD OF VENUS AND MAIN-PERIOD OF SATURN
From 05/10/1991 to 13/12/1991
Net benefic 50.87%, Net malefic 49.13%

Note: The following results of the inter-period planet are in addition to those given under the main- and sub-period planets.

Courage
You will be adventurous, courageous and will have much fighting.

Marriage and Marital Relationship
You may not be passionate and may not have connections with unworthy persons. There may not be danger or ill health to your partner. You may not suffer from separation from your partner. Your partner may not be sickly or not short-tempered. You may not have loss of vitality. You may get a shrewd partner. You may not have an unhappy marriage.

Longevity
You may be long-lived.

Gains and Income
You will be wealthy. You will gain in all your attempts. You will have increased earnings. You will

get success over your enemies. You will perform good deeds and command respect. You will engage perseveringly in work. You will be humorous, witty, intelligent, influential, popular, famous, luxurious, learned, contended and industrious. You will have a excellent position for inflow of money. You may gain from dealings connected with fire, flame or mining. You can expect to gain from your paternal grandfather.

To mitigate any evil influences or to strengthen the benefic aspects of this period of Ketu, you are advised to pray to the God Ganesha, wear cat's eye, use deep red colour and/or operate on number 9.

Index